Kanji Memorization Drills

Version Two

Workbook of Exercises

for the Mastery of

1,208 Kanji

A Supplement to the

"Learn to Read in Japanese" Series

by Roger Lake

Kanji Memorization Drills

Version Two

Introduction

This second version of *Kanji Memorization Drills* consists of a set of exercises designed to teach a total of 1,208 kanji and their pronunciations. Before you dive in, I recommend that you first work through our Japanese Readers, *Learn to Read in Japanese,* Volumes I and II. Once you are familiar with that material, you may want to alternate between practicing with this workbook and revisiting the Readers.

On each of the following pages, you will see three columns. In the **first column**, there is a kanji character followed by a small number that denotes the number of pronunciations that you should try to learn for that character. In the **second column**, you will see that kanji's unique listing number, taken from the Kanji Catalogue that is included in the Reader. Also in the second column, there are mnemonics (which I also call CUES in the Catalogue) that approximate the Japanese pronunciations and help students to remember them. Finally, in the **third column**, there are sample Japanese words that contain the actual kanji readings.

Where feasible, I have sorted the kanji into informal groups of similar characters and arranged those characters so that they fit within the confines of a single page, to make it easier for students to compare them.

In order to use this book productively, I suggest that you use **three tools**: 1) an index card, roughly 3 x 5 inches in size, 2) a pen with a fine point and 3) an eraser tool. The purpose of the index card is to conceal the second and third columns while you test yourself on the pronunciations of the kanji in the first column. The purpose of the pen is to make small erasable dots in the margin to the left of any characters whose pronunciations you cannot readily recall. The purpose of the eraser tool is to erase those dots after you have successfully re-tested yourself on the missed kanji.

After experimenting with erasure methods, I've concluded that it's probably best to use the "Pentel Presto Jumbo Correction Pen Fine Point" for the eraser tool. The fluid in its tank flows easily, it lasts for a long time, it can be applied precisely to the areas that you want to erase, and it will keep your book in good condition even after many erasures. If you ever feel that the pages in this volume need to be replaced, you can purchase a replacement book from our PDF store at https://japaneseaudiolessons.com, print it, and staple the pages together in groups of about 24 pages (assuming two-sided printing). Please be aware that we offer a 50% discount to owners of our printed books who purchase PDF versions of the same books – see the details at our PDF store at japaneseaudiolessons.com.

To use this book productively, please begin by placing the index card to the right of the first column on a page, concealing the "answers" in the second and third columns. Take note of the number of pronunciations that you are expected to know for the kanji in the first column (indicated by the small numbers that follow each character) and try to recall those pronunciations from memory. Check your answers by referring to the mnemonics in the second column and the sample vocabulary in the third column. If you are not able to remember every pronunciation for a given character, place a small **dot** in the margin to its left, about 5 mm outside the box surrounding the printed text, and move on to the next entry. After you complete a page in this way, you will probably see one or more dots in the left margin, denoting kanji that require further testing.

Next, starting at the top of the page again, do a **one-dot page review**, testing yourself on only dotted kanji. Try to recall the pronunciations for all the kanji with dots on that page while they are still fresh in your memory. If you are still unable to provide correct answers for every dotted kanji on the page, repeat the process until you get perfect results, but don't erase the dots yet. Turn the page and continue testing yourself in this way on subsequent pages until you finish the chapter, which is usually six pages in length.

After you complete a chapter, turn back to its first page and conduct a **one-dot chapter review**, testing yourself again on the kanji with dots. If there are still one-dot kanji whose pronunciations you cannot fully recall, add **second dots** in the margin to the left of those characters and continue your testing on any additional one-dot kanji in the chapter, adding second dots to the characters wherever necessary.

After you complete this one-dot chapter review, return to the first page of the chapter and perform a **two-dot chapter review**, testing yourself on only kanji with two dots. If there are still kanji whose pronunciations you cannot fully identify on this round, add a third dot next to them. If necessary, keep conducting additional chapter reviews (for example, you can test yourself on kanji with three dots and four dots, etc.) until you have achieved correct results for all the characters in the chapter.

After you have achieved perfect responses for all the kanji on a given page, use the correction pen to erase the dots on that page, to preserve your book for future use. If you haven't used the correction pen for a while, you may have to squeeze the tube and rub the tip on the paper surface to get the white fluid flowing. Although the fluid is nontoxic, it is difficult to remove after it dries, so try not to spill it on your clothes or hands. Make only *vertical* strokes over the dots that you want to erase, to avoid accidentally covering the printed material on the right. Apply the minimum amount of fluid needed to cover the dots. Wait a few seconds and then use the index card to blot the fluid. After erasing the dots, move on to the next page.

When testing yourself on kanji with a large number of pronunciations and deciding whether to place dots next to them, you can choose to be either strict or lenient in your grading. It may seem unreasonable to expect yourself to remember as many as 13 readings for a single character, and perhaps your primary goal at this stage should be merely to learn to recognize each kanji's shape and recall at least a few of its pronunciations. Of course, it's best to try to remember all of the readings if you can.

As you use this book, you will find it helpful to consult the Kanji Catalogue that is included in *Learn to Read in Japanese,* Vol. II, or the one that is included in the stand-alone *Core Kanji* book. For example, on p. 1-1, in the second column next to kanji # 175, you will see "正 (correct) laws," and you may want to look up that kanji's **DESCRIPTION** in the Catalogue to understand why the radical 正 is used to mean "correct." In addition, the Pronunciation Index in the Catalogue is useful for looking up characters when you want to compare them to the ones you are currently studying.

Please note that some kanji are pronounced in two ways that, at first glance, appear identical. For example, on page 2-9, in the listing for kanji # 297, you will find two similar mnemonics in the second column: **Toe**s and **To**rtoise. To understand why I've employed these two almost interchangeable mnemonics ("toe" and "to") for this character, please refer to the sample words in the third column. These illustrate that sometimes this kanji is pronounced "tou" and sometimes "to," which are two distinct pronunciations to Japanese ears.

Please be aware of **rendaku**, a phenomenon that can affect the pronunciations of kanji in compound words when the kanji appear in the middle or at the end of a word. Kanji pronunciations that contain the consonants in the following table can change as shown here:

ch → j	(e.g., chi → ji)	k → g	(e.g., koto → goto)
f → b	(e.g., fun → bun)	s → z	(e.g., sushi → zushi)
f → p	(e.g., fuku → puku)	sh → j	(e.g., sha → ja)
h → b	(e.g., hito → bito)	t → d	(e.g., toki → doki)
h → p	(e.g., hai → pai)	ts → z	(e.g., tsukai → zukai)

As a result of rendaku, a few kanji in this book have more possible pronunciations than the numbers in their first columns indicate. For example, on page 2-9, next to kanji # 298, the number "3" appears in the first column, indicating that there are three mnemonics in the second column (**Ha**waiian, **Hats** and **Ho**le), but in the last column you will see *four* pronunciations, contained in the sample words "happyou," "hatsumei," "shuppatsu" and "hossa," meaning that "patsu" has been omitted from the mnemonics column. The reason for the omission is that I elected not to invent a fourth mnemonic for this character, since the "hatsu" pronunciation implies the "patsu" reading (h → p). Generally, however, the book supplies mnemonics for almost all of the rendaku-driven pronunciations that are associated with the kanji.

I hope that the drills in this volume will help you to achieve Japanese reading fluency.

Roger Lake

July 1, 2025

Kanji Memorization Drills, Version Two

Chapter 1

食 5		^398. I went to this 白 (white) **Ta**vern by the **Sho**re, where I 食べた **ta**beta (ate) 良 (good) food and drank **Koo**l-Aid, after which they **Sho**wed-**Coo**kies for dessert, but I lost my appetite after I realized I had dropped my **Jeep-Key**s Light Years away	食べる taberu = to eat; 食感 shokkan = texture of food; 食う kuu = to eat (rough speech); 食事 shokuji = meal; 餌食 ejiki = victim, prey
飯 2		^400. **Han**sel cooked this 食 (meal), including ご飯 go**han** (cooked rice), but it's **Messy**, and it gets an F; we're also marking it with this X	ご飯 gohan = meal, cooked rice; 残飯 zanpan = leftover food; 冷や飯 hiyameshi = cold rice
反 4		^680. **Han**sel was に反対 ni **han**tai (in opposition to) the witch, and he had a plan to wash her with **Soap** in a **Tan**k in **Hon**duras, but the plan was poor, and Gretel gave it this grade of F and marked it with this X	反対 hantai = opposition, the reverse; 反り返る sorikaeru = to bend back or warp; 反物 tanmono = cloth, textile; 謀反 muhon = mutiny, rebellion
阪 2		^1005. when a ß (Greek) team played **Sakka**a (soccer) in 大阪 oo**saka** (Osaka), **Han**sel was in 反 (opposition, i.e., on the opposing team)	大阪 oosaka = Osaka, large hill; 阪神 hanshin = Osaka and Kobe
販 1		^1199. **Han**sel wanted a career in 販売 **han**bai (marketing) so that he could fill up this 貝 (money chest), but he got this F on his final exam, and Gretel also marked it with this X	販売 hanbai = sales, marketing; 自働販売機 jidouhanbaiki = vending machine
坂 1		^1130. we don't mind playing **Sakka**a (soccer) on this 土 (soil), but you get this F and this X for making us play on a steep 坂 **saka** (slope)	坂 saka = slope, hill; 下り坂 kudarizaka = downward slope
板 3		^1166. I cut down this **Ban**ana 木 (tree) to make an 板 **ita** (wooden board) to cut Italian **Pan** (bread) on, but my teacher graded my work with this F and marked it with this X	看板 kanban = signboard; 板 ita = wooden board, metal plate; 鉄板焼き teppanyaki = food grilled on an iron griddle
返 2		^356. when I got this F on my paper and had it marked with this X, I put it on this snail and 返した **kae**shita (returned it) to the teacher, but the teacher **C**alled-**Esther**, my mother, and sent the paper back to us on a **Hen**	返す kaesu = to return an item; 寝返る negaeru = to betray; 返事 henji = reply
避 2		^802. a **Sa**laryman wants to **Hea**l this snail and 避ける **sa**keru (avoid) side-effects, and he uses this 辛 (needle) to inject the snail with the medicine in the 口 (box) under this lean-to (LBN = lean-to, box, needle)	避ける sakeru = to avoid; 避難 hinan = taking refuge
壁 3		^1051. I **C**alled-**Ben** Franklin and asked him to **Help-the-Ki**ng by inventing a 壁 **kabe** (wall) for the castle, since birds are **Peck**ing the old one, and he came up with this defensive design using this lean-to with a double roof, 口 (boxes) and 辛 (needles) like these, plus 土 (soil) like this (LBN = lean-to, box, needle)	壁 kabe = wall; 壁画 hekiga = mural painting; 絶壁 zeppeki = cliff
症 1		^1085. if you are in this 病 (sick) bed, the 正 (honest) thing to do is to **Show** a doctor a list of your 症状 **shou**jou (symptoms)	症状 shoujou = symptoms, condition of a patient; 感染症 kansenshou = infectious disease
政 1		^175. 政治家 **sei**jika (politicans) should pass 正 (correct) laws to ensure that dancers like this can find **Safe** places to practice	政治 seiji = politics, government; 政治家 seijika = politician
延 3		^842. an **E**ngineer who is always 正 (correct) visited **No**rway, and he had to request an 延期 **en**ki (postponement) of his appointments because this 3X snail on which he traveled was so slow, but later he won a **No**bel prize	延期 enki = postponement; 引き延ばす hikinobasu = to delay; 延床面積 nobeyuka menseki = total floor area
誕 1		^1122. this 延 [engineer who is always 正 (correct)] 言 (spoke) and had a **Tan**trum after we forgot his 誕生日 **tan**joubi (birthday) and made him ride on this slow 3x snail	誕生する tanjou suru = to be born; 誕生日 tanjoubi = birthday
証 3		^1150. it's 正 (correct) to 言 (say) that we should **Show** 証明 **shou**mei (identification) before we start our **Aca**demic studies at the **Aca**demy-of-**S**heep-**F**arming	証明 shoumei = proof, identification; 証す akasu = to prove or verify; 証 akashi = proof, certificate

供 5	^486. this man, who is staying in a **Do**py-**Mo**tel in **Kyou**to, tilts his hat back in order to watch as 子供 ko**domo** (children) play in these plants above this hill, and he offers them **Koo**l-Aid in exchange for getting **Tomo**grams, or at least **Sonar** exams	子供 kodomo = child; 提供する teikyou suru = to offer, provide, sponsor; 供物 kumotsu = offering; お供する otomo suru = to accompany; 供える sonaeru = to offer at an altar
共 2	^969. these plants on this hill are 共に **tomo** ni (together), and they are located outside of a **Tomo**graphy center in **Kyou**to	共に tomo ni = together; 共同の kyoudou no = cooperative, communal; 共感 kyoukan = sympathy; 共通の kyoutsuu no = common, mutual
洪 1	^1119. due to this water from a 洪水 **kou**zui (flood) at a **Cour**thouse, we had to climb up onto this hill 共 (together) and find shelter in these plants	洪水 kouzui = flood
基 2	^1198. this drone is powered by this **Motor** at the bottom, and our surveillance around **Kiev** will 基ずく **moto**zuku (be based on) it	基ずく motozuku = to be based on; に基づいて ni motozuite = based on, according to; 基準 kijun = criterion, standard; 基盤 kiban = foundation, basis; 基金 kikin = fund
寒 2	^507. when it's 寒い **samu**i (cold), this **Samu**rai's wife, who lives in **Kan**sas and sports this bad haircut and this corset, maneuvers around these patches of ice	寒い samui = cold atmosphere; 寒気 kanki = a chill; this can also be pronounced "samuke"
同 2	^339. this line above this box in this two-sided lean-to, which is 同じ **ona**ji (the same) on the left and on the right, represents an **Old-Na**pkin that was used to wrap a **Dough**nut	同じ onaji = the same; 同情 doujou = sympathy, pity
洞 2	^963. I found this two-sided lean-to, containing this cloth above a box next to this stream inside a 洞穴 **hora**ana (cave), but it was a **Home-for-Ra**ts that like to feast on **Dough**nuts	洞穴 horaana = cave, den; 洞窟 doukutsu = cave, grotto; 洞察 dousatsu = insight, discernment
胴 1	^1191. when this 月 (moon) is full, I somehow feel 同 (sympathy) for hungry people, and so I eat **Dough**nuts like the one that was previously wrapped in this napkin, and that's why my 胴体 **dou**tai (torso) is so large	胴体 doutai = body, torso
捕 3	^670. this guy on the left, who keeps this truncated 犬 (dog) behind this 用 (fence), has a **Toe** protruding from a **Ho**le in his sock, but he is kneeling in order to get a leash from the **Tsui**tcase-(suitcase)-in-his-**Car**, and he will take the 犬 (dog) out to 捕る **to**ru (catch) a burglar	捕る toru = to catch; 捕らえる toraeru = to arrest, capture or understand; 捕虜 horyo = prisoner of war, captive; 捕まえる tsukamaeru = to capture or catch
補 2	^995. this happy Jimmy with two lips is a 候補 kou**ho** (candidate), and he keeps this truncated 犬 (dog) behind this 用 (fence) at his **Ho**me to impress the voters, while some of **O**prah's-**G**eese-take-a-**Nap**	補佐 hosa = aid, help; 補給する hokyuu suru = to supply or supplement; 候補 kouho = candidate; 補う oginau = to supplement or compensate for
舎 2	^745. a **Car**penter came from the 田舎 ina**ka** (countryside), where he lived in this **Sha**bbby house containing this 土 (soil) and this 口 (box)	田舎 inaka = rural area, hometown; 校舎 kousha = school building
捨 2	^594. **Su**perman is this person who is crawling toward this **Sha**bby house in order to 捨てる **su**teru (throw away) this 土 (soil) that is defiling this 口 (box)	捨てる suteru = to throw away; 四捨五入する shishagonyuu suru = to round to the nearest whole number
説 3	^439. this 兄 (older brother), who is wearing these rabbit ears because he is **Z**any, 言 (speaks) and 説明する **setsu**mei suru (explains) about how he **Set-up-a-Su**per farm, where he grows **T**omatoes	遊説 yuuzei = election campaign; 説明 setsumei = explanation; 小説 shousetsu = novel; 演説 enzetsu = a speech; 説く toku = to explain, persuade, preach
税 1	^708. while harvesting this 禾 (ripe grain), 兄 (older brother) put on these rabbit ears and acted **Z**any, until he realized that he would have to pay 税金 **zei**kin (taxes) on the grain	税金 zeikin = tax, duty

Kanji	Mnemonic	Vocabulary
浴 3	^256. this bathroom in the **Yu**kon near the **A**rctic with water vapor rising from the roof and this spring of water outside is a good place to 浴びる **a**biru (bathe), after which one can put on a 浴衣 **yu**kata (summer robe) and eat **Y**ogurt-and-**Coo**kies	浴衣 yukata = summer kimono; 浴びる abiru = to bathe; 浴室 yokushitsu = bathroom
容 1	^296. after receiving this bad haircut, I fled to **Yo**semite, explored its 内容 nai**you** (contents) and bathed in this bathroom	内容 naiyou = content
欲 3	^535. this bathroom with water vapor rising from it and this oil derrick outside are attached to our **H**otel at **Yo**semite, and we tell the waiters in the restaurant that we 欲しい **ho**shii (desire) **Y**ogurt-and-**Coo**kies	欲しい hoshii = to desire; 欲求 yokkyuu = desire; 欲張り yokubari = greed; 食欲 shokuyoku = appetite
裕 1	^660. this happy Jimmy with these two lips acquired 裕福 **yuu**fuku (wealth) and decided to buy this 浴 (bathroom) in the **Yu**kon	裕福 yuufuku = wealth
溶 2	^815. after getting this bad haircut, I fled to **Yo**semite, where I used a **T**orch to 溶ける **to**keru (melt) some snow into water like this, before bathing in this bathroom	溶岩 yougan = lava; 溶ける tokeru = to melt or dissolve, intransitive; 溶かす tokasu = to melt or dissolve, transitive
然 2	^611. as a **Z**en monk sits on this three-legged bench with a rocker bottom, watching his **N**egative-**N**ephew play with this 犬 (dog) near a fire, he looks out at 自然 shi**zen** (Nature) and sees it as 天然 ten**nen** (natural)	全然 zenzen = not at all; 自然 shizen = nature; 当然 touzen = justly; 天然 tennen = natural
黙 2	^836. this sincere guy in **Dama**scus was sitting with this 犬 (dog), and this fire was hot, so he wanted **More-Koo**l-Aid, but he 黙った **dama**tta (kept silent)	黙る damaru = to keep silent; 沈黙 chinmoku = silence
熱 3	^65. 九 (nine) vegetables which were slashed after being grown in this 土 (soil) walking on 土 (soil) are being cooked by this fire **At-Su**perman's house and are 熱い **atsu**i (hot); they will **Net-Su**perman a profit when he sells them **N**ext door	熱い atsui = hot (objects); 熱 netsu = fever; 熱心に nesshin ni = enthusiastically
勢 4	^110. this 土 (soil) at the upper left walks on these lopsided legs across more 土 (soil) towards a **Z**any guy who uses a **S**aber to slash 九 (nine) kinds of vegetables with 力 (force) before **S**elling them to 大勢の oo**zei** no (many) **I**cky-**O**gres	大勢 oozei = many people; 勢力 seiryoku = power, influence; 伊勢崎 isesaki = a city in Japan; 勢い ikioi = power, energy
貴 2	^643. I keep 貴重な **ki**chou na (valuable) things, including my **K**eys and my **To**asted-**To**rtillas, in this three-drawer 貝 (money chest), and the 中 symbol above the chest reminds me that my valuables are 中 (inside)	貴重な kichou na = valuable; 貴ぶ toutobu = to value, respect
遺 2	^1037. my father keeps only dried **E**els 中 (inside) this 貝 (money chest), which will be his 遺産 **i**san (legacy) to me, together with a **Yu**kon-**Ea**gle and this snail, none of which is very 貴 (valuable)	遺産 isan = inheritance, legacy, heritage; 遺言 yuigon = will, deathbed instructions
男 4	^109. this 男性 **dan**sei (man), who is wearing an **Otto**man-era-**Coat**, exercises this 力 (force) by **Dan**cing in this 田 (rice paddy) with **Nan**cy Pelosi, who is **O**ld	男の子 otoko no ko = boy; 男性 dansei = man; 長男 chounan = first-born son; 正男 Masao = a boy's given name
湧 1	^903. this マ (mother) and this 男 (male), who is her son, open a valve, and this **W**ater 湧く **wa**ku (gushes out)	湧く waku = to gush out, well up, appear
染 4	^774. a **Sen**ator visited **So**malia in a **Jee**p, where he saw some **Sheep**, 九 (nine) bodies of water like this and many 木 (trees) like this, but 汚染 o**sen** (pollution) was a problem	感染 kansen = contagion, infection; 汚染 osen = pollution; 染まる somaru = to be dyed or stained, to be influenced; 馴染む najimu = to adapt or become accustomed to; 染み込む shimikomu = to soak into or penetrate
雑 3	^785. 九 (nine) 木 (trees) like this surround this net where **Z**ach's-**Tsu**itcase (suitcase) was stored in a 複雑な fuku**zatsu** na (complicated) **Z**one in **Z**ambia	複雑な fukuzatsu na = complicated; 雑巾 zoukin = dust cloth, cleaning cloth; 雑誌 zasshi = magazine

諦 1	^804. people 言 (say) that a cook who 立 (stands) on slippery floors should wear spikes like these on her shoes, but **Achilles'-Ra**ck of lamb was ruined because this 巾 (Bo Peep) 諦めた **akira**meta (gave up) on that advice and switched to ordinary shoes	諦める akirameru = to give up
締 3	^1173. this 巾 (Bo Peep) on the lower right, who 立 (stands) on slippery floors wearing these spikes on her shoes, and this 糸 (skeet shooter) fell in love, and **She-Marrie**d him, but sometimes she slides around in spite of her spikes, so he went out to his **Jee**p and got a harness made out of a **Shee**t to 締める **shi**meru (fasten) her to the ceiling	取締役 torishimariyaku = a representative director (a director chosen by a board to represent it); 戸締まり tojimari = door fastening; 締める shimeru = to fasten (seatbelt), tie (necktie), strangle, tighten (transitive); 締まる shimaru = to tighten (intransitive); 締め切り shimekiri = closing, deadline
敵 2	^881. this dancer on the right deals with her 敵 **teki** (enemies), who are **Techies**, by hiring an 古 (old) sentry to sit in this lean-to and use this 立 (bell) to make loud sounds, and she will also **Ca**ll-a-**T**alented-**Ki**ng for help	敵 teki = enemy, opponent; 素敵な suteki na = great, wonderful; 敵 kataki = enemy, rival
摘 2	^1083. this person on the left is a **Techie** who is kneeling, even though it might damage his **Tsu**it (suit), in order to 指摘する shi**teki** suru (point out) that this 古 (old) sentry in this two-sided lean-to is using this 立 (bell) to make loud sounds	指摘 shiteki = pointing out, identification; 摘む tsumu = to pick tea, cotton, etc.
踊 2	^366. this 止 (hesitant) squarehead goes behind this 用 (fence), removes the **Yo**ke from this マ (mammoth) and 踊る **odo**ru (dances) with it, which leaves a distinctive **Odor** of mammoth on the squarehead	舞踊 buyou = dancing; 踊る odoru = to dance
路 3	^525. this 止 (hesitant) squarehead and this dancer with a ponytail who leaps over this box are **Ro**aming on a 道路 dou**ro** (road) in **Michi**gan, looking for a **Jee**p	道路 douro = road; 路子 Michiko = a female given name; 旅路 tabiji = journey
距 1	^717. this 止 (hesitant) squarehead will carry this swing set to **Kyo**to, which is a long 距離 **kyo**ri (distance) away	距離 kyori = distance, range
跳 2	^1084. this 止 (hesitant) squarehead has 踊 (danced) with a 兆 (trillion) partners, including Prince **Ha**rry and **To**lstoy, but he only knows how to 跳ねる **ha**neru (hop)	跳ねる haneru = to jump or hop, to splash; 跳ぶ tobu = to jump or leap; 跳び箱 tobibako = a vaulting box
跡 2	^1111. this 止 (hesitant) squarehead on the left is a **Selfish-Ki**ng who has been developing an **Ato**mic bomb with help from this four-legged hen, which has 跡 **ato** (traces) of radiation on its feathers	奇跡 kiseki = miracle, wonder, marvel; 跡 ato = trace, track, ruin
貿 1	^85. I have this backpack and this 刀 (sword) on top of this three-drawer 貝 (money chest), and I would like to 貿易する **bou**eki suru (trade) them for a **Bow**ling ball	貿易 boueki = trade
留 4	^71. this backpack and this 刀 (sword) were **Re**united at this 田 (rice paddy) in **To**kyo where **To**ads-**Do**ze after their owner, a local **Ru**ler who had been 留守 **ru**su (absent from home) with the backpack, came back	留学 ryuugaku = foreign study; 留める tomeru = to fasten, button or attach; 留まる todomaru = to stay; 留守 rusu = absence from home
細 4	^220. a **Home-schooled-So**ldier, who is just a **Boy-So**ldier, and who is in a **Coma**, is **Si**lent as this 糸 (skeet shooter) shoots at this 細い **hoso**i (narrow) 田 (rice paddy) where he is hiding, leaving trails of smoke which are 細い **koma**kai (small)	細い hosoi = thin; 心細い kokorobosoi = downhearted; 細かい komakai = minute, small; 詳細 shousai = details
畑 2	^889. in **Ha**waii-a-**Tall-Ke**nnedy sets this 火 (fire) in this 畑 **hatake** (field) after the harvest, and he pays a **Harbor-Tax** when he ships his crops	畑 hatake = field for cultivation or field of expertise; 田畑 tahata = field (crops)
倍 1	^269. this man is tilting his hat in order to examine this 立 (bell) on this 口 (box) which he wants to **Buy** and then resell it for 倍増 **bai**zou (double) the price	三倍の sanbai no = three times as much; 倍増する baizou suru = to double

護 1		^1163. a 看護婦 kan**go**fu (nurse) heard a **Gho**st 言 (speak) from this net on this 又 (table) under these hanging plants	弁護士 bengoshi = lawyer; 看護婦 kangofu = female nurse
獲 2		^947. this woman on the left contorts her body in order to view some **E**ggs stored in this net under these plants on this 又 (table), which she hopes to 獲得する **kaku**toku suru (obtain) from **K**arl-the-**Koo**l-Aid vendor, who is also in the egg business	獲物 emono = game (hunting) or catch (fishing); 獲得する kakutoku suru = to win or obtain
犯 2		^901. when **Han**sel walks with Gretel, he **Occa**sionally sees her contorting her body like this to avoid snakes like this one, and he attacks the 犯人 **han**nin (culprits)	犯人 hannin = criminal, culprit; 犯す okasu = to violate, to commit (e.g., a crime)
猿 2		^1055. this woman is contorting herself to support **Saru**man's scheme to train 猿 **saru** (monkeys) to work as **En**tertainers in Middle Earth, taking them out of this 土 (soil) where they live, keeping them in boxes like this, and giving them names that start with エ and Y, like Eric and Yolanda	猿 saru = monkey; 日本猿 nihonzaru = Japanese macaque; 類人猿 ruijin'en = ape
遠 3		^351. this snail carries an **En**gineer who designed this megaphone with two lips which is hidden under this 土 (soil), and although it scares **Toa**ds and **Doe**s, he uses it to speak to 遠い **too**i (distant) people	遠慮 enryo = reserve; 遠い tooi = far; 待ち遠しい machidooshii = long for, look forward to
園 3		^279. an **En**gineer is using this megaphone with two lips to tell children playing in this 土 (soil) above this 口 (box) in this enclosed 公園 kou**en** (park) to enter the **Zone**-to-the-**North**, and have **Sono**grams done	公園 kouen = a park; 花園 hanazono = a flower garden; 竹の園 takenosono = a bamboo garden
環 1		^718. this 王 (king) visited **Kan**sas, where three eyes like these are common, and he used this megaphone to address people about the 環境 **kan**kyou (environment)	環境 kankyou = environment, surroundings
隙 1		^879. this ß (Greek) person bakes **Superior-Qui**che like the kind they make in Athens in this 日 (oven), which rotates on this 小 (rod) and spins out these four flames through 隙間 **suki**ma (gaps) in its sides	隙間 sukima = gap, hole; 隙 suki = gap, opening, carelessness, inattentiveness
原 3		^888. **Gen**ghis placed this 小 (small) 白 (white) spinning oven in this lean-to a 野原 no**hara** (field), where no one would **Hara**ss him without a **Warra**nt	原因 gen'in = cause; 野原 nohara = field; 海原 unabara = ocean; 小笠原 Ogasawara = an island group south of Japan
願 2		^94. losing his head has had a **Nega**tive effect on this 小 (small) 白 (white) guy in this lean-to, and he 願う **nega**u (begs) **Gan**dalf to find it	願う negau = to wish or beg; 願望 ganbou = wish, longing
真 3		^101. this cabinet on this table contains strings for **Ma**'s-(Mother's)-**Koto** (Japanese harp), and it has a **Ma**chine with this **Shin**y antenna at the top, which delivers 真実の **shin**jitsu no (true) news	真 makoto = truth, sincerity; 真面目な majime na = sincere; 真ん中 mannaka = middle; 真っ直ぐ massugu = straight; 写真 shashin = photograph; 真実 shinjitsu = truth; 真理 shinri = truth
慎 2		^632. the man on the left is a 慎重な **shin**chou na (prudent) **Shin**to priest who draws himself up to his full height like this as he seeks this 真 (truth), and he digs through boxes of **Tsu**its-(suits)-**Tsu**its-and-**Shee**ts	慎重 shinchou = careful, prudent; 慎む tsutsushimu = to be discreet, to refrain from
具 1		^100. I keep 道具 dou**gu** (tools) in this cabinet on this table, together with the **Goo** that I use to grease them	道具 dougu = tool; 具体的に gutaiteki ni = con-cretely; 具合 guai = condition
通 4		^365. this マ (mammoth) on this 用 (fence) 通う **kayo**u (commutes) on this snail to its job at a lakeside hotel, where other マ (mammoths) 通る **too**ru (pass through) the lobby **To**wing **Tsu**itcases (suitcases), **D**olphins swim by, and the staff **Call-Yo**gis to teach yoga	通る tooru = to pass through; 通り toori = street, way; 通学する tsuugaku suru = to commute to school; 通り doori = in accordance with, avenue; 通う kayou = to commute
樋 3		^1143. this snail 通 (passes through) a 木 (wood) 雨樋 ama**doi** (gutter) and carries this **Toy** マ (mammoth) on a 用 (fence), but it can't **Hear** us because it has **Doi**lies stuffed into its ears	樋 toi = a gutter; 樋口 Higuchi = a family name; 雨樋 amadoi = a rain gutter

Kanji	Mnemonic	Vocabulary
再 3	^1032. a **Sci**entist made this model of a rice paddy with a handle and strong legs and was hoping to get some 円 (yen) for it, but a woman who was eating **Foo**d-on-a-**Tata**mi mat wouldn't buy it, even though he asked her 再び **futata**bi (again), and he felt **Sad**	再会する saikai suru = to meet again; 再開する saikai suru = to reopen or resume; 再三 saisan = many times, again and again; 再び futatabi = again; 再来年 sarainen = the year after next
構 3	^141. people used this 木 (wood) when they built this 結構な kek**kou** na (fine) **Cour**thouse with this 井 (well) and this 再 (model of a rice paddy with a handle) in the lobby; since they 構う **kama**u (care about) quality, they consulted the **Kama** Sutra, spent a lot of 円 (yen), and strengthened the building so that it would provide protection from **Gamma** rays	結構 kekkou = fine, splendid, considerably; 構う kamau = to mind or care about; 心構え kokorogamae = a mental attitude
講 1	^1027. when a woman 言 (spoke) and gave a 講義 **kou**gi (lecture) in this **Cour**thouse with this 井 (well) and this 再 (rice paddy model with a handle), her explanations seemed 構 (fine) to me	講義 kougi = lecture; 講堂 koudou = auditorium
織 3	^753. this 糸 (skeet shooter) is shooting at a 組織 so**shiki** (organization) of **Ori**ental **Or**thodontists who buy **Sheep**-in-**Ki**ev and work on their teeth with halberds like this, and that is the source of this plaintive 音 (sound)	羽織 haori = short jacket worn over kimono; 織る oru = to weave; 組織 soshiki = organization
職 2	^696. I listen to 音 (sounds) with this 耳 (ear) while carrying this halberd, and it may **Shock**-yo**U** to learn that my 職業 **shoku**gyou (occupation) is military musician, but wait until you see my **Show**	職業 shokugyou = occupation; 就職する shuushoku suru = to get a job; 職権 shokken = authority
身 2	^651. when 自 (myself) climbs onto this rickety chair, people from my 出身 shus**shin** (birthplace) try to support me by driving this **Shin**y sword into the ground, so that my 身 **mi** (body) doesn't fall down, and they feed me **Meals**	身長 shinchou = a person's height; 出身 shusshin = birthplace, hometown, alma mater; 身 mi = body, person, e.g., 一人身 hitori mi = one person
射 2	^932. a **Shah** tells this kneeling sunny guy on the right to stop chewing gum for a moment and deliver a 注射 chuu**sha** (injection) into the **Ear** of this 身 (body) on the left	反射 hansha = reflection; 注射 chuusha = injection; 射る iru = to hit or shoot (an arrow)
牙 3	^921. when the **King-of-Bagh**dad invited a **Gue**st to his hanging **Gar**dens, he wore this helmet with a visor designed to hide his 牙 **kiba** (fangs)	牙 kiba = fang, tusk; 象牙 zouge = ivory; 牙城 gajou = stronghold
邪 2	^796. the guy on the left is a **Ze**sty **Ja**zz performer from ß (Greece) with this clarinet emerging from under his visor, and he is testing the visor to see if it might prevent 風邪 ka**ze** (upper respiratory infections)	風邪 kaze = upper respiratory infection; 無邪気 mujaki = innocence
雅 2	^922. when I went to **Meet-a-Yankee**, I noticed a **Gambler** in this net, wearing 優雅な yuu**ga** na (elegant) robes and sporting these large 牙 (fangs)	雅びた miyabita = gracious, elegant, refined; 優雅な yuuga na = elegant; 温雅 onga = graceful, affable
型 2	^1116. this リ Ri uses a **Cata**pult which is attached to this tower on the upper left to send **Cake** to prisoners who are being held in this 土 (soil), and he always insists on using proper 型 **kata** (form) when doing so	型 kata = form (e.g., dance), posture, style; 髪型 kamigata = hair style (this can also be written 髪形); 典型的 tenkeiteki = typical
研 2	^442. **Ken** is a researcher who does 研究 **ken**kyuu (research) into kidney 石 (stones) like this in this research tower, and this keeps him on his **Toes**	研究 kenkyuu = research; 研ぐ togu = to sharpen, to wash rice
餅 2	^743. a researcher is celebrating the New Year by putting these rabbit ears on this research tower, and he wants to 食 (eat) **More-Cheese** with his 餅 **mochi** (Japanese rice cake), so he asks a **Ba**ker to add some	餅 mochi = Japanese rice cake; 煎餅 senbei = rice cracker
隅 1	^79. the roots of this 田 (rice paddy) are growing more vigorously in the right upper 隅 **sumi** (inside corner) of this pot, since they are trying to avoid this ß (Greek) observer **Sumis**u-san (Mr. Smith) on the left	引き出しの隅 hikidashi no sumi = inside corner of a drawer
遇 1	^1120. a **Goo**se 遭遇した sou**guu** shita (encountered) this 田 (rice paddy) with asymmetrical roots in this pot that was riding on this snail, and it ate the snail	遭遇する souguu suru = to encounter; 待遇 taiguu = treatment (of customer), salary and benefits

Chapter 2

富 3		^939. this **Foo**lish guy with a bad haircut has 豊富な hou**fu** na (abundant) 田 (rice paddies) like this one and also **To**mato fields, but he has to keep this napkin over this 口 (mouth) to avoid bragging about them, and he has to employ guards with **Tommy** guns to protect his 富 **tomi** (wealth)	富士山 fujisan = Mt. Fuji; 豊富な houfu na = abundant; 富む tomu = to be rich or prosper; 富 tomi = wealth
福 1		^661. this Shah had the 福 **fuku** (good luck) to find this 田 (rice paddy) in **Fuku**oka, but he doesn't want to talk about it before completing the sale, so he keeps this napkin over this 口 (mouth)	福 fuku = good luck, fortune; 幸福 koufuku = happiness
副 1		^1206. リ Ri might buy this 田 (rice paddy) in **Fuku**oka, but he has put this napkin over his 口 (mouth), since he's not allowed to talk about it yet, and a 副産物 **fuku**sanbutsu (byproduct) of his silence is that he seems to be sulking	副作用 fukusayou = a side-effect; 副産物 fukusanbutsu = a byproduct; 副住職 fukujuushoku = vice-priest
幅 1		^1185. this 巾 (Bo Peep) is a **Ha**waiian-**Bar**ber with this napkin over this 口 (mouth) which prevents her from complaining about the 幅 **haba** (width) of this 田 (rice paddy) next to her shop	幅 haba = width
頭 4		^93. this 口 (square) on the left represents an 頭 **atama** (head) that was removed from this platform on the right for repair after he was **A**ttacked-by-his-**Ma** (mother) at the **Zoo**, for stepping on her **Toe**s while she was **Cash**ing-a-check-for-a-**Ra**bbi, and he is resting on this stand on the left, covered by this napkin	頭 atama = head; 頭痛 zutsuu = headache; 牛五頭 ushi gotou = five cows; 頭文字 kashira moji = first character of a word
領 1		^1126. Pope **Leo** is missing his 頭 (head), and he is living in this 令 (house with a wobbly table) while he waits for the 大統領 daitou**ryou** (president) to find it	領土 ryoudo = territory; 大統領 daitouryou = president of a country
頼 3		^98. in response to an 依頼 i**rai** (request), a **Ta**ll-**Nor**wegian makes this 束 (promise) to a **Ta**ll-**Yorks**hire man to retrieve the head that is missing from this platform on the right, but first he wants to finish his **Rice**	頼む tanomu = to request, beg, ask, entrust to; 頼る tayoru = to rely on, depend on; 依頼 irai = request, commission
頑 1		^622. **Gan**dalf is a 頑固な **gan**ko na (stubborn) wizard who sometimes loses his 頭 (head), but he always 頑張る **gan**baru (does his best), since he operates from this reliable 元 (base)	頑張る ganbaru = to persevere, to do one's best; 頑丈 ganjou = sturdy, strong; 頑固な ganko na = stubborn
頂 3		^783. Margaret **Cho** used this 丁 (nail) to fasten an **I**talian-**Dark**-**Kimono** that she wore when she climbed to an 頂 **itada**ki (summit) to retrieve a 頭 (head) that a friend had lost, and then she performed an **I**talian-**Dance**	登頂する touchou suru = to climb to the summit; 頂 itadaki = peak, summit; 頂く itadaku = to humbly receive
額 2		^791. this 客 (customer), who is trying to get her 頭 (head) back, offers to exchange a 金額 kin**gaku** (sum of money), a **Gall**on-of-**Kool**-Aid, and some **Hebrew**-**Tiles** for it	金額 kingaku = a sum of money; 額 hitai = forehead
頬 2		^890. after this 夫 (husband) on the left lost his head from the platform on the right, he was disoriented and walked into these flames; in addition his 頬 **hoo** (cheeks) were stung by **Hor**nets, and Santa said "**Ho**-**Ho**" when he saw him	頬 hoo = cheek; 頬張る hoobaru = to stuff one's cheeks or fill one's mouth with food; 頬 hoho = cheek
頃 2		^96. this ヒ (hero) on the left, who is a **Coro**ner, is examining this headless guy on the right, who was found near a merry-**Go**-**Ro**und, because he has to conduct an autopsy	頃 koro = approximate time, often pronounced goro
題 1		^454. the 話題 wa**dai** (topic) of today's discussion is this headless boatman who will ferry me in this boat by the light of this lantern across the River Styx after I **Die**; this sounds like a real 問題 mon**dai** (problem)	話題 wadai = topic; 問題 mondai = problem
首 2		^56. this head with antennae, supported by a narrow 首 **kubi** (neck) above this 目 (body), peers over the wall of its **Cubi**cle and **Shoos** co-workers away	首 kubi = neck; 首相 shushou = prime minister
道 3		^349. this snail is carrying this 首 (neck) to its **Dor**mitory, which is infested with **Toa**ds, but there is a bottle-首 (neck) in this 道 **michi** (street) in **Michi**gan	道路 douro = road; 神道 shintou = a Japanese religion; 道 michi = street

Kanji		Mnemonic	Vocabulary
祖 3		^272. this Shah, who uses a **Jeep** to bring hay to his sheep, which say **Baa**, is praying at the tomb of his 祖父 __so__fu (grandfather), which resembles this 目 (**So**lar panel)	お祖父さん ojiisan = grandfather; お祖母さん obaasan = grandmother; 祖父 sofu = grandfather; 祖母 sobo = grandmother; 祖先 sosen = ancestor; 先祖 senzo = ancestor
組 4		^752. this **So**lar panel will provide electricity to mix the **Ko**ol-Aid for a **Cool-Mee**ting organized by a 組 **kumi** (group) of 糸 (skeet shooters) like this, who will shoot **Gummy** snacks into the crowd	組織 soshiki = organization; 組む kumu = to assemble, unite, pair, fold (arms or legs), make (a plan); 組 kumi (or gumi) = group, team, school class; 番組 bangumi = TV or radio program
助 3		^108. a **Tall-Su**perintendent of schools, whose name is **Jo**nah, uses the electricity from this tall solar panel to maximize this 力 (force), and he is able to 助ける **tasu**keru (help) people obtain **Su**perior-**Ke**ttles	助ける tasukeru = to help; 助手 joshu = assistant; 飲み助 nomisuke = heavy drinker
畳 3		^876. a **Tall-Talented-Me**diator came to this 田 (rice paddy), complimented our **Ta**rnished-**Ta**pestries, and asked **Jo**an of Arc to bring this solar panel out from under this 畳 **tatami** mat	畳 tatami = tatami mat; 畳む tatamu = to fold; 六畳 rokujou = six tatami mats
狙 1		^948. this woman on the left contorts her body as she tries to hide behind this solar panel, since a **Ne**gative-**Ra**scal 狙っている **nera**tte iru (is aiming) at her	狙う nerau = to aim
査 1		^860. after this 木 (tree) was allowed to grow over this solar panel, blocking its sunlight, **Sa**msung conducted a 調査 chou**sa** (investigation)	検査 kensa = investigation, examination; 調査 chousa = investigation, survey, analysis; 巡査 junsa = patrolman
呼 2		^428. I stood under this kneeling burning telephone pole, opened this 口 (mouth) and 呼んだ **yo**nda (called out) to say that a **Yo**gi was pouring **Co**la on the fire	呼ぶ yobu = to call out, to summon; 呼吸 kokyuu = breathing, respiration
宇 1		^897. in Uganda they place what look like bad haircuts like this over kneeling telephone poles like this to conceal detectors that search the sky for 宇宙人 **u**chuujin (space aliens)	宇宙 uchuu = universe, cosmos, space
芋 1		^1102. when I'm eating 芋 **imo** (potatoes) and see these plants sprouting from the top of this kneeling telephone pole, I experience positive **Emo**tions	芋 imo = potato; じゃが芋 jagaimo = Irish potato (usually written ジャガイモ)
側 3		^490. this man on the left tilts his hat back, but it is difficult to see this リ Ri, who is on the opposite 側 **gawa** (side) of this 貝 (money chest), and there is a **Gaudy-Wagon** 側に **soba** ni (close by), at which they are both able to buy **Soba** (noodles) **Soak**ed in broth	右側 migigawa = right side; 側に soba ni = close to; however, 側 soba is usually written そば; 側面 sokumen = side, aspect
測 2		^1031. リ Ri made a 推測 sui**soku** (assumption) that the man with a slanted hat was still standing on the opposite 側 (side) of this 貝 (money chest), but the man had left to attend a **Hacka**thon, and that allowed this water to pour in, so that the 貝 (chest) and リ Ri got **Soak**ed	測る hakaru = to measure or gauge (usually written 計る hakaru); 推測 suisoku = an assumption or guess; 予測 yosoku = a prediction or supposition
的 2		^45. this giant hook attaches to a 白 (white) **Te**chie with the 目的 moku**teki** (purpose) of dragging him offstage for having stepped on his **Ma**'s-(Mother's)-**Toe**s, causing her to shed this tear	目的 mokuteki = purpose; 自動的な jidouteki na = automatic; 的 mato = target
約 1		^225. this giant hook, made from a **Ya**k horn, grabs this 糸 (skeet shooter) and binds him to his 契約 kei**yaku** (contract), causing him to shed this tear	予約 yoyaku = reservation; 約束 yakusoku = promise
均 1		^988. at our **Kin**dergarten, we plow this 土 (soil) with this hook and grow plants like these, but our results are only 平均 hei**kin** (average)	平均 heikin = average, mean
匂 1		^949. on the lower left, this is a **Ne**onatologist who is a ヒ (hero) and who likes to fish with hooks like this, but she has a fishy 匂い **nio**i (scent)	匂う niou = to smell of; 匂い nioi = fragrance, scent; **Note:** niou and nioi can also be written 臭う and 臭い

天 2	^189. in the **Ama**zon, the 天 **ama** (sky) is like this **Ten**t over a 大 (big) forest	天の川 ama no gawa = Milky Way; 天気 tenki = weather
夫 4	^614. during the **Otto**man empire, an 夫 **otto** (husband) was often a 人 (person) with two pairs of arms like these who wasted **Foo**d and **Foo**lishly drank lots of **Boo**ze	夫 otto = husband; 夫婦 fuufu = married couple; 水夫 suifu = sailor; 大丈夫 daijoubu = all right
実 4	^195. this 夫 (husband) with an extra pair of arms is a **Jittery-Su**perstar with this bad haircut and a **Jee**p who raises 実の **jitsu** no (real) 木の実 kino**mi** (nuts) and has **Mea**ls with **Mino**taurs	実は jitsu wa = as a matter of fact; 実行 jikkou = practice, action, deed, implementation; 木の実 kinomi = nut, fruit, berry; 実る minoru = to bear fruit or ripen
漢 1	^197. Chinese 夫 (husbands) come from across this water, they are fond of these plants, they often wear glasses like these, they have 大 (big) ideas, and they print 漢字 **kan**ji (Chinese characters) on their **Can**dy wrappers	漢字 kanji = Chinese character
難 5	^198. **Nan**cy Pelosi's 夫 (husband is this 漢 (Chinese) person wearing these glasses who wants to assist some cats in this net, which is 難しい **muzukashii** (difficult) to penetrate; he wants to **Mu**zzle-**Zu**ckerberg's-**Cat**, which is inside the net, and help another **Gato** (male cat, in Spanish), a **Gata** (female cat, in Spanish), and his **Nie**ce-from-**Ku**wait	困難 konnan = difficulty; 難しい muzukashii = difficult; 有難う arigatou = thank you; 有難い arigatai = grateful, usually written ありがたい; 難い nikui = difficult, used as a suffix, usually written にくい
嘆 2	^792. I **Nag**-my-**Gu**ests to learn 漢 (kanji) like this, but they use 口 (mouths) to 嘆く **nage**ku (lament) the difficulty of the task and would rather work on their **Tan**s	嘆く nageku = to lament, grieve; 感嘆する kantan suru = to admire or be astonished at
登 3	^297. this TV set, which is covered by this napkin and these two bench hats, and is supported by these **To**es, is displaying a **Tor**toise that can 登る **nobo**ru (climb) like **Nobo**dy else	登頂する touchou suru = to reach the summit; 登山 tozan = mountain climbing; 登る noboru = to climb
発 3	^298. this **Ha**waiian guy with these lopsided legs who is wearing these two bench **Hat**s gives a 発表 **ha**ppyou (presentation) with this right leg extended, but the sock on this right foot has a **Ho**le in it	発表 happyou = presentation; 発明 hatsumei = invention; 出発する shuppatsu suru = to depart; 発作 hossa = attack or fit, e.g., 心臓発作 shinzou hossa = heart attack
祭 3	^377. as they admired this spinning nail under this flying carpet and this peaked roof, which is decorated for a **Sc**ientific 祭 **matsuri** (festival), a **Ma**tador-and-**Su**perman sat on a **Mat**-that-**Su**perman-had-**Re**paired and enjoyed seeing this three-legged bench and this pizza slice on the roof	祭日 saijitsu = holiday; 祭る matsuru = to worship; 祭 matsuri = festival
際 3	^379. this 祭 (festival) has a 国際 koku**sai** (international) flavor, with exhibits on ß (Greek) **Sc**ience and **Ge**eky-**Wa**rriors, and it is **Ke**enly-**Wa**tched by the world	国際 kokusai = international; 手際 tegiwa = skill; 際立つ kiwadatsu = to stand out or be conspicuous
察 2	^896. a **Sat**isfied-**Su**perintendent from the 警察 kei**satsu** (police) visited this 祭 (festival) where he received this bad haircut, and then he was *dis*satisfied and a little **Sad**	警察 keisatsu = police; 観察 kansatsu = observation; 察知する sacchi suru = to perceive
責 2	^772. this 貝 (money chest) belongs to a **Se**lfish-**K**ing who allows an owl to sit on this perch; the owl has **seki**nin 責任 (responsibility) for **Se**lling pardons and puts the proceeds in the money chest	責任 sekinin = responsibility; 責める semeru = to accuse, reproach, torment
積 3	^931. a **Se**lfish-**K**ing, who 積む **tsu**mu (accumulates) this 禾 (ripe grain) and wants to **Se**ll it, sets up this owl's perch on this 貝 (money chest) overlooking the grain so that an owl can take 責 (responsibility) for **Tsu**pervising (supervising) the sales	面積 menseki = area; 積極 sekkyoku = positive, progressive; 積もる tsumoru = to pile up (intransitive); 積む tsumu = to heap up, accumulate, load (transitive)

乗₂		^509. **Joan of Arc** is waiting because she wants to be a 乗客 **jou**kyaku (passenger) on this stream-lined vehicle in this 木 (tree) with a roof, but when she tries to 乗る **no**ru (board), there is **No** space	乗客 joukyaku = passenger; 乗る noru = to get aboard or ride
垂₂		^799. this streamlined 車 (car) without wheels, which has three projections on the front and on the back, is lying on its side with its hubcaps aligned 垂直に **sui**choku ni (vertically), and it is based on advanced **Sui**dish (Swedish) technology, allowing it to run on these hubcaps and to serve as a **Taxi**	垂直 suichoku = vertical, perpendicular; 垂れる tareru = to hang, droop, dangle, sag, lower
睡₁		^800. during 睡眠 **sui**min (sleep), I dreamed that these 目 (eyes) saw this streamlined **Sui**dish (Swedish) 車 (car) without wheels lying on its side with its hubcaps aligned 垂 (vertically)	睡眠 suimin = sleep
定₃		^455. **Joan of Arc** had a 予定 yo**tei** (plan) to mount this **Ta**ser on this foot and hide from **Sadda**m under this bad haircut	勘定 kanjou = bill, check, calculation; 予定 yotei = plan; 定年 teinen = retirement age; 定める sadameru = to decide or prescribe
是₂		^1035. a **Ze**alous policeman who has this taser mounted on this foot sits in this 日 (sun) and says that 是非とも **ze**hitomo (by all means) he will use this taser **Corre**ctly	是非とも zehitomo = by all means; 是等 korera = these (usually written これら)
提₁		^1156. this guy kneels in order to advise this policeman sitting in this 日 (sun) that the use of this **Ta**ser mounted on this foot is unethical and that he should 提出する **tei**shutsu suru (hand in) his resignation	提出する teishutsu suru = to hand in or submit; 前提 zentei = premise, prerequisite
旋₁		^913. the 方 (honorable person) on the left is a **Sen**ator who 旋回する **sen**kai suru (turns) to see this crutch and this taser mounted on this foot, suggesting that he needs to work on health care and law enforcement	旋回 senkai = rotation, turning
疑₂		^978. this ヒ (hero), this マ Ma (Mother), and this Native American chief are a family traveling in an Uber-Taxi-to-**Ga**mble, and they plan to hunt **Gee**se with this taser that they have mounted on Ma's 足 (foot), which some people 疑う **utaga**u (doubt) is a good idea	疑う utagau = to doubt or suspect; 疑問 gimon = a question or doubt; 疑惑 giwaku = a suspicion or doubt
務₂		^518. this マ (mother) who balances on this nail with her left hip extended, this dancer, and a guy with this 力 (force) are a family who work at a 事務所 ji**mu**sho (office) on the **Moon**, to which they ride on **Tsu**ki-(moon)-**To**boggans and then **tsuto**meru 務める (discharge their duties)	公務員 koumuin = public servant; 事務所 jimusho = office; 務める tsutomeru = to discharge one's duty
得₃		^706. this man on the left carries Eggs in one of his hats, he thinks that cooking them in this 日 (sun) above this dance floor with this 寸 (sunny guy) is Uber and **To**tally-**Coo**l, and they hope to make a 得 **toku** (profit) from this activity	得る eru = to get, earn, understand, receive something; あり得る arieru = it's possible (this can also be pronounced ariuru); なし得る nashieru = to be able to do (this can also be pronounced nashiuru); 得 toku = gain, profit; 得意 tokui = pride, strong point
樹₂		^1089. this 士 (man) stands under this (tree) and makes **Ju**ice and **Qui**che with 豆 (beans) like this, and he has inserted himself into this 村 (village) that contains 樹木 **ju**moku (trees)	樹木 jumoku = trees; 直樹 naoki = a man's given name
酎₁		^1099. this kneeling sunny guy on the right was drinking 酒 (sake) while **Che**wing this gum, but after he drank 焼酎 shou**chuu** (Japanese liquor) as well, he dropped the gum on the ground	焼酎 shouchuu = a Japanese spirit distilled from sweet potatoes, rice, etc.
尊₂		^1208. this 寸 (kneeling sunny guy) has dropped his gum, he's drinking this modified 酒 (sake, to which he's added these rabbit ears), he works for **Son**y, he eats **To**asted-**To**rtillas and he 尊敬する **son**kei suru (respects) everyone	尊重する sonchou suru = to respect or value; 尊敬する sonkei suru = to respect; 尊い toutoi = sacred, important, valuable

村 2	^131. my **Son** painted a **Mura**l which depicts a 村 **mura** (village), with this 木 (tree) on the left and this kneeling sunny guy on the right; the sunny guy has dropped this piece of gum on the ground	村長 sonchou = village mayor; 村 mura = village
対 2	^674. this sunny kneeling guy, who chews this gum, 対する **tai** suru (opposes) **Tire** stops like this because he thinks they cause damage, and he marks them all with X's like this, but a **Tsui**te (sweet) parking lot attendant 対決する **tai**ketsu suru (confronts) him about this practice	絶対に zettai ni = absolutely, by any means; 対 tsui = pair, e.g., 対の tsui no = in a pair
様 2	^136. **Yolanda** 様 **sama** (very honorable Yolanda) will jump down from this 木 (tree) to rescue this 王 (king) wearing rabbit ears who is drowning in this 水 (water) because she is a good **Samaritan**	様子 yousu = condition, state; お客様 okyakusama = very honorable customer
泉 2	^252. this **Senator** 白 (White) bathed in an 温泉 on**sen** (hot spring) which was supplied by this 水 (water) from a natural 泉 **izumi** (spring), where **Eagles-are-Zooming**	温泉 onsen = hot spring; 泉 izumi = spring (of water)
線 1	^228. this **Senator** 白 (White) is drowning in this 水 (water), and this 糸 (skeet shooter) shoots a 線 **sen** (line) to save him	線 sen = line; 二番線 nibansen = Track Number Two
暴 3	^1021. when **Boys** are **Ab**andoned, they go to **Bars-to-get-Kool**-Aid and then sit 共 (together) in this 水 (water) under this 日 (sun) and threaten to become 乱暴 ran**bou** (violent)	乱暴な ranbou na = violent or disorderly; 暴れる abareru = to become violent; 暴露 bakuro = exposure or revelation
爆 1	^1022. I was sitting in a **Bar-drinking-Kool**-Aid when a 暴 (violent) person set off a 爆弾 **baku**dan (bomb) and started this 火 (fire)	爆弾 bakudan = bomb; 原爆 genbaku = atomic bomb
膝 1	^861. this 人 (person) squeezed himself between this 木 (tree) and this 水 (water) and then fell onto his 膝 **hiza** (knees) by the light of this 月 (moon), and his wife said, "**He's-A** little drunk"	膝 hiza = knee, lap
途 2	^378. under this peaked roof and this stool, this spinning 丁 (nail) carried by this snail revolves like a **Tornado** 途中 **to**chuu (on the way) to the **Zoo**	途中 tochuu = on the way; 一途に ichizu ni = wholeheartedly
余 2	^637. I was sitting on this stool above this spinning 丁 (nail) under this peaked roof in the **Ama**zon, 途 (on the way) to pick up some **Yo**gurt, when I realized that we already had a 余分 **yo**bun (surplus) of milk products	余り amari = surplus, rest; 余計 yokei = excessive, all the more; 余分 yobun = surplus, extra
斜 2	^910. when **Nancy's-Nanny** encountered the **Shah**, she asked him for these two cans of food from this 斜めの **nana**me no (slanted) shelf, but he said that her request was 余 (excessive)	斜めの naname no = diagonal, oblique; 斜面 shamen = slope, slanting surface
除 3	^646. since this ß (Greek) guy is 余 (excessively) interested in Empress **Jo**sephine, he drives to see her but ends up parking in the **No-Zone**, from which a tow truck 除く **nozo**ku (removes) his **Jee**p	削除する sakujo suru = to delete, eliminate; 除く nozoku = to remove; 掃除する souji suru = to clean
徐 1	^904. this man with two hats told Empress **Jo**sephine that her spending on hats was 余 (excessive), advised her to 徐行する **jo**kou suru (slow down) her shopping and offered her one of his hats	徐々に jojo ni = gradually, step by step; 徐行する jokou suru = to slow down
塗 2	^1041. I have this 余 (spinning nail structure) that I use for 余 (surplus) **T**omatoes, and it's sitting on this pile of 土 (soil) and exposed to this water, but I want to 塗る **nu**ru (paint) the top so that it will look **New**	塗装 tosou = a coat of paint; 塗る nuru = to paint, plaster, spread, smear
橋 2	^139. we built a 橋 **hashi** (bridge) using **Hashi** (chopsticks) made of 木 (wood) like this in **Kyou**to, and it was so 高 (tall) that it reached this 天 (sky)	橋 hashi = bridge; 新橋 Shinbashi = Tokyo district; 歩道橋 hodoukyou = pedestrian bridge
高 3	^19. these two **Tall-Cans** have been stacked to help create this 高い **takai** (tall) **Courthouse** in **Dakha**, with this tire stop at the top	高い takai = high, tall, expensive; 高校 koukou = high school; 円高 endaka = rise in the yen's value

量 2		^1061. Pope **Le**o, who is this sincere guy wearing these bifocals, **Har**vests-**Ca**rnations, and when he has 大量 tai**ryou** (a large amount), he arranges them on this rug in this 日 (sun)	量 ryou = quantity; 大量 tairyou = large amount; 量る hakaru = to weigh
忘 2		^310. during a **War**-in-the-**Su**ez Canal, I was sitting at this 亡 (shaky table) on my patrol **Bo**at studying a map, and I 忘れた **wasu**reta (forgot) to take medication for this 心 (heart)	忘れる wasureru = to forget; 忘年会 bounenkai = end-of-year party
亡 4		^585. we bought this shaky table in **Na**rnia, but if we seat **Bo**no and **Mo**ses at it, it might fall on them, and they might 亡くなる **na**kunaru (die), causing our **Na**sty-**Ki**ng to get mad	亡くなる nakunaru = to die; 死亡 shibou = death; 金の亡者 kane no mouja = a money-grubbing person; 亡骸 nakigara = a corpse
忙 2		^586. this man on the left is an **Iso**lated-**Ga**mbler on a **Bo**at, he draws himself up to his full height like this as he tries to stabilize this 亡 (shaky table) without any help just before a card game, and this makes him feel 忙しい **isoga**shii (busy)	忙しい isogashii = busy; 多忙 tabou = very busy
望 3		^664. this 王 (king) has a 志望 shi**bou** (ambition) to have his **Bo**nes buried on this 月 (moon) after his 亡 (death), but when he summons scientists to his palace to discuss this, they park in the **No-Zo**ne next to the **Mo**at and get towed	希望 kibou = hope; 志望 shibou = ambition; 望み nozomi = hope, dream, wish; 所望 shomou = desire, wish, request
看 1		^1164. 三 (three) ノ (no)-nonsense people with good 目 (eyes) like this went to **Kan**sas to train as 看護婦 **kan**gofu (nurses)	看板 kanban = signboard; 看護婦 kangofu = female nurse
支 3		^26. this 士 (man) has spread a **Sh**eet on this 又 (table) at our 支社 **shi**sha (branch office), and he stands on it all day, trying to sell **Sa**lty-**Sa**ndwiches, ever since we sent him a **Tsu**itcase-(suitcase)-of-**Ca**ffeine	支社 shisha = branch office; 支える sasaeru = to support; 差し支え sashitsukae = hindrance, inconvenience, trouble
枝 2		^128. my **Ex**cellent-**Da**ughter works at this 支 (branch office), where she makes art from 枝 **eda** (branches) of this 木 (tree) amd delivers it to customers in a **Je**ep	枝 eda = branch; 爪楊枝 tsumayouji = toothpick
妓 1		^1121. this 女 (female) who is drinking **Co**la at this 支 (branch office) is a 舞妓 mai**ko** (apprentice geisha)	舞妓 maiko = an apprentice geisha, a dancing girl; 芸妓 geiko = 芸者 geisha
技 2		^1133. this **Ge**ek (an unfashionable or eccentric person) went down onto his knees at this 支 (branch office) after a **Wa**tercooler-got-**Za**pped by a power surge, since we had asked him to fix it, knowing that he has 技術 **gi**jutsu (skill) in repairing things	技術 gijutsu = technology, technique, skill; 競技 kyougi = competition; 技 waza = skill, technique
地 2		^503. this **Ji**ttery scorpion lives in this 土 (soil) under the 地 **chi** (ground), where it eats **Che**ese	地震 jishin = earthquake; 地下鉄 chikatetsu = subway
池 2		^504. this scorpion drank this water from the 池 **ike** (pond) on **Ike**'s (Eisenhower's) farm and ate his **Che**ese	池 ike = pond; 乾電池 kandenchi = battery
他 2		^505. ordinary men with flat hats ride in unmarked vehicles, but this 他の **hoka** no (other) man with this slanted hat rides in a **Ho**pped-up-**Ca**r marked with scorpion decals like this and hangs out in **Ta**verns, which is why he is considered a 他人 **ta**nin (outsider)	他の hoka no = another (undefined) object; 他人 ta'nin = other people, outsiders
施 3		^1067. this 方 (honorable person) uses this crutch and has to use a **Se**gway to get around, but she can **Ho**ld-the-**Do**or-for-a-**Co**-worker while he carries a **Sh**eep that has been stung by this scorpion into a treatment 施設 **shi**setsu (facility)	お布施 ofuse = alms or offerings (e.g., given to monks); 施す hodokosu = to donate, perform, give time; 施設 shisetsu = facility, institution, equipment
点 3		^29. **Ta**rzan removes this cannon from this **Tsu**itcase (suitcase) and uses this hot fire to 点ける **tsu**keru (ignite) it to signal the start of a **Te**nnis match	点てる tateru = to perform the tea ceremony; 点く tsuku = to turn on, intransitive; 点ける tsukeru = to turn on, transitive; 点 ten = score; 百点 hyakuten = 100 points
店 2		^493. this is a **Mi**serable 店 **mise** (store) under this lean-to, where people come to buy water pumped from this well by a 店員 **ten**'in (store clerk) who plays **Te**nnis	店 mise = store; 店員 ten'in = store clerk; 喫茶店 kissaten = coffee shop

Chapter 3

Kanji	Mnemonic	Vocabulary
京 2	^514. a Key-that-a-Yogi gave me fits this 口 (box, or house) on this 小 (small) hill in 京都 **kyou**to (Kyoto), which features a Ca**ve** under ground and this tire stop on the roof	京都 kyouto = Kyoto; 東京 toukyou = Tokyo; 京阪 keihan = Kyoto-Osaka
涼 2	^515. when this rain falls in this 京 (Kyoto), it gets 涼しい **suzu**shii (cool), and Pope **Leo** goes out to buy **Sou**venirs-from-the-**Zoo**	涼風 ryoufuu = a cool breeze; 涼しい suzushii = cool
景 2	^516. when this 日 (sun) shines above this 京 (Kyouto), the 景色 **ke**shiki (scenery) is lovely, and we drink from a **Keg** and eat **Ca**ke	景色 keshiki = view, scenery; 風景 fuukei = view, scenery, landscape
停 1	^627. this man on the left is a **Tai**lor who sits next to this 口 (box) containing thread, which is protected by this tire stop, tilts his hat back in order to see better, and sews with this 丁 (nail) under this roof at a バス停 basu**tei** (bus stop)	バス停 basutei = bus stop; 各駅停車 kakuekiteisha = local train
就 2	^974. I went to this 京 (Kyoto) in order to 就職する **shuu**shoku suru (find employment) and to buy a **Shoe** to put on this 犬 (dog)'s bent right leg, and I brought the footwear home in a **Tsui**tcase (suitcase)	就職する shuushoku suru = to find employment; 就く tsuku = to set out, obtain a position
蹴 1	^975. this 止 (hesitant) squarehead, who wears **Ke**ds (a brand of shoes), 蹴る **ke**ru (kicks) balls in this 京 (Kyoto), and this disabled 犬 (dog) chases them	蹴る keru = to kick; 蹴飛ばす ketobasu = to kick away, to refuse curtly
象 2	^906. when you go to see the 象 **zou** (elephant) **Show**, there is a **Zo**ne that you can visit where you will find 色 (colorful) 家 (houses) like this	対象 taishou = an object; 印象 inshou = impression; 象 zou = elephant
像 1	^907. this man on the left uses his 想像 sou**zou** (imagination) to think of a **Zo**ne where 象 (elephants) like this can be protected, and he tilts his hat back in order to search for one	想像 souzou = imagination; 仏像 butsuzou = image or statue of Buddha
家 5	^405. this **Ye**llow 豚 (pig) lives in this 家 **ie** (house), which is only a **Ca**bin, where people make Uber-**Chee**se, drink from **Ke**gs and grow **Ya**ms	家 ie = house; 家族 kazoku = family; 家 uchi = home; 田中家 tanakake = the Tanaka family; 公家 kuge= the Imperial Court; 家主 yanushi = landlord
隊 1	^726. a ß (Greek) 軍隊 gun**tai** (army) keeps a **Ti**ger as a pet in this 家 (house), and its ears protrude from the roof	軍隊 guntai = army; 兵隊 heitai = soldier
走 2	^450. after smoking **Hashi**sh in the **So**viet Union, this guy with soil on his feet like this could really 走る **hashi**ru (run)	走る hashiru = to run; 脱走 dassou = desertion, escape
徒 1	^451. after he finishes his **To**ast, a 生徒 sei**to** (student) 走 (runs) after his teacher on the left, who lends him one of his two hats, and they go to school	生徒 seito = student; 信徒 shinto = follower, believer
起 2	^452. if I'm camping in **O**hio and this 己 (snake) appears at the end of this foot, I 起きる **o**kiru (get up), grab my **Ke**ys and 走 (run)	起こる okoru = to occur, to happen; 起立する kiritsu suru = to stand up; 縁起 engi = omen, luck
越 4	^453. a **Co**ast Guardsman has 引っ越した hik**ko**shita (moved his residence), and he 走 (runs) with this hoe and this halberd, since he has to 越える **ko**eru (go across) town in order to **E**mbark with his **Co-Shi**pmates, carrying some **E**tchings-from-**Su**dan	越える koeru = to go across, to exceed (this can also be spelled 超える koeru); 越権 ekken = going beyond authority, abuse of confidence; 三越 Mitsukoshi = name of a department store; 超越する chouetsu suru = to stand out or transcend
超 2	^621. a 走 (runner) who is 超 **chou** (super) fast was **Cho**sen to carry this 刀 (sword) on this 口 (box) in a parade in **Co**lombia	超人的 choujinteki = superhuman; 超満員 chouman'in = overcrowded; 超える koeru = to go across, to exceed (this can also be spelled 越える koeru)
趣 2	^715. when I 走 (run) after alligators and 取 (take) their eggs, I often encounter **O**ld-**M**osquitoes-in-**Mucky** swamps and lose my **Sho**es, but this activity is my 趣味 **shu**mi (hobby)	趣がある omomuki ga aru = it's tasteful; 趣味 shumi = hobby, taste

経₄	^224. this 糸 (skeet shooter) gets some 経験 **kei**ken (experience) by shooting toward this dog groomer's 又 (table) on this 土 (soil) in **Kyou**to, where the dogs wear dog **Tag**s, sit in **Cage**s, and **Help** themselves to dog food	経文 kyoumon = sutras, scriptures; 経つ tatsu = to elapse or pass, referring to time; 経験 keiken = experience; 経る heru = to pass (time), to go through or by way of
軽₃	^289. a **Cat-on-the-Roof** of this 車 (car) watches as I sit at this 又 (table) on this 土 (soil) and eat **Carro**ts and **Cak**e; after I finish, my body still feels 軽い **karu**i (light)	軽い karui = light; 尻軽な shirigaru na = frivolous, of loose morals; 軽やか karoyaka = light, easy, minor; 軽自動車 keijidousha = a lightweight car
怪₃	^1024. this man on the left is an **Aya**tollah who is 怪しい **aya**shii (doubtful) whether this dog grooming business is suitable for his dog, and he draws himself up to his full height when he sees that this 又 (table) holds a **Keg** of beer, the room is full of this 土 (soil), and the owner is out flying **Ki**tes	怪しい ayashii = suspicious, doubtful; 怪我 kega = serious injury, often written けが; 怪物 kaibutsu = monster
径₁	^1097. this man on the left keeps dogs in **Cage**s, where he also stores his extra hats, above this 又 (dog groomer's table) on this 土 (soil), and the cages have narrow 直径 chok**kei** (diameters)	直径 chokkei = diameter; 半径 hankei = radius
雨₅	^261. in **Ame**rica, the amount of 雨 **ame** (rain) that is seen on window panes like these varies depending on the location, and the same is true in the **Ama**zon, over the **Salt-mines-of-Mexico**, and in Uganda and the **Yu**kon	大雨 ooame = heavy rain; 雨傘 amagasa = Japanese umbrella; 小雨 kosame = light rain or drizzle; 雨量 uryou = amount of rain; 梅雨 tsuyu = rainy season
雪₃	^262. since there are these three layers of ice on the ground, this 雨 (rain) must be 雪 **yuki** (snow), which some of our **Settlement's-Super** pioneers say is **Yu**cky, and that's why they are **Book**ing vacations in Florida	新雪 shinsetsu = new snow; 雪 yuki = snow; 吹雪 fubuki = snowstorm
雲₂	^264. these 二 (two) ム (cows) belong to Governor **Cuomo**, and the 雲 **kumo** (clouds) suggest that this 雨 (rain) is coming, so **Un**doubtedly he should put them back in the barn	雲 kumo = cloud; 雨雲 amagumo = rain cloud; 雲海 unkai = sea of clouds
漏₂	^740. **Moses** lived in this lean-to with a double roof, but after this 雨 (rain) penetrated inside and this water accumulated outside, he had to 漏らす **mo**rasu (let out) some water and, when that failed, **Row** his boat to safety	漏らす morasu = to let out, to omit; 漏電 rouden = electrical short circuit; 漏水 rousui = water leak
雰₂	^1201. this 雨 (rain) is going to fall any 分 (minute) now, but we are having **Fun**, and the rain won't spoil the 雰囲気 **fu**'inki (ambience) of our party, where already some **Foo**ls are staring at me	雰囲気 fu'inki (a colloquial way of saying fun'iki) = atmosphere, ambience, mood
当₃	^31. this is a tool with a three-pronged switch and three **Toe**s which will 当然 **tou**zen (naturally) divide objects in an 当たり前の **a**tarimae no (reasonable) way, and it can also be used to **Attach Art** to a bulletin board	本当 hontou = truth; 当り atari = per, apiece, used as a suffix (this can also be written 当たり); 手当て teate = medical treatment
急₂	^312. this **Cute** fish is **Isolated** from the others, but he has a lot of 心 (heart), and 急に **kyuu** ni (suddenly) he can 急ぐ **iso**gu (hurry)	急に kyuu ni = suddenly; 急ぐ isogu = to hurry
席₂	^496. before feeding the baby, I put him in this infant 席 **seki** (seat) on top of this stool belonging to a **Secretary** inside this lean-to, but he has a **Seki** (cough) and can't eat	寄席 yose = an entertainment hall; 席 seki = seat; 出席 shusseki suru = to attend; 座席 zaseki = the seat of a chair
座₂	^497. these two 人 (people) 座る **suwa**ru (sit) on this 土 (soil) in this lean-to, which is a restaurant in **Za**mbia, and they are served **Sou**p-and-**Wa**ter	座布団 zabuton = floor cushion for sitting; 座る suwaru = to sit on a zabuton
卒₃	^27. **Sot**tish-**Su**perman wore this double-breasted kimono to his 卒業 **sotsu**gyou (graduation), where he sang a **Solo** and **To**asted-**Zo**oey	卒業 sotsugyou = graduation; 卒倒する sottou suru = to faint or swoon; 何卒 nanitozo = I beg you, kindly, by all means

Kanji	Mnemonic	Meanings
寝 2	^372. this person with this bad haircut **ne**ru 寝る (sleeps) on this bench, but first she sits at this cloth-covered 又 (table), says her **Shin**to prayers and arranges this long hair to the left so that it won't get tangled in her **N**ecklace	寝室 shinshitsu = bedroom; 寝る neru = to go to bed, to sleep
帰 2	^566. as this リ Ri watches, a **Cat-E**nters his home, and he will 帰る **kae**ru (return), riding this elephant, with this long hair streaming to the left, to **K**ick the intruder out	帰る kaeru = to return home; 帰宅 kitaku = a return to one's home
婦 1	^1165. when this 婦人 **fu**jin (woman) with this long hair 帰 (returns), she will give **Foo**d to this elephant	婦人 fujin = woman; 看護婦 kangofu = female nurse; 新婦 shinpu = a bride
掃 2	^645. this guy on the left will 帰 (return home), 掃く **ha**ku (sweep) the house, get on his knees, and use **S**oap to 掃除する **sou**ji suru (clean) the floors in the front **H**all	掃除する souji suru = to clean; 掃く haku = to sweep; 掃き集める hakiatsumeru = to sweep up together
浸 3	^797. a **Shin**to priest with this long hair flowing to the left saw this water and realized that his shrine had 浸水した **shin**sui shita (flooded), but he was able to save a **Tsu**itcase (suitcase) and a **Hii**ta (heater) by placing them onto this table covered by a cloth	浸水する shinsui suru = to be flooded; 浸かる tsukaru = to be soaked in; 浸す hitasu = to soak, dip or drench
緑 2	^227. this 糸 (skeet shooter) fires at this 緑 **midori** (green) flag which is flying from a **Miniature-D**ory floating in this 水 (water), while Pope **Leo-drinks-Kool-Aid** and 緑茶 **ryoku**cha (green tea)	緑 midori = green; 緑茶 ryokucha = green tea
縁 1	^1023. this 糸 (skeet shooter) shoots at this 緑 (green) flag flying from this 家 (house), which he thinks is a good 縁起 **en**gi (omen), suggesting that **E**ntertainers are inside	縁起 engi = omen, sign of luck, origin, causation
録 1	^999. if you pay this 緑 (green) 金 (money) to a **R**obotic-**Kool**-Aid dispenser, it will mix some Kool-Aid for you, and it will also make a 記録 ki**roku** (record) of the transaction	記録 kiroku = a record; 録音 rokuon = a sound recording; 登録 touroku = registration, enrollment
親 3	^383. when 親 **oya** (parents) say **Oya**suminasai (good night) to their kids, they should 見 (look) at their beds and check for **Shin**y needles like this and for **Shii**te-**T**affy	親 oya = parent; 両親 ryoushin = parents; 親しい shitashii = intimate, close
新 4	^389. I use this 新しい **atara**shii (new) **N**eedle, which is **Shin**y, and this pair of **Ar**abian pliers to **Attack-R**ats	新潟 Niigata = a city on Honshu Island; 新聞 shinbun = newspaper; 新たな arata na = new, fresh; 新しい atarashii = new, fresh
売 3	^425. we 売る **u**ru (sell) this **U**gandan 士 (soldier) statue mounted on this roof with lopsided legs, which you may also **Buy** from our 販売機 han**bai**ki (vending machines) located near the **Ur**inals in the bathrooms	売る uru = to sell; 販売 hanbai = sales; 読売 Yomiuri = name of a newspaper
読 5	^432. if we want people to 読む **yo**mu (read) our books, we need to 売 (sell) them 言 (words) like this, and we can borrow some good words from a **Do**cument about **Do**es and **T**oads that attend **Yo**ga-**Mee**tings led by **Yo**gis	読書 dokusho = reading; 読解 dokkai = reading comprehension; 句読点 kutouten = punctuation marks; 読む yomu = to read; 読売 Yomiuri = name of a newspaper
志 3	^1145. this 士 (man) has this 心 **Kokoro**-(heart)-set-on-**Za**mbia, and in particular he has this **Kokoro**-set-on-**Za**mbian-**Sh**eep, since his 志望 **shi**bou (ambition) is to help **Sh**eep with heart problems	志す kokorozasu = to intend or aspire to; 志 kokorozashi = ambition, wish, goal; 志望 shibou = ambition, wish, goal
誌 1	^786. this 士 (man) uses 言 (words) well, and he writes articles about 心 (heart) problems in **Sh**eep for a 雑誌 zas**shi** (magazine)	雑誌 zasshi = magazine; 週刊誌 shuukanshi = weekly magazine
続 2	^226. **Z**ombies-in-**Ku**wait 売 (sell) skeets to this 糸 (skeet shooter), who stores them in his **Tsu**itcase-(suitcase)-at-the-**Zoo** and 続く **tsuzu**ku (continues) to fire them at this 士 (man) on this roof with lopsided legs	接続 setsuzoku = connection; 続く tsuzuku = to continue, intransitive

Kanji	Mnemonic	Readings
険₂	^196. this horizontally-placed **Ke**g-is-stuck-in-**Wa**ter inside this washing machine, and this roof is too 険しい **kewa**shii (steep) to allow this ß (Greek) guy named **Ken** to climb up, grab this handle and fix it	険しい kewashii = steep; 危険 kiken = danger
験₁	^382. **Ken** and this 馬 (horse) have arrived to visit Barbie, and he will 経験する kei**ken** suru (experience) this stuck-keg problem when he does his laundry	試験 shiken = examination; 経験 keiken = experience
検₁	^859. **Ken** climbs this 木 (tree) in order to 検査する **ken**sa suru (inspect) a keg which is stuck in this 大 (big) washing machine under this steep roof	検査 kensa = investigation, examination; 探検 tanken = exploration, expedition (this can also be written 探険 tanken)
将₂	^374. this 寸 (kneeling sunny guy) is a **Commie** (Communist), and after he picks up this gum, he wants to **Show** us life as it will be in the 将来 **shou**rai (future), after the Revolution, when all workers will have benches and barbecue grates like these	女将 okami = mistress, landlady, hostess, proprietress; 将来 shourai = the future
受₃	^577. when you 受ける **u**keru (take) a cooking exam in **U**ganda or in the **U.K.**, you must cook on this barbecue grate located on this rack on this 又 (table), on which you may also keep a bottle of lemon **Ju**ice for seasoning	受ける ukeru = to receive, to take or pass an exam or class; 受付 uketsuke = reception; 受験する juken suru = to take an exam
授₂	^578. this guy on the left is a 教授 kyou**ju** (professor) who drinks **Ju**ice in his 授業 **ju**gyou (class), and he kneels to watch his students 受 (take) an exam about the animals living in the **San-Diego-Zoo**	教授 kyouju = a professor; 授業 jugyou = class instruction; 授ける sazukeru = to give or grant
鶏₂	^754. in the **Niwa**-(garden)-a-鳥-**Tori** (bird) was barbecued by this 夫 (husband) on a grate like this, and it was a 鶏 **niwatori** (chicken) that he kept in a **Cage**	鶏 niwatori = chicken; 鶏肉 keiniku = chicken meat
瞬₂	^773. on certain 夕 (evenings) during the 年 (year), this 目 (eye) watches people take exams on knees like this to become **Master-Tata**mi makers and win barbecue grates like this as prizes, and if the eye looks away 瞬間的に **shun**kanteki ni (momentarily), some people may cheat, but if they are caught, they are **Shun**ned	瞬く matataku = to blink or twinkle; 瞬く間に matataku ma ni = in an instant; 瞬間 shunkan = moment; 瞬間的に shunkanteki ni = momentarily
揺₂	^852. this guy on the left was barbecuing some **Yu**cca on this grill in **Yo**semite when this 舌 (tongue) emerging from this 山 (mountain) began to talk, startling him so that he 揺れた **yu**reta (shook) and fell to his knees like this	揺れる yureru = to sway or shake; 動揺 douyou = uneasiness, agitation
君₂	^419. "Hey 君 **kimi** (you)! A **Cun**ning person has stabbed **Kimmy** with this trident, and this 口 (mouth) is wide open."	石田君 ishida kun = young man Ishida; 君 kimi = you (informal male speech)
群₃	^929. I saw 君 (you) in a **Mo**vie, painting a **Mural** of a 群れ **mu**re (herd) of 羊 (sheep) like this, and waving a **Gun**	群れ mure = herd, crowd, group; 群がる muragaru = to flock or throng; 群衆 gunshuu = group of people, crowd, mob
究₁	^112. when their 研究 ken**kyuu** (research) on this soaring **Cu**ban bird was done, the spirits of these 九 kyuu (nine) 研究者 ken**kyuu**sha (researchers) soared too	研究 kenkyuu = research or study
空₆	^248. this **Super**-sized **Albatross** with two lopsided legs, whose **Mood**-is-**Nasty**, rebounds from this 空いている **a**ite iru (vacant) 工 (crafted object) **Cooling** tower near the 空港 **kuu**kou (airport) in **Cara**cas and **Soar**s into the 空 **sora** (sky)	空く suku = to become empty; 空く aku = to become vacant; 空しい munashii = empty, fruitless; 空港 kuukou = airport; 空 kara = empty; 空 sora = sky; 夜空 yozora = night sky
窓₂	^311. when I was living in a **Mars-Do**me, I sat on a **So**fa, looked through a 窓 **mado** (window) and saw this ム (cow) bird with these two lopsided legs and this big 心 (heart)	窓 mado = window; 同窓会 dousoukai = reunion of graduates
突₃	^868. this soaring bird with two lopsided legs appeared 突然に **totsu**zen ni (suddenly), hovered over this 大 (big) guy and offered to **Tote-Su**perman's **Tsui**tcase (suitcase) to **To**lstoy's house	突然の totsuzen no = abrupt or sudden; 突き当たり tsukiatari = dead end; 突破する toppa suru = to break through

義 1		^1028. I attended a 講義 kou**gi** (lecture) about people who grasp halberds like this with 手 (hands) like this to attack **Gee**se and truncated 羊 (sheep) like this	義理 giri = moral debt, limited duty to the outside world; 義務 gimu = unlimited duty to the emperor, ancestors and descendants; 講義 kougi = lecture
議 1		^438. I 言 (spoke) at a 会議 kai**gi** (meeting) about the **Gee**se and the truncated 羊 (sheep) that are polluting our garden, and I held this halberd with this 手 (hand) to show that I was serious	会議 kaigi = meeting
我 3		^862. this reminds us of General **Wa**shington, who always kept this 手 (hand) on this halberd; he was a **Warrior-Re**bel who had the gift of **Ga**b, and he used to say, "我が国 **wa**gakuni (our country) is going to win"	我が国 wagakuni = one's country; 我 ware = self; 我ら warera = we; 我慢 gaman = patience, endurance, tolerance
素 4		^712. **Su**perman 素早く **su**bayaku (speedily) **So**ared up and dropped this owl's perch onto this 糸 (skeet shooter), but after pulling it off using **Shee**pdogs-and-**Ro**pes, we **So**ld it	素早い subayai = nimble, speedy; 素麺 soumen = fine white noodles; 素人 shirouto = amateur; 要素 youso = component, factor
緊 1		^732. this 糸 (skeet shooter) is trying to juggle this inoperable 巨 (swing set) and this 又 (table) at a **Kin**dergarten, and there is a lot of 緊張 **kin**chou (tension) among the onlooking teachers	緊張 kinchou = tension
喫 2		^192. this 大 (big) guy juggles this owl's perch and this 刀 (sword) while using this 口 (mouth) to smoke cigarettes that he made in **Ki**ev, using a **Kit**-that-he-got-from-**Su**perman, and he often smokes them at a 喫茶店 **ki**ssaten (coffee shop)	喫煙 kitsuen = smoking; 喫茶店 kissaten = coffee house
手 5		^23. when **Ted Shoo**ed away a **Ta**rantula at the **Zoo**, his **Ma** (mother) noticed that this 手 **te** (hand) has six fingers	右手 migi te = right hand; 派手 hade = flashy, colorful; 運転手 untenshu = driver; 下手 heta = unskillful; 上手 jouzu = skillful; 上手い umai = delicious, skillful (usually written うまい)
毛 3		^688. **Mo**ses was this right-wing guy, since the base of this 手 (hand) extends to the right, who wore **Ke**ds (a brand of shoes), slept under a 毛布 **mou**fu (blanket) with **Ge**ckos, and had lots of 毛 **ke** (hair)	毛布 moufu = blanket; 毛 ke = hair, fur, wool; 胸毛 munage = chest hair
妻 2		^237. my 妻 **tsuma** (wife) is this 女 (female) and a **Tsu**per-(super)-**Ma** (mother) who is a **Sci**entist, and she wears this cross and this comb in her hair	妻 tsuma = wife; 稲妻 inazuma = lightning; 夫妻 fusai = married couple
要 3		^238. because she has three eyes like these, this 女 (female) **Cana**dian-**Me**rmaid knows all of the 必要 hitsu**you** (necessary) things that her family 要る **i**ru (needs) to eat, such as **Yo**gurt and **Ee**ls	肝心要 kanjin kaname = the main point; 要するに you suru ni = in short; 必要 hitsuyou = necessary; 要る iru = to need
腰 2		^884. this 女 (female) with these three eyes had a **Cobra-bite-her-Shee**pdog on the 腰 **koshi** (waist), and she is wandering under this 月 (moon), searching for some **Yo**gurt which she says is 要 (necessary) for treating the wound	腰 koshi = low back, waist, hip; 及び腰 oyobigoshi = a bent back; 腰痛 youtsuu = low back pain
数 4		^639. this 女 (female), who lives in a **Ca**sino-**Zo**ne near a **Ca**lifornia-**Zoo**, carries this 米 (rice) to this dancer, who lives at the **Zoo**, and asks her to 数える **kazo**eru (count) the 数 **kazu** (number) of grains in it, since the dancer is **Su**per at 数学 **suu**gaku (mathematics)	数える kazoeru = to count; 数 kazu = number; 人数 ninzuu = number of people; 数字 suuji = numeral, figure; 数学 suugaku = mathematics
姿 2		^763. this 女 (female) has diabetes and worries about what will happen 次 (next) if her blood sugar gets too low, so she keeps **Sugar-Ta**blets handy, runs with her **Shee**p, and maintains a good body 姿 **sugata** (shape)	姿 sugata = figure, shape, condition; 容姿 youshi = appearance, looks; 姿勢 shisei = posture, stance
威 1		^915. this 女 (woman) with this flat hat enjoys tremendous 権威 ken'**i** (authority), and she finds it **Ea**sy to avoid 脅威 kyou**i** (threats) by hiding in this lean-to, with this big halberd by her side	権威 ken'i = authority

桜₁	^984. when this 女 (female) said that these three 桜 **sakura** (cherry) flowers were blooming on this 木 (tree), a **S**alaryman-turned-off-his-**Kuura**a (cooler, or air conditioner) and went out to see them	桜の花 sakura no hana = cherry blossoms; 夜桜見物 yozakura kenbutsu = going out to look at cherry blossoms in the evening
卵₂	^28. I will eat these two 卵 **tamago** (eggs) with **Tama**les-and-**Goat** cheese on my **Ran**ch	卵 tamago = egg; ゆで卵 yudetamago = boiled egg; 卵黄 ran'ou = egg yolk
迎₂	^358. these two **Moonies-Ca**ll out to potential donors as they ride on this snail to the station, where they will 迎える **mukae**ru (greet and welcome) a colleague **Gai**ly	迎える mukaeru = to greet/welcome; 歓迎する kangei suru = to welcome
印₂	^1046. a **Shi**ite-is-**Ru**shing up this ladder to get some **Ink** for this seal, which he'll use to add a 印 **shirushi** (symbol) to his document	印 shirushi = sign, symbol, indication; 矢印 yajirushi = arrow (on a map or sign); 印鑑 inkan = signature seal
節₃	^1048. we **Set**-up-a-**Su**per farm during the spring 季節 ki**setsu** (season) in order to grow 竹 (bamboo) like this to make 良 (good) seals like this one, and we also **Sell-Che**ese so that we can buy **Food-for-our-Sheep**	季節 kisetsu = season; 関節 kansetsu = joint (e.g., knee); 節約する setsuyaku suru = to economize; お節料理 osechi ryouri = food served during the New Year's holidays; 節 fushi = knot (wood), joint (body), melody
童₁	^1094. this sincere guy wearing bifocals, who is a 児童 ji**dou** (child), 立 (stands) as he eats a **Dough**nut	児童 jidou = child; 童話 douwa = fairy tale
飛₂	^574. when these two propellers start spinning like **Torna**dos, you will **Hear** a whirring sound, and 升 (one thousand and ten) 飛行機 hikouki (airplanes) will start to 飛ぶ **to**bu (fly)	飛ぶ tobu = to fly; 飛行機 hikouki = airplane
束₃	^99. this 木 (tree) is surrounded by **Tan**Bark, which sometimes gets **Soak**ed by sprinklers, and it was given these glasses and a 花束 hana**taba** (bouquet) as a reward for producing a **Tsu**itcase-(suitcase)-full-of-**Ca**shew nuts	花束 hanataba = a bouquet; 約束 yakusoku = promise, appointment; 束の間 tsuka no ma = moment
速₃	^359. this 束 (bundle), which resembles a 木 (tree) wearing glasses, is 速い **haya**i (fast), in spite of riding on a snail, since his glasses allow him to see far ahead and avoid obstacles; he is heading to Prince **Harry's-Yacht**, where he will **Soak** in the tub with **Sumi**su-san (Mr. Smith)	速い hayai = fast; 速達 sokutatsu = express mail; 早速 sassoku = immediately; 速やかな sumiyaka na = swift
早₄	^34. Prince **Harry's-Yacht** features this spinning top that was **Sold** in **Sa**pporo and spins 早い **haya**i (early) in the morning when no one is **Watch**ing	早い hayai = early; 素早い subayai = speedy, nimble; 早退 soutai = leaving early; 早速 sassoku = immediately, sudden; 早稲田 Waseda = a university in Shinjuku
草₂	^909. some **Cool-Saxophone** players got up 早 (early) and were playing music in this 草 **kusa** (grass) when a **Soldier** joined them	草 kusa = grass; 仕草 shigusa gesture, mannerism; 草原 sougen = grasslands, prairie; 草履 zouri = Japanese sandals
卓₂	^620. sitting at a 食卓 shoku**taku** (dining table) while drinking **Tap**-water-and-**Kool**-Aid, Tarzan thinks about how to fix this broken wagon wheel	食卓 shokutaku = dining table; 卓球 takkyuu = pingpong
七₃	^20. **Nancy's-Nanny** gave her 七 **nana** (seven) bites of **Sheep-Chee**se for taking a **Nap-with-Norma**	七つ nanatsu = seven items; 七時 shichiji = 7:00; 七日 nanoka = 7th of the month, seven days
宅₁	^21. in this 宅 **taku** (home), 七 (seven) **Tall**-people-are-**Coo**ped up under this roof, and they all wear slanted hats like this	お宅 otaku = your honorable home; 帰宅 kitaku = the return home
番₁	^328. someone has drawn a slash over the 米 (rice) at the top, suggesting that it is the 番 **ban** (turn) of this 田 (paddy) in **Ban**gladesh to supply rice	番 ban = a turn or number; 一番 ichiban = number one; 番号 bangou = number
翻₁	^1087. a guy from **Hon**duras wrote a book saying that these 羽 (feathers) from his country are 番 (number) one, and he 翻訳した **hon**'yaku shita (translated) his book into English	翻訳 hon'yaku = translation

Chapter 4

足 4	^449. I tripped on an **Ash**y ashcan and landed on this knee cap on my 足 **ashi** (leg), causing this taser to discharge, and the **Acci**dent 足りた **tar**ita (sufficed) to keep me from going to work at the **Tax** office; I then saw an Uber car and used this foot to kick water at it to **Soak**-the-Uber, but my efforts were 不足 fu**soku** (insufficient)		足 ashi = leg or foot; 足立 Adachi = a ward in Tokyo; 足りる tariru = to suffice; 不足 fusoku = insufficient; 満足 manzoku = satisfaction
皿 1	^567. I put left-over food on 皿 **sara** (plates) and cover it with **Saran** wrap taken from these three rolls		皿 sara = plate, dish or saucer; 大皿 oozara = large dish
血 4	^747. when I add this **Ketchup-to-the-Soup** in this 皿 (dish), or to my **Chee**rios, I'm careful not to spill it in my **Jeep** or on my **Ke**ds (a brand of shoes), and I'm reminded of the 血 **chi** (blood) that was formerly offered to the gods as part of religious rites		血圧 ketsuatsu = blood pressure; 血 chi = blood; 鼻血 hanaji = a nosebleed; 血管 kekkan = blood vessel
衆 1	^930. when I saw this 血 (blood) and these two swords in a 群衆 gun**shuu** (crowd), I ducked into a **Shoe** store and said TY (thank you) to the owner		群衆 gunshuu = group of people, crowd, mob
猛 1	^953. this woman on the left is contorting her body while anxiously approaching this 子 (child) named **Mo**ses, who is sitting in cold water in this 皿 (dish), trying to cope with a 猛暑 **mou**sho (heat wave)		猛暑 mousho = fierce heat, heat wave; 猛勉強 moubenkyou = studying extra hard; 猛犬 mouken = savage dog
盛 4	^1018. **Mo**ses was a **Sakkaa** (soccer) player, but now he and **Joan** of Arc are having a lot of 成 (success) like this with a factory that makes 皿 (dishes) like this and 盛んだ **saka**n da (is thriving), selling its products at **Sa**feway stores		盛る moru = to fill or pile up; 盛ん sakan = active, enthusiastic, energetic, thriving; 繁盛 hanjou = success or prosperity; 盛大 seidai = grandiose, pompous, thriving, successful
盆 1	^1167. I bought this 皿 (dish) at お盆 O**bon** (a Buddhist festival), and as a **Bonus** the seller helped me to 分 (understand) how it was made		お盆 Obon = a Buddhist festival devoted to ancestor worship; 盆踊り bonodori = a dance performed at Obon
塩 2	^60. a **Shii**te-**Or**phan who lives in this 土 (soil) helps us to break this 口 (block) of 塩 **shio** (salt) with this crutch, and after it trickles into this 皿 (bowl), we **En**joy eating it		塩 shio = salt; 塩分 enbun = salt content
温 3	^257. **Ata**turk-with-a-**Tan** is the **Own**er of this 皿 (bowl) of **N**utritious-**Koo**l-Aid which is getting 温かい **atata**kai (warm) under this 日 (sun) and emitting this water vapor		温かい atatakai = warm (water, etc.); 温度 ondo = temperature; 温泉 onsen = hot spring; 温もり nukumori = warmth
明 8	^154. when this 日 (sun) and this 月 (moon) shine together, the sky is 明るい **aka**rui (bright), and we can expect someone to come to the **Aca**demy 明日 **ashi**ta (tomorrow) and give an **Ash**y ashtray, **A-Key**, **A-Ke**ttle and some Anchovies to **May**, our **Mean** cat, who will **Meow** in response		明るい akarui = bright, cheerful; 明日 ashita = tomorrow; 明らかな akiraka na = obvious; 有明 ariake = dawn; 明日 asu = tomorrow; 説明 setsumei = explanation; 明朝体 minchoutai = Ming dynasty, or Ming-style font; 明日 myounichi = tomorrow
艦 1	^737. this 船 (boat) is equipped with two **Cann**ons firing these crutches and shells, and it appears to be a 軍艦 gun**kan** (battleship) fighting over this 皿 (dish)		軍艦 gunkan = warship, battleship
百 3	^47. Himalayan-**Yak** owners traveled in 百 **hyaku** (100) **O**range limousines like this as they ate **Heal**ing-**Yam**s		百 hyaku = 100; 三百 sanbyaku = 300; 八百 happyaku = 800; 八百屋 ya'oya = green grocer; 百科 hyakka = many objects
宿 3	^491. 百 (one hundred) guys with bad haircuts like this showed up as this man at the lower left tilted his hat back in order to examine his 宿題 **shuku**dai (homework); the guys, who are wearing **Shoes**-from-**Ku**wait, are staying at the 宿 **yado** (inn), in the **Yard**-by-the-**Door**, and next to the **Juke**box		宿題 shukudai = homework; 宿 yado = inn; 新宿 Shinjuku = a ward in Tokyo
勤 2	^517. this sincere guy wearing these glasses rides on a **Tsu**ki-(moon)-**To**boggan to the place where he 勤めている **tsuto**mete iru (is being employed), and he expends this 力 (force) taking care of these plants at a moon **Kin**dergarten		勤める tsutomeru = to be employed; 通勤する tsuukin suru = to commute to work

Kanji	Story	Vocabulary
会 4	^293. the **Kai**ser wants to buy these 二 (two) ム (cows) under this peaked roof, but first he will 会う **a**u (meet) a **Gu**ide who is an **E**xpert on cows and who will take him to a 会議 **kai**gi (meeting) with the seller in **A**frica	会議 kaigi = meeting; 運送会社 unsougaisha = moving company; 会得する etoku suru = to grasp, understand, master; 会う au = to meet someone
絵 2	^223. this 糸 (skeet shooter) will attend this 会 (meeting) to shoot paint at a 絵画 **kai**ga (painting) of the **Kai**ser, and he hopes to produce an **E**xcellent 絵 **e** (picture)	絵画 kaiga = painting; 絵本 ehon = picture book
転 2	^285. these 二 (two) ム (cows) were struck by this 車 (vehicle), which is a 自転車 jitensha (bicycle), after its rider had a **Coro**nary (heart attack) in **Ten**nessee	転ぶ korobu = to fall; 自転車 jitensha = bicycle
伝 3	^345. these 二 (two) ム (cows) collided with this man, even though he had tilted his hat back to improve his vision, and he sustained a **Den**tal injury, his **Tsu**it-(suit)-was-**T**attered, and his **Tsu**itcase-(suitcase)-was-**Da**maged, but he delivered his 伝言 **den**gon (message) anyway	伝言 dengon = message; 伝える tsutaeru = to convey or hand down; 手伝う tetsudau = to help
芸 1	^1056. I'm playing a computer **G**ame in which I teach these 二 (two) ム (cows) to perform 芸 **gei** (tricks) with plants like this	芸 gei = art or craft, animal trick; 芸術 geijutsu = art; 芸者 geisha = female entertainer
汚 4	^467. this kangaroo from **O**osutorariya (Australia) jumps away from this water which is 汚水 **o**sui (sewage), causing me to spill **Y**ogurt-made-from-**Goat**'s milk and 汚す **yogo**su (soil) my clothes; the kangaroo also bumps into a **Kit**ten-**Ana**tomy book and gets it 汚い **kitana**i (dirty), and it spills a **Kega** (keg of) beer	汚水 osui = sewage; 汚す yogosu = to soil; 汚い kitanai = dirty; 汚す kegasu = to sully or disgrace
写 2	^468. this kangaroo flooded the darkroom under this roof while trying to 写す **utsu**su (copy) some 写真 **sha**shin (photos) of people **U**tilizing-**S**upermarkets, which he wanted to take back to his **Sha**bby house, and now he's standing in this water	写す utsusu = to copy; 写真 shashin = photograph; 青写真 aojashin = blueprint
号 1	^470. this 口 (mouth) at the top represents a 番号 ban**gou** (number, i.e., the number "0") which this kangaroo wears on his uniform, and he scores **Goa**ls	番号 bangou = number; 信号 shingou = traffic light
与 2	^1070. after this kangaroo got **Att**acked, it jumped into this pool of **Y**ogurt, so let's 与える **ata**eru (give) it credit for quick thinking	与える ataeru = to give, award, cause; 賞与 shouyo = reward, bonus
考 2	^469. this **Kanga**roo is this 者 (person) who 考える **kanga**eru (thinks) about how to **Co**pe with the cuts that he gets from these scissors, but he continues to play with them	考える kangaeru = to think; 思考 shikou = consideration, thought
老 3	^1065. this **O**ld 者 (person) is a 老人 **rou**jin (elderly person) who has ヒ (hearing loss) and employs **Ro**bots to prepare her **Fo**od	老いる o'iru = to grow old; 老人 roujin = elderly person; 老ける fukeru = to age or lose one's youthful appearance
鬼 2	^1168. this 鬼 **oni** (devil) wears this pointy hat and these bifocals, stands on these lopsided tentacles, and is **Own**ing this ム (cow) which he plans to **Kee**p	鬼 oni = devil, cruel person; 殺人鬼 satsujinki = killer, cutthroat
魅 1	^1169. this 鬼 (devil) is looking into this 未 (future) to try to determine what his next **Mea**l will be, a question that he finds 魅力的 **mi**ryokuteki (fascinating)	魅力 miryoku = attractiveness, charm; 魅力的 miryokuteki = fascinating, charming
送 2	^348. this person wearing this hat with two antennae is an **Occ**ultist who rides on this snail while she 送る **oku**ru (sends out) **S**ordid electronic messages	送る okuru = to send, or to drop off; 放送 housou = broadcast
咲 2	^193. this occultist, who wears this hat with two antennae, uses this 口 (mouth) to ask **Z**achory to harvest some flowers that have 咲いた **sa**ita (blossomed) and put them in our **S**alads	早咲き hayazaki = early blooming; 咲く saku = to blossom
関 3	^701. this occultist, who wears this hat with two antennae, is thinking of passing through this gate in order to pursue a 関係 **kan**kei (relationship) in **Kan**sas, but she has a **Seki** (cough) and finally decides to **C**all-a-**Ca**b and return	関係 kankei = relationship; 関所 sekisho = checkpoint; 関わる kakawaru = to be involved
割 4	^562. this リ Ri plays a **S**axophone while this guy with this bad haircut on the left, who is a **Warrior**, carries this owl's perch and **Wal**ks on this 口 (tomb) with his **C**ats, trying to 割る **wa**ru (break) the tomb	時間を割く jikan wo saku = to make time for; 割に wari ni = relatively; 割る waru = to break glass and wood, transitive; 分割する bunkatsu suru = to divide or split

風 5	^479. when a 台風 tai**fuu** (typhoon) occurs, it creates 風 **kaze** (wind) which may blow these **Foo**lish hat-wearing 虫 (insects) into our **Foo**d or damage the **Caze**tte (cassette) collection from **Kaza**khstan which we keep in the **Car**	台風 taifuu = typhoon; 扇風機 senpuuki = an electric fan; 風呂 furo = hot bath; (春)風 shunpu = a spring breeze; 風 kaze = wind; 風向き kazamuki = wind direction; 風邪 kaze = upper respiratory infection
凧 1	^767. 巾 (Bo Peep) eats **Taco**s while she stands under this wind and flies her 凧 **tako** (kite)	凧 tako = kite
嵐 1	^1128. an **Ara**b-who-is-a-**Shi**ite visited this 山 (mountain), and was caught in an 嵐 **arashi** (storm) with strong 風 (winds) like this	嵐 arashi = storm
南 2	^388. in this weather station with this antenna, which is located near the **Mina**ret-of-**Mic**key's mosque, this compass needle points 南 **minami** (south), rather than north, according to his **Nan**ny	南 minami = south; 南米 nanbei = South America
厳 3	^902. **Gen**ghis, who has big 耳 (ears) like this, lives with this dancer under this lean-to, where he bounces on this diving board, and they **Keep-Bee**s like these up on the roof, which they frighten with a **Gon**g, since they are 厳しい **kibi**shii (strict) with them	厳格な genkaku na = stern, strict; 厳しい kibishii = stern, rigid, strict; 荘厳な sougon na = solemn
教 3	^187. **OSHA-In**forms and 教える **oshi**eru (teaches) this 子 (child) and this dancer in **Kyou**to that they should stay out of this 土 (soil), not play with these scisssors and not eat **Old-Soy** sauce	教える oshieru = to teach; 教室 kyoushitsu = classroom; 教わる osowaru = to be taught
昨 3	^41. 昨日 **ki**nou (yesterday) someone used this serrated axe to **Ki**ll a **Tor**toise and then left its body in a **Sack** out in this 日 (sun)	昨日 kinou = yesterday; 一昨日 ototoi = the day before yesterday, usually written おととい; 昨晩 sakuban = last night
作 3	^482. this man on the left is tilting his hat back in order to examine the blade on this serrated axe that he carried in his **Tsu**itcase-(suitcase)-from-**Ku**wait to 作る **tsuku**ru (make) a 作品 **saku**hin (creation), which he keeps in a **Sack** whenever he is playing the **Sa**xophone	作る tsukuru = to make; 作文 sakubun = written composition; 作家 sakka = writer; 発作 hossa = attack or fit, e.g., 心臓発作 shinzou hossa = heart attack
段 1	^559. a **Dan**cer uses these 階段 kai**dan** (stairs) to climb up and down and give food to this π (yak) on this 又 (table)	階段 kaidan = stairs; 段々 dandan = gradually; 普段 fudan = usual, every day
暇 2	^803. this 日 (sun) shines on this ladder in the **Hima**layas, which we climb to place this **C**arton of コ (corn) on this 又 (table), when we have 暇 **hima** (free time)	暇 hima = free time; 休暇 kyuuka = vacation, day off
興 3	^693. in **Kyou**to you can find this store which is raised on two legs, with 同 (identical) 段 (stairs) on both sides to the top of the building, where there are **Co**la machines, and since I have a 興味 **kyou**mi (interest) in **Old-Coa**ts, I buy them there	興味 kyoumi = interest; 興奮 koufun = excitement; 興す okosu = to revive, to raise up
付 5	^132. this man on the left, whose name is **Put**in, tilts his hat back to speak to this **Foo**lish kneeling sunny guy who accompanied him to the **Zoo**, where this piece of gum 付(いた) **tsu**ita (adhered), first to their **Tsu**it**Ke**is (suitcase) and later to their **Tsu**its (suits)	貼付 tenpu = pasting; 寄付 kifu = donation; 事付け kotozuke = message; 植付 uetsuke = planting; 付く tsuku = to adhere, intransitive
符 2	^133. this man with a slanted hat, whose name is **Put**in, **Foo**lishly clamped some 切符 kip**pu** (tickets) together using these 竹 (bamboo) clamps and this gum, and now they 付 (adhere) to each other	切符 kippu = ticket; 護符 gofu = talisman, charm
腐 2	^722. we were eating a **Cool-Sa**lad in this restaurant when we noticed that this 肉 (meat) that was 付 (adhering) to this ceiling was beginning to 腐る **kusa**ru (spoil), and we warned the owners about their **Foo**d storage practices	腐る kusaru = to rot, spoil, be corrupted; 豆腐 toufu = bean curd
府 1	^1004. our 政府 sei**fu** (government) stores **Foo**d under lean-tos like this, but the food tends to 付 (adhere) together when it rains	政府 seifu = government; 京都府 kyoutofu = Kyouto prefecture

酒 4	^465. while I was drinking 酒 **sake** made from this water and eating **Qui**che in this basement in this house, a **Sa**laryman-opened-a-**Ke**g on the 西 (west) side, so I put on my **Sho**es and went outside to play **Sakkaa** (soccer)	お神酒 omiki = sake offered to the gods; 酒 sake = alcoholic beverage; 冷酒 hiyazake = cold sake, but this is usually pronounced "reishu"; 日本酒 nihonshu = Japanese sake; 酒屋 sakaya = liquor store; 居酒屋 izakaya = a bar or pub
配 3	^466. a **Cool-Bar**maid named **Hei**di has brought a **Pie** to this house containing 酒 (sake), but she sees this 己 (snake) outside, and she 心配する shin**pai** suru (worries) that it may bite	配る kubaru = to deliver, distribute, hand out; 宅配便 takuhaibin = home delivery; 心配する shinpai suru = to worry
昼 2	^49. since it gets so hot at 昼 **hiru** (noon), the **Heat-has-Ru**ined this gas pump on a platform under this double roof, where I **Chew** my 昼食 **chuu**shoku (lunch)	昼 hiru = noon; 真っ昼間 mappiruma = broad daylight; 昼食 chuushoku = lunch
届 2	^74. the 由 (reason) that I can't 届ける **todo**keru (deliver) this unit is that the **Tokyo-Do**me collapsed on me, I'm stuck under this double roof, and I'm drinking water from a **Tokyo-Do**me-**Ke**ttle	届ける todokeru = to deliver, transitive; 届 todoke = registration, notification
民 2	^375. this leaning woman, who is a 市民 shi**min** (citizen), is squeezed into this lean-to with a double roof, which is why she is **Mean** and complains about **Taxi-Meters**	市民 shimin = citizen; 民 tami = the people, a nation
眠 2	^376. this 目 (eye) of this 民 (citizen) is wide open, and she can't 眠る **nemu**ru (sleep), because her **Neighbors'-Mu**sic affects her rest, and this makes her **Mean**	眠る nemuru = to sleep; 睡眠を取る suimin wo toru = to get some sleep
泥 2	^819. although she is a 尼 (nun), **Dorothy** went on a **Da**te with the Scarecrow under this reinforced lean-to, but he was this ヒ (heel) who threw this water at her and, on top of that, he was a 泥棒 **doro**bou (thief)	泥棒 dorobou = thief; 泥水 deisui = muddy water, red-light district; 泥酔する deisui suru = to get dead drunk
尻 1	^827. when these 九 (nine) **Sheep-Rea**lized that it was raining, they all sheltered their 尻 **shiri** (buttocks) under this heavy-duty lean-to	お尻 oshiri = buttocks
局 1	^867. the **Kyoto-Kool-Aid** club is located in this double-roofed lean-to next to the 郵便局 yuubin**kyoku** (post office), and this 可 (cute) person is inside it	郵便局 yuubinkyoku = post office; 結局 kekkyoku = after all
殿 2	^1080. a **Den**tist plans to enlarge this lean-to with a double roof until it's a 宮殿 kyuu**den** (palace) where she can live 共 (together) with this π (yak) on this 又 (table), and she says that this is all **To**tally-**Nor**mal	宮殿 kyuuden = palace; 殿様 tonosama = daimyo, feudal lord
居 2	^809. I have an 古 (old) 住居 juu**kyo** (residence) in **Kyo**to, which is this lean-to with a double roof, and my life is **Easy**	住居 juukyo = dwelling; 居間 ima = living room
告 2	^429. this 口 (mouth) speaks 広告 kou**koku** (advertisements), and the person above it holds out this shield to demonstrate that drinking **Co**ke, and wearing the right **Tsu**it (suit), can shield us from unpopularity	広告 koukoku = advertisement; 告げる tsugeru = to inform
造 2	^1108. this person with this big 口 (mouth), is traveling on this snail with a **Tsu**itcase-(suitcase)-from-**Ku**wait and holding out this shield as he heads to the Canal **Zo**ne, where he plans to 製造する sei**zou** suru (manufacture) shields like this one	造る tsukuru = to create or make (usually written 作る); 製造 seizou = manufacture
先 3	^422. this **Sen**ator, who used to be a 先生 **sen**sei (teacher), is standing on this platform with these lopsided legs at the **Ma**ll and holding this shield, which he keeps in a **Sa**ck-that-he-bought-in-**In**dia, to shield himself from accusations about things that happened 先ほど **saki**hodo (a while ago)	先生 sensei = teacher; 先ず mazu = first of all; 先 saki = tip, point, first, future; 先に saki ni = ahead, formerly, beyond
洗 2	^423. this **Sen**ator, who returned from Saudi **Ara**bia 先 (previously), where there is a water shortage, stands on this platform with these lopsided legs, holds this shield out to this water on the left and 洗う **ara**u (washes) it	洗濯 sentaku = laundry; 洗う arau = to wash
光 4	^448. after the **Hick-Karl Meets** his friend the **Hick-Carrie**, who is feeling **Cold**, they light this fire that 光る **hika**ru (shines) on this platform on lopsided legs	光る hikaru = to shine, glitter, stand out; 光成 mitsunari = a male name; 光 hikari = light; 日光 nikkou = sunlight

金 6	^301. my teacher at this **Kin**dergarten drinks **Gin**, she knows 全 (everything) about the **Con**go, she uses a **Gon**g to tell us when recess is finished, and she gave me these two pieces of お金 u**kane** (money) that are lying on the ground floor to buy some **Can**adian-**E**ggs and **Can**aries	金属 kinzoku = metal; 賃金 chingin = wages; 金剛力 kongouriki = superhuman strength; 黄金 ougon = gold; お金 okane = money; 金物 kanamono = hardware
銀 1	^302. I went to the 銀行 **gin**kou (bank) to get this 金 (money) for some 良 (good) **Gin**	銀 gin = silver; 銀行 ginkou = bank
鉄 2	^304. I paid this 金 (money) for this 大 (big) 牛 (cow) in **Te**xas, and it needed a **Te**tanus-shot-which-**Su**perman gave it via a 鉄 **tetsu** (iron) needle	鉄砲 teppou = gun; 豆鉄砲 mamedeppou = peashooter; 地下鉄 chikatetsu = subway
銭 2	^744. our **Sen**ator thought that **Zen**-was-**Ea**sy and that one doesn't need 金 (gold) like this and halberds like this to attain enlightenment, so he didn't bring any 金銭 kin**sen** (money) to his first temple visit	金銭 kinsen = money; 一銭 issen = 0.01 yen; 小銭 kozeni = coin, small change
釘 1	^825. I paid 金 (money) for 釘 **kugi** (nails) like this to build a shed for my **Cool-Gee**se	釘 kugi = nail or peg; 釘付けになる kugizuke ni naru = to be unable to take one's eyes from
針 2	^1138. Prince **Harry** paid this 金 (money) to a **Shin**to priest for 十 (ten) 針 **hari** (needles)	針 hari = needle; 方針 houshin = a policy, principle or direction; 秒針 byoushin = the second hand on a clock
綿 2	^1189. this 巾 (Bo Peep) **Walks-Tal**l, and all of the **Men** admire her outfit made from this 白 (white) 綿 **men** (cotton) 糸 (thread)	綿 wata = cotton; 綿 men = cotton; 木綿 momen = cotton; 綿密 menmitsu = detailed, meticulous
止 4	^173. we put up this barrier so that cars will 止まる **to**maru (stop) before they run into our **To**mato and **Ya**m farm, but **Sheep** can enter through the side **Door**	止める tomeru = to stop, transitive; 止める yameru = to stop doing something, to give up; 中止する chuushi suru = to cancel; 通行止め tsuukoudome = road closed
正 4	^174. if a car 止 (stops) and everything is 正しい **tada**shii (correct), a **Taxi-Da**rts up, and the driver places this cap on top of this 止 (barrier), **Show**ing that it is **Sa**fe for the car to proceed to the **Massa**ge parlor	正しい tadashii = correct; 正直な shoujiki na = honest; 正確 seikaku = precise, accurate; 正夢 masayume = a dream come true
東 2	^508. in a **Hideous-Gash** on the 東 **higashi** (east) side of this 木 (tree) in 東京 **tou**kyou (Tokyo), there is a family of tree **Toa**ds that watches this 日 (sun) rise	東 higashi = east; 東京 toukyou = Tokyo
練 2	^229. this 糸 (skeet shooter) in Wyoming 練習 **ren**shuu suru (practices) shooting 東 (east), since that's where its enemy the **Rent** collector lives in Nebraska	練習する renshuu suru = to practice; 練る neru = to knead or plan carefully
易 3	^402. a **Yankee-Saw** these streamers under this 日 (sun) and told Edward-the-King that life is 易しい **yasa**shii (Easy)	易しい yasashii = easy; 貿易 boueki = trade; 安易な an'i na = easy
場 2	^403. **Joan** of **Arc** has a **Bar** on this patch of 土 (soil) which is a nice 場所 **ba**sho (place), and her life is 易 (easy)	会場 kaijou = site of an event; 場所 basho = place
湯 2	^404. in the **Yu**kon, **To**ads love this cool water and have 易 (easy) lives, but they don't like 湯 **yu** (hot water)	お湯 oyu = honorable hot water; 熱湯 nettou = boiling water
揚 2	^768. this guy has to kneel for his **A**gricultural research in **Yo**semite, but his work is 易 (easy), and he often finds time to 揚げる **age**ru (fly) kites	揚げる ageru = to hoist, to fly a kite, to fry in deep fat; 抑揚 yokuyou = intonation
陽 1	^891. if you live in β (Greece), spend a lot of time in the 太陽 tai**you** (sun) and eat a lot of **Yo**gurt, life seems 易 (easy)	太陽 taiyou = the sun; 陽性の yousei no = cheerful, positive
湾 1	^1016. when I visited 台湾 Tai**wan** and **Wan**dered over to this water, I saw this four-legged hen flying over this 弓 (bow)	湾 wan = gulf, bay; 台湾 taiwan = Taiwan
弓 2	^1044. I 引 (pulled) the string on this 弓 **yumi** (bow) at a **You**th-**Mee**ting when I visited **Cu**ba	弓 yumi = bow; 弓道 kyuudou = archery

白 3	^44. this ray of light from this 日 (sun) shines on 白い **shiro**i (white) **Shee**p-that-**Roa**m at a **Shee**p-**Ran**ch near the **Harbor-in-Ku**wait	白い shiroi = white; 白髪 shiraga = grey or white hair; 白髪 hakuhatsu = grey or white hair; 潔白 keppaku = innocence
泊 2	^46. I 泊まつた **to**matta (spent the night) in a 白 (white) hotel by this water near the **Harbor-in-Ku**wait and listened to the croaking of the **To**ads	二泊 nihaku = a two-night stay; 三泊 sanpaku = a three-night stay; 泊まる tomaru = to stay overnight
習 2	^472. a 白 (white) bird was using these feathers to 習う **nara**u (learn) to fly when a **Na**sty-**Ra**scal threw a **Shoe** at it	習う narau = to learn; 練習 renshuu = practice; 習字 shuuji = calligraphy practice
皆 3	^597. 皆 **mina** (everyone), including these two ヒ (heroes), has brought a **Ki**te and is sitting on this 白 (white) snowy hill in **Mina**sota (Minnesota), or **Minna**sota, as some spell it	皆目 kaimoku = utterly, alto-gether; 皆 mina = everyone; 皆様 minnasama = very honorable everyone
階 1	^598. this ß (Greek) guy, who lives on the 三階 san**kai** (third floor) of our building, is bringing a **Ki**te to these two seated ヒ (heroes) on a 白 (white) hill	階段 kaidan = stairs; 四階 yonkai = the fourth floor
激 2	^1147. when we lived in a 白 (white) house by this water, we had a 過激 ka**geki** (aggressive) **Ha**waiian-**Gue**st who was a dancer like this and whom we thought was an 方 (honorable person), but she stole our **Guest-Key**	激しい hageshii = fierce, tempestuous, crowded (traffic), frequent (change); 過激 kageki = aggressive, radical
寿 3	^607. **Su**perman saw this 寸 (sunny guy) sitting in the shade of this elongated owl's perch, and he suggested that they pick up this gum and go get some 寿司 **su**shi with some **Ju**ice, but the sunny guy was practicing for his **Koto**-(Japanese harp)-recital-at-**Buck**ingham Palace	寿司 sushi = raw fish slices on rice; 寿命 jumyou = lifespan, longevity; 寿 kotobuki = congratulations, felicitations (given at weddings, New Year's, etc.)
帽 1	^243. this 巾 (Bo Peep) is trying to decide between these two 帽子 **bou**shi (hats)	帽子 boushi = hat
布 2	^687. I'm about to get a **New-No**se from a plastic surgeon, but I don't want to look **Foo**lish, so I plan to hug this friend 巾 (Bo Peep) and keep my face covered with 布 **nuno** (cloth) until the swelling goes down	布 nuno = cloth; 布団 futon = floor cushion, Japanese bedding; 毛布 moufu = blanket; 昆布 konbu = kelp; 頒布 hanpu = distribution
怖 2	^463. this guy on the left is a **Koa**la, and I **Foo**lishly hug this 巾 (Bo Peep) because I'm 怖い **kowa**i (scared), while the koala draws himself up to his full height indignantly	怖い kowai = afraid, scary; 恐怖 kyoufu = fear, horror
希 1	^663. I hug my friend 巾 (Bo Peep) in **Ki**ev, while this mysterious X hovers overhead, and we have some 希望 **ki**bou (hope) that the X will turn out to be a good omen	希望 kibou = hope
常 2	^683. these three old boys on this roof watched this 巾 (Bo Peep) with this big 口 (mouth) as she spun around looking for **Joa**n of Arc to help with a 非常 hi**jou** (emergency), but Joan's life **Tsoon**-(soon)-**E**nded	非常 hijou = emergency; 非常な hijou na = extreme, great; 通常 tsuujou = usual; 常に tsune ni = always, continually
帯 2	^1012. **O**prah-drank-**Beer** with this 巾 (Bo Peep) while standing under this roof below this cloud-covered 山 (mountain) in **Thai**land, and afterwards her 帯 **obi** (sash) no longer reached around her	帯 obi = a kimono sash; 携帯電話 keitai denwa = cellular phone; 所帯 shotai = household, family
滞 2	^1013. in **Thai**land, I 滞在した **tai**zai shita (stayed) at a hot springs inn and, when I heard that a **T**ornado-had-blown-the-**D**oor-off-a-**Cour**thouse, I accidentally dropped this 帯 (phone) into this water	滞在する taizai suru = to stay (at a hotel, etc.); 滞る todokooru = to stagnate, be delayed or be overdue
爪 2	^647. my **Tsu**ma (wife) has long 爪 **tsume** (nails) like this, and she uses them to open **Tsu**metai (cold) cartons of milk	爪楊枝 tsumayouji = toothpick; 爪 tsume = nail, claw
孤 1	^723. this 子 ko (child) lives in 孤独 **ko**doku (isolation) and uses this hammer and his long 爪 (nails) like this to open ears of **Cor**n	孤独 kodoku = solitude, isolation; 孤児 koji = orphan

Chapter 5

族 ₁	^115. this 家族 ka**zoku** (family) of these disabled Native American 方 (honorable people) drinks mostly beer, but **Zoo**ey-drinks-**Kool**-Aid	家族 kazoku = family
旅 ₂	^116. this 方 (honorable person) named Pope **Leo** and this companion who carries this crutch will 旅行する **ryo**kou suru (travel) and are taking this first step on their 旅 **tabi** (trip) with their **Tabby** cat	旅行する ryokou suru = to travel; 旅 tabi = trip, travel
派 ₂	^764. Prince **Harry** has been 派遣された **ha**ken sareta (sent) on a 旅 (trip) by his **Pa** (father), and he is waiting for a boat in this lean-to by this water	派手 hade = showy, gaudy, colorful; 立派な rippa na = splendid, impressive
脈 ₁	^770. this person is about to step out from this lean-to under the light of this 月 (moon) on a journey to get some **Miami-Kool**-Aid, and he feels his 脈 **myaku** (veins) throbbing in anticipation	脈 myaku = pulse or vein; 山脈 sanmyaku = mountain range; 動脈 doumyaku = artery
年 ₂	^177. my **Negative-Nephew** has been sitting here, with this knee protruding to the left, for a 年 **nen** (year), holding this crutch, playing with his **Toy-Sheep** and waiting for help	三年 sannen = three years; 今年 kotoshi = this year
牛 ₂	^205. a Guatemalan-**You**th, who is an **Us**her-at-an-Indian theatre, owns this 牛 **ushi** (cow) with one horn that is bigger than the other	牛肉 gyuuniku = beef; 牛 ushi = cow
午 ₁	^207. this 牛 (cow) hides her head in the 午後 go**go** (afternoon), when the **Golden** sun shines brightest	午前 gozen = in the morning; 午後 gogo = in the afternoon
許 ₂	^1141. **You-Ru**ined the class at **Kyo**to University when you 言 (said) that everyone had 許可 **kyo**ka (permission) to show up at 午 (noon)	許す yurusu = to forgive, accept, permit; 免許 menkyo = a license
生 ₁₂	^208. after this 牛 (cow) 生まれる **u**mareru (is born), it stands on this platform and watches out for **Eagles** and **Fool**ish **Hack**ers who might want to **Kill** it, including **Joe Nama**th, who is **N**asty and **O**ld, but they play it **Safe** when they go to **Sho**ws by taking **U**ber and sharing expenses with **Yo**gis-from-India	生きる ikiru = to live; 芝生 shibafu = lawn; 生える haeru = to grow or sprout; 芽生え mebae = budding; 生地 kiji = material, cloth, texture; 誕生日 tanjoubi = birthday; 生 nama = raw; 生る naru = to bear fruit; 生い茂る oishigeru = to grow thickly; 先生 sensei = teacher; 一生 isshou = a lifetime; 生まれる umareru = to be born; 弥生時代 yayoi jidai = the Yayoi era
乾 ₂	^290. this zebra with this crutch is lurking outside this **California-Wagon**, so let's stay inside, where 乾いている **kawa**ite iru (it's dry), and we can eat from **Cans**	乾く kawaku = to get dry; 乾電池 kandenchi = dry cell battery
朝 ₃	^291. I'm sitting in this California wagon in the early 朝 **asa** (morning), watching this 月 (moon) fade away, feeling **Sad** that I was **Cho**sen for early morning watch duty, and hoping that the day will get warm **ASAP** (as soon as possible)	今朝 kesa = this morning; 朝食 choushoku = breakfast; 朝 asa = morning
韓 ₁	^655. in 韓国 **kan**koku (S. Korea), I rode in this wagon which was pulled by a **Kan**garoo, and that was 違 (different) from what I expected	韓国 kankoku = S. Korea
毎 ₂	^336. 毎日 **mai**nichi (every day), Michael Jackson grabs this crutch, loads the **Goats**-into-the-**Toyota**, and goes out to this 田 (rice paddy)	毎週 maishuu = every week; 三日毎に mikka goto ni = every three days
海 ₄	^337. 毎 (every) year I go to the 海 **umi** (ocean) to watch **Uber-Military** exercises with the **Kai**ser near this water, but the show seems **A**rtificial, and I am **Una**ffected by it	海 umi = ocean; 海外 kaigai = overseas; 海女 ama = fisherwoman, female pearl diver; 海原 unabara = ocean
悔 ₃	^675. this man on the left is a **Kai**ser who feels 後悔 kou**kai** (regret) because 毎 (every) day he forgets to bring **Kool**-Aid to his **Cool-Ya**k, and this is 悔しい **kuya**shii (mortifying), but he stands erect and proud like this anyway	後悔 koukai = regret; 悔い kui = regret; 悔しい kuyashii = vexing, mortifying

浮 4	^671. when an Uber car runs into a barbecue grate like this, falls into a river and 浮かぶ **u**kabu (floats) in water like this, even 子 (children) like this say, "Uber-was-**Wa**rned" and "they are hiring **Foo**lish drivers," but other people say, "Uber-is-the-**Key** to our economy"		浮かぶ ukabu = to float, intransitive; 浮気 uwaki = extra-marital affair; 浮浪者 furousha = a vagrant; 浮世 ukiyo = floating world
乳 4	^186. this 子 (child) at this mother's breast is staying warm near this barbecue grate and drinking 乳 **chichi** (milk) in **Nyuu**yooku (New York), while **Chichi** (my father) looks on and eats Uber crackers and **Chee**se		牛乳 gyuunyuu = cow's milk; 乳 chichi = milk; 乳母 uba = wet nurse; 乳首 chikubi = nipple
札 3	^735. a **Foo**lish-**Da**d needs some 札 **satsu** (bank notes), so he pawns his **Sa**xophone while mom nurses their baby at this breast next to this 木 (tree) and reads a **Sat**isfying-**Su**perman novel		値札 nefuda = price tag; 札幌 Sapporo = a city in Hokkaido; 千円札 sen'en satsu = 1,000 yen bill
融 1	^987. on the lower left, this is the floor plan of a house in the **Yu**kon, with a wall missing at the bottom, which promotes a sense of 融合 **yuu**gou (fusion) between the inside and the outside but allows 虫 (insects) like this Tarantula to get in, and the occupants must keep napkins like this over 口 mouths like this to avoid screaming		金融 kin'yuu = finance, loaning money; 融合 yuugou = fusion, adhesion, blending
遊 2	^360. this 方 (honorable person) on the left is an **Asso**ciate salesman from the **Yu**kon who 遊ぶ **aso**bu (plays) on this snail with this 子 (child) who uses this crutch		遊ぶ asobu = to play; 遊園地 yuuenchi = playground
称 1	^1123. this guy on the right, who is 小 (small) and carries this crutch and who has the 通称 tsuu**shou** (nickname) of **Sho**rty, is celebrating the harvest of 禾 (ripe grain)		対称 taishou = symmetry; 対称的な taishouteki na = symmetrical; 通称 tsuushou = a nickname or alias
飾 3	^1203. this 巾 (Bo Peep), who uses this crutch, lives in **Chica**go but just got back from **Kaza**khstan, and if you invite her to a 食 (meal) like this she will **Shock-yoU** by offering to 飾る **kazu**ru (decorate) your house		葛飾 katsushika = a ward in Tokyo; 飾る kazaru = to decorate; 装飾 soushoku = decoration
疲 2	^370. this Straight Arrow 疲れた **tsuka**reta (got tired) from working in the **Heat** and is sleeping in this sick bed, and he left his **Tsu**it-(suit)-in-the-**Car**		疲労 hirou = fatigue, weariness; 疲れる tsukareru = to get tired
彼 2	^371. this man on the left works at a **Ca**lifornia-**Re**staurant where he wears these two hats, as a cook, cooking with **Cano**la oil, and as a waiter, serving this Straight Arrow whom he refers to as 彼 **kare** (he)		彼 kare = he; 彼女 kanojo = she
皮 2	^833. this Straight Arrow works at a **Car-Wa**sh, he has thin 皮 **kawa** (skin), and he **Hea**rs everything that people say about him		皮 kawa = skin, peel; 毛皮 kegawa = fur; 皮膚 hifu = skin
破 3	^837. this 皮 (Straight Arrow) was in **Ha**waii when he tripped on this 石 (stone), and his **Ya**k-skin-**Boo**ts 破れた **yabu**reta (tore) apart, so that he couldn't go to a **Party**		読破する dokuha suru = to finish reading a book; 破る yaburu = to break, tear or violate; 突破する toppa suru = to break through
波 4	^878. a 津波 tsu**nami** of **Wa**ter like this struck this 皮 (Straight Arrow), who had just eaten a **Na**sty **Mea**l with Prince **Har**ry and his **Pa** (father)		阿波踊り Awa'odori = a type of Bon dance; 津波 tsunami = tidal wave; 波止場 hatoba = pier; 音波 onpa = sound wave
箱 1	^142. I have my 目 (eye) on this 木 (tree) and this 竹 (bamboo), which I will use to make 箱 **hako** (boxes) for storing my **Ha**t-and-my-**Coa**t		箱 hako = box; 靴箱 kutsubako = shoe box
相 5	^787. I have my 目 (eye) on this 木 (tree) by the **Sho**re, under which I plan to listen to **Sou**l music and drink **I**ced tea while I 相談する **sou**dan suru (consult) with **Su**perman about the next **Sa**ga I will write		首相 shushou = prime minister; 相談 soudan = consultation, advice; 相手 aite = opponent or partner; 相撲 sumou = sumo wrestling; 相模原 Sagamihara = a city
想 3	^905. during the **So**viet era, a **So**ldier with an **O**ld-**Mo**torcycle, who had some 想像 **sou**zou (imagination) and this 心 (heart) of courage, had his 目 (eye) on this 木 (tree), and he climbed it to find a way to escape		愛想がいい aiso ga ii = sociable; 想像 souzou = imagination; 想う omou = to imagine or contemplate

人 6	^13. I met a 人 **hito** (person) with long legs like these, and **He-Told** me that he smoked **To**bacco with **Nin**jas and wore **Jean**s when he wanted to look **Rea**lly **Natural**	人 hito = person; 恋人 koibito = lover; 玄人 kurouto = expert, professional; 素人 shirouto = amateur; 人間 ningen = human being; 日本人 nihonjin = Japanese person; 一人 hitori = 1 person; 大人 otona = adult
入 4	^14. this 人 (person) with this wind-swept hair 入る **hai**ru (enters) **Hei**di's house to give her some fruit from **Nyuu**yooku (New York) that was **Irradi**ated to kill germs, but Heidi is **Irri**tated by this	入る hairu = to enter; 入学 nyuugaku = entering a school; 入れる ireru = to put into; 気に入る ki ni iru = to like; 入口 iriguchi = entrance
込 2	^357. many people 入 (enter) this snail bus in order to **Com**mute to work, but it 込む **ko**mu (gets crowded), often **Comi**cally so	む komu = to get crowded; 申込書 moushikomisho = application form
八 4	^15. at the time we were leaving to see this Eiffel tower, 八 **hachi** (eight) chicks were **Hatchi**ng from **Yo**lks on our **Yacht** in the **Harbor**	八 hachi = eight; 八日 youka = the 8th of the month, eight days; 八つ yattsu = eight items; 八百 happyaku = eight hundred
久 3	^30. this **Cute** dancer asked for a man's salad, but she waited until after **His-Salad** had been left outside the **Cool**er 久しぶり **hisa**shiburi (for a long time)	永久に eikyuu ni = forever, permanently; 久しぶり hisashiburi = after a long time; 屋久島 Yakushima = an island south of Kyushu
大 5	^188. this 大きい **oo**kii (big) 人 (person) is **Ti**red and **O**verweight, and he lives on a **Di**et of **O**rganic-**T**omatoes near a **Yama** (mountain)	大変 taihen = terrible; 大きい ookii = big; 大学 daigaku = university; 大人 otona = adult; 大和 yamato = ancient Japan
火 3	^443. this 人 (person) was surrounded by these flames and feeling the **Heat** from a 火 **hi** (fire), until a **Yankee-Kennedy** drove by in a **Car** and rescued him	火 hi = fire; 花火 hanabi = fireworks; 火曜日 kayoubi = Tuesday; 火傷 yakedo = a burn injury, usually spelled やけど; 火事 kaji = fire
文 4	^25. some **Monks** told **Moses** that Daniel **Boone**'s business is **Boomi**ng, but Daniel sits on this tire stop all day with these X (legs crossed) and expresses 文句 monku (complaints) about the world	文句 monku = complaint; 文字 moji = letter, character; 文 bun = sentence; 文化 bunka = culture; 恋文 koibumi = love letter
斉 1	^952. this 文 (culture) of worshipping this truncated moon is **Sa**tanic, and if you cross its adherents, they will attack you 一斉に is**sei** ni (all at once)	一斉に issei ni = all at once, at the same time, all together
済 3	^259. a **Sci**entist known for her 文 (culture), who graduated **Su**mma cum laude, is still trying to 済ます **su**masu (finish) her dissertation on 月 (moon) phenomena, and she is happy to discover this truncated moon shining near this ocean in **Zai**re (the former name of the Congo)	救済 kyuusai = help, rescue, relief; 済む sumu = to end (intransitive), to manage, to do without; 済ます sumasu = to finish, transitive; 経済 keizai = economy
黒 2	^76. this fire started under this sincere guy wearing bifocals, and he was about to turn 黒い **kuro**i (black), but **Kooky-Roy** Rogers put out the flames with a can of **Coke**	黒い kuroi = black; 目黒 Meguro = a ward in Tokyo; 黒板 kokuban = blackboard
魚 3	^80. we have a **Sack-of-Cana**dian 魚 **sakana** (fish) like this that we caught in the **Uber-Ocean**; they are covered with scales like these, each of them has four legs like these, and we will use them to make fish **Gyoza**	魚 sakana = fish; 小魚 kozakana = small fish; 魚 uo = fish; 金魚 kingyo = goldfish
漁 2	^685. Pope **Leo** looked at this water, saw this 魚 (fish) and decided to start a 漁業 **gyo**gyou (fishing business) to sell fish **Gyoza**	漁 ryou = fishing; 漁師 ryoushi = fisherman; 漁業 gyogyou = fishing business
馬 3	^958. this 馬 **uma** (horse) with this flowing mane and this long tail belongs to an **Ugandan-Man** who works in a **Bar** at a **Mall**	馬 uma = horse; 競馬 keiba = horse racing; 絵馬 ema = a drawing or painting of a horse
徴 1	^784. this man with two hats will join this 王 (king) on this 山 (mountain), where they will watch this dancer named Margaret **Cho**, who has 特徴 toku**chou** (special features), and give her one of his hats	特徴 tokuchou = characteristic, special feature

Kanji	Mnemonic	Vocabulary
類₁	^97. a 大 (big) harvest of this 米 (rice) came in, and we want King **Lou**is to look at some 書類 sho**rui** (documents) about the harvest, but his head is missing from this platform	書類 shorui = documents; 衣類 irui = clothes; 種類 shurui = variety
米₄	^326. a **Yog**i-in-the-**Ne**therlands can arrange these 米 **kome** (uncooked rice) grains into an eight-sided **Com**et like this, **Ba**ke them in an oven and feed them to **Mi**ce	米酢 yonezu = rice vinegar; 米 kome = uncooked rice; 餅米 mochigome = glutinous rice; 米国 beikoku = U.S.A.; 白米 hakumai = white rice
来₄	^327. the **Co**ders who 来る **ku**ru (come) for dinner 来週 **rai**shuu (next week) will get **Qui**che, **Koo**l-Aid and this 米 (**Ri**ce), and they can park their cars against tire stops like this	来ない konai = will not come; 来ます kimasu = will come; 来る kuru = will come; 来年 rainen = next year
隣₂	^329. this **Wrink**led ß (Greek) named **Tobias-of-Nari**ta lives 学校の隣 gakkou no **tonari** (next door to a school) and sits with this bent knee in the 夕 (evenings), sorting through this 米 (rice)	隣人 rinjin = neighbor; 隣 tonari = next door
料₁	^512. Pope **Le**o puts this 米 (uncooked rice) into these two containers on this shelf to use in creating 料理 **ryou**ri (cuisine)	料理 ryouri = cuisine; 無料 muryou = free of charge; 料金 ryoukin = fee
奥₂	^532. this 米 (uncooked rice) is being stored in this **Oak** box on this two-legged table, and an 奥さん **oku**san (honorable wife) pushes this lever at the top that **O**pens the box	奥さん okusan = someone else's wife; 奥義 ougi = secrets, mysteries
歯₂	^533. after the **Har**vest, we put this 米 (uncooked rice) in this box and put this 止 (stop) sign at the top to stop **Shee**p from chewing it with their 歯 **ha** (teeth)	歯 ha = tooth; 虫歯 mushiba = decayed tooth; 歯科 shika = dentistry
精₂	^847. a **Sai**lor saw this 青 (blue) 米 (rice) at a food **Show**, and the color was so bizarre that it caused him to have 精神的な **sei**shinteki na (mental) problems	精神 seishin = mind, soul, spirit; 精神的な seishinteki na = spiritual, mental; 精進料理 shoujin ryouri = vegetarian cuisine, as eaten by Buddhist monks
粉₃	^1104. **Con**an O'Brien 分 (understands) that this 米 (rice) can be made into 粉 **kona** (flour), but he spills it onto his **Coat** while trying to be **Fun**ny	粉 kona = flour, powder; 小麦粉 komugiko = wheat flour; 花粉 kafun = pollen
粒₂	^1135. I was 立 (standing) around looking at 粒 **tsubu** (grains) of this 米 (rice) that had fallen onto my **Tsu**pervisor's-(supervisor's)-**Boo**ts, and I realized that I could sweep them up and **Reu**se them	粒 tsubu = grains, drops, counter for tiny particles; 雨粒 amatsubu = raindrop; 粒子 ryuushi = a particle or grain
矢₁	^1045. this Native American chief guards his **Y**ard with 弓矢 yumi**ya** (bows and arrows)	矢 ya = arrow; 矢印 yajirushi = arrow (on a map or sign); 弓矢 yumiya = bow and arrow
知₃	^323. this Native American **Chi**ef is a veterinary dentist with a **Jee**p who specializes in **Shee**p, and he 知る **shi**ru (knows) a lot about 口 (mouths) like this	知識 chishiki = knowledge; ご存知 gozonji = to honorably know; 知る shiru = to know; 知らせる shiraseru = to inform
短₂	^324. this Native American chief is a **Midget-with-a-Jeep-Car**; he has a good **Tan**, but he is too 短い **mijika**i (short) to see over this TV set	短い mijikai = short (object); 長短 choutan = length
医₁	^325. this Native American chief is an 医者 **i**sha (doctor) with **Ea**gle eyes, staring out of this storefront clinic, which is open on one side	医者 isha = medical doctor
喉₂	^794. this man in the middle is an ear, nose & throat doctor who takes care of Native American patients like this in ユ (the Yukon) and who knows a lot about the 口 (mouth) and the 喉 **nodo** (throat), and he tilts his hat back like this to examine patients, but his bedside manner is **Cold**, and as a result on some days he earns **No-Dough** (money)	耳鼻咽喉科 jibiinkouka = ear, nose and throat specialty; 喉 nodo = throat
候₁	^996. this man on the left slants his hat back to examine this unicorn horn and tells this Native American chief that he should move to ユ (the Yukon), where he can use the horn and work as a prison guard, but the chief says that the 気候 ki**kou** (climate) up there is too **Cold**	気候 kikou = climate; 天候 tenkou = weather; 候補 kouho = candidate

建 4		^363. before they 建てる <u>ta</u>teru (erect) a **Ta**xi garage for a **Tall-Te**chie who is a **Cone**head, **Ken** and Barbie must review their plans 3x and 書 (write) them down	建てる tateru = to build; 建て date = story or floor (of a building); 建立 konryuu = act of building a temple or monument, etc.; 建築 kenchiku = architecture
健 2		^811. this man with a slanted hat is named **Ken**, he works as an 建 (architect) with Barbie, and they are **Su**ing **Co**ca Cola over the effects of its beverage on their 健康 <u>ken</u>kou (health)	健康 kenkou = health; 健やか sukoyaka = vigorous, healthy, sound
庭 2		^495. this 王 (king) likes to ride on this 3x snail in this lean-to in his 庭 <u>niwa</u> (garden), where he is guarded with **Ta**sers and surrounded by **Kneel**ing-**Wa**rlords	庭園 teien = formal Japanese garden; 庭 niwa = garden; 裏庭 uraniwa = back yard
廻 1		^692. I'm stuck in this box traveling on the back of this 3x snail in the **Ne**therlands, 回 (rotating) back and forth and wondering whether my next life can be predicted, according to the doctrine of 輪廻 rin<u>ne</u> (samsara)	輪廻 rinne = samsara, cycle of death and rebirth
嫌 4		^817. this 女 (female) on the left is staring at this split 木 (tree) that has been patched together with this trident, and 嫌いです <u>kira</u>i desu (she doesn't like it), but her husband **Gen**ghis takes off his **Iya**hon (earphones), grabs a key from his **Key-Ra**ck, and goes out to talk to **Ken** and Barbie about the situation	機嫌 kigen = mood, feeling; 嫌な iya na = unpleasant, disgusting; 嫌い kirai = to hate; 嫌悪 ken'o = hatred, disgust
謙 1		^965. although **Ken** and Barbie repaired this tree using this trident, they are aware that some people 嫌 (hate) the job they did, and their 謙虚 <u>ken</u>kyo (modesty) enables them to 言 (say) that their work wasn't perfect	謙虚 kenkyo = modesty
煎 2		^650. when our **Sen**ator came here 前 (before) the election, we 煎じていた <u>sen</u>jite ita (were boiling) water over this fire and 煎っていた <u>i</u>tte ita (were roasting) **Ee**ls	煎じる senjiru = to boil; 煎る iru = to roast or toast
焦 3		^750. **Asse**s (donkeys) in **Co**lombia are put into this net and suspended over this fire as part of a **Show**, you can be sure that they will 焦る <u>ase</u>ru (be eager) to escape before they 焦げる <u>ko</u>geru (get burned)	焦る aseru = to be in a hurry, be impatient, anxious & eager; 焦げる kogeru = to be scorched or burned; 焦点 shouten = focus, central issue
無 3		^583. a **Moo**ney says that it's 無理 <u>mu</u>ri (impossible) for **Boo**zers to escape from this cage above these flames, unless they have a **Na**zi friend to open the door	無理 muri = impossible, unreasonable; 無事 buji = safety, peace, health, good condition; 無くす nakusu = to lose
撫 2		^846. this man on the left was once a **Na**zi and a **Boo**zer, but he 無 (lost) everything that he owned, and now he kneels to 撫でる <u>na</u>deru (rub) the heads of stray animals that he meets	撫でる naderu = to rub or stroke; 愛撫 aibu = a caress
照 3		^822. this 口 (Television set) displays a **Show** featuring a **De**butante who fights with this 刀 (sword), and this 日 (sun) and this fire are being used to 照らす <u>te</u>rasu (illuminate) the stage	照る teru = to shine; 対照的に taishouteki ni = diametrically opposite; 日照り hideri = dry weather, drought
能 1		^616. this ム (cow) on this 月 (moon) has the 能力 <u>nou</u>ryoku (ability) ヒ (hear) what we say and to ヒ (heal) our illnesses, but her **No**se is stuffy, and she cannot smell us	能力 nouryoku = ability; 有能 yuunou = able, competent
態 1		^960. my **Thai** friend has 能 (ability) and a good 心 (heart) like this, as well as a good 態度 <u>tai</u>do (attitude)	態度 taido = attitude; 変態 hentai = pervert or perversion, metamorphosis (insect)
了 1		^760. Pope **Leo** was born without arms, but his 了承 <u>ryou</u>shou (understanding) was profound from the beginning	終了 shuuryou = ending, termination; 了承 ryoushou = acknowledgement, understanding
蒸 2		^1101. when **Joa**n of Arc was in the **Moo**d to eat these Y (yams) growing on these plants, she asked this 了 (child without arms) to help her 蒸す <u>mu</u>su (steam) them over this fire and arrange them in a pyramidal shape like this, after which she ate them as フ (food)	蒸気 jouki = vapor, steam; 蒸す musu = to steam, to be hot and humid; 蒸し暑い mushiatsui = hot and humid

木 6		^118. when you return with your **Gui**tar and take out your house **Key**, this 木 **ki** (tree) in the front yard reminds you to buy **More-Koo**l-Aid, but not the **Boring-Koo**l-Aid, since that's no better than **Co**la, and to **Mow** the lawn	六本木 roppongi = district in Tokyo; 木の実 kinomi = nut, fruit, berry; 木曜日 mokuyoubi = Thursday; 土木 doboku = public works, civil engineering; 木の葉 konoha = leaf; 木綿 momen = cotton
末 3		^119. people on **Sue**de **Mats** sit around this tree with two pairs of branches, which are longer at the top because it's **Magic** and can reach for the sky on 週末 shuu**matsu** (weekends)	末っ子 suekko = youngest child; 週末 shuumatsu = weekend; 末期 makki = the hour of death
存 2		^462. when I'm in the **Zon**e, I hug this 子 (child), who plays games that are made by **Son**y, as I 存じる **zon**jiru (humbly know)	存じる zonjiru = to humbly know; 存在 sonzai = existence, presence
右 3		^457. I use my 右 **migi** (right) hand to hug food and bring it to this 口 (mouth), but some **Mean-Gees**e and an **U**ber strike in the **Yu**kon are making it hard for me to focus on eating	右側 migigawa = right side; 右折 usetsu = right turn; 左右 sayuu = left and right
若 3		^461. when I was 若い **wakai** (young), I played **Whack-A**-mole with **Jack** Nicholson under these plants on the 右 (right) side of our house, and we whacked the moles as we **K**neeled-in-the-**Yard**	若い wakai = young; 若年 jakunen = youth, an early age; 般若 hannya = prajna, wisdom
在 2		^1014. this person hugging this 土 (soil) may be expressing the **Zeit**geist (spirit of the Age) of certain people at the 現在 gen**zai** (present time), who are embracing **A**griculture	現在 genzai = nowadays, present time; 在る aru = to exist, usually written ある
有 3		^460. **A**rthur, an **A**ristocrat from the **Yu**kon, symbolically hugs this 有名 **yuu**mei (famous) 月 (moon) which 有る **aru** (exists), and he says 有難う **ari**gatou (thank you)	有る aru = to exist (usually written ある); 有難う arigatou = thank you; 有名 yuumei = famous
書 2		^415. I'm grasping this brush with this three-fingered hand to 書く **ka**ku (write) a story in this 土 (soil) on this 日 (cabinet) about a **Ca**rpenter who starred in a Broadway **Show**	書く kaku = to write; 辞書 jisho = dictionary
事 3		^416. this test sheet, this rectangular answer book and this brush being held by this three-fingered hand will be used for a test covering 事 **koto** (intangible things), such as **Ko**to (Japanese harp) music, **Ghost-To**es and **Ji**had	事 koto = intangible thing, matter; 仕事 shigoto = work; 用事 youji = errand
律 2		^417. this man on the left doesn't pay his taxes, and the **Rea**son-he-**Cheat**s is that he thinks that the tax 法律 hou**ritsu** (laws) written on these two sheets of paper, impaled on this rod being held by this three-fingered hand, are just **Writt**en-**Suggest**ions, but if he is caught, he will have to forfeit one of his two hats	律儀な richigi na = conscientious; 法律 houritsu = law
津 3		^877. a 津波 **tsu**nami of water like this struck a calligrapher as he was writing messages with this brush on these two sheets of paper at a **Shin**to shrine, causing the brush to perforate them and soaking his **Tsu**it (suit), before going on to strike a **Zoo**	興味津々 kyoumi shinshin = very interesting; 津波 tsunami = tidal wave; 宮津 Miyazu = a town in Kyoto Prefecture
筆 3		^1091. a **Fo**olish-**D**ebutante grasps this 竹 (bamboo) handle at the top of a 筆 **fude** (brush), **Hits**-yo**U** with it and bruises your **Heel**	筆 fude = writing brush; 毛筆 mouhitsu = writing (painting) brush; 鉛筆 enpitsu = pencil; 筆者 hissha = writer
棚 2		^742. a cowboy in Mon**Tana** who wears a ban**Dana** had a surplus of these 月 (moons), so he used 木 (wood) to build a 棚 **tana** (shelf) on which to store them	棚 tana = shelf; 戸棚 todana = cupboard
崩 2		^973. I'm **Co**oped-up-in-a-**Zoo** on this 山 (mountain), and this is my **Ho**me, but if these two 月 (moons) drift apart, the mountain and the zoo will 崩れる **kuzu**reru (collapse	崩れる kuzureru = to collapse, be destroyed; 崩壊 houkai = collapse, crumbling, decay
争 2		^936. an **A**rab-**So**ldier from **So**malia 争う **araso**u (fights) this fish-headed monster and stabs it with this trident	争う arasou = to fight, dispute or compete; 戦争 sensou = war
静 3		^418. the sky is 青 (blue), and it's 静か **shizu**ka (quiet), now that a **Sheep**-herder-from-**Zu**rich has stabbed this fish monster with this trident, and **Joan** of Arc is **Safe**	静か shizuka = quiet, serene; 静脈 joumyaku = vein; 安静 ansei = rest

Chapter 6

質 2		^86. I bought these two pairs of pliers with money from this three-drawer 貝 (money chest) and was told that they have 品質 hin**shitsu** (product quality), but my 質問 **shitsu**mon (question) is, will you give me some **Sheets** of paper that I can wrap them in, in exchange for some **Sheep-Cheese**?	質問 shitsumon = question; 品質 hinshitsu = product quality; 質屋 shichiya = pawnshop
近 2		^390. this snail is an electrician with a **Cheap-Car** who carries this pair of pliers that he uses on wires that are 近い **chika**i (near) the **Kin**dergarten where he works	近い chikai = close; 身近 mijika = close at hand, closely related; 近所 kinjo = neighborhood; 最近 saikin = recently
所 3		^391. after **T**olstoy-had-a-**Coro**nary (heart attack), **J**onah used these pliers to fix up his 所 **tokoro** (Place) for a **Show**	所 tokoro = place; 台所 daidokoro = kitchen; 近所 kinjo = neighborhood; 場所 basho = place
断 3		^704. this **Tall** pair of pliers is blocking access to this shelf full of this 米 (rice) which was intended to be the payment for a koto (Japanese harp), but the **Koto-is-Warm** and covered with **Dan**druff, and therefore the pliers 断る **kotowa**ru (refuse) to accept it	断つ tatsu = to cut off, discontinue; 断る kotowaru = to refuse; 中断 chuudan = interruption
継 2		^635. this 糸 (skeet shooter) is making this 米 (rice) into **Ts**oup (soup) on this shelf in the **C**ave where he lives, but one day he will 継ぐ **tsu**gu (inherit) the title of Chief Skeet Shooter	継ぐ tsugu = to succeed to, to inherit; 継承する keishou suru = to succeed to
兵 2		^917. a 兵隊 **hei**tai (soldier), who was using these pliers to create defensive barriers using **Hay**wire, put them on this platform with legs, and the Lone Ranger said "**Hi-Yo** Silver" when he saw them	兵隊 heitai = soldier; 兵庫県 hyougoken = Hyogo prefecture
浜 2		^766. a lifeguard bought some **Ham-at-the-Ma**ll and ate it in this chair near this water at the 海浜 kai**hin** (seaside), but seabird attacks **Hin**dered his enjoyment of the meal	浜辺 hamabe = beach; 海浜 kaihin = seaside
折 3		^892. this person kneels in order to pick up this giant pair of pliers, which she uses to hand **O**reo cookies to her customers in the **Ori**ent, after she **Set-up-a-Sup**er business there, but sometimes the cookies 折れる **o**reru (break)	折れる oreru = to break, intransitive; 時折 tokiori = once in awhile; 骨折する kossetsu suru = to break a bone
祈 2		^955. this Shah carries these pliers when he 祈る **ino**ru (prays) for **Inn**ocent people in **Ki**ev, since they remind him to be practical in his requests	祈る inoru = to pray; 祈願 kigan = a prayer or supplication
喜 2		^599. this nurse 喜ぶ **yoroko**bu (gets delighted) in the **Yoro**pean-(European)-city-of-**Co**logne when she gets a **Key** to the city	喜ぶ yorokobu = to be delighted; 喜劇 kigeki = comedy
嬉 1		^600. this 女 (female) 喜 (nurse) is 嬉しい **ure**shii (pleased) about her patient with kidney failure, who is starting to excrete **Ure**a (urea is a major component of urine)	嬉しい ureshii = pleased
任 2		^483. this man on the left tilts his hat back to examine this 王 (**Maca**roni) which he plans to 任せる **maka**seru (entrust) to a 主任 shu**nin** (foreman) who is a **Nin**ja	任せる makaseru = to entrust; 主任 shunin = foreman
王 1		^1077. when an **O**ld 主 (master) met the 王様 **ou**sama (king), he removed his tiny cap	王様 ousama = king; 女王 jo'ou = queen
悠 1		^985. this man with a slanted hat on the left and this dancer on the right have good 心 (hearts) like this, but they keep this **U**nicorn horn between them, for the sake of keeping things 悠々 **yuu**yuu (quiet or calm)	悠々 yuuyuu = quiet, calm, leisurely; 悠長 yuuchou = leisurely, slow, deliberate, easy-going; 悠久の yuukyuu no = eternal
修 3		^1049. this guy on the left is **Osa**ma bin Laden, who is tilting his hat back to show his face to this dancer with this 参 (rocker-bottom) **Sho**e, whom he wants to recruit for 修行 **shu**gyou (training), but the dancer always keeps this unicorn horn between them and is prepared to **Shoot** him	修める osameru = to learn or master; 修理 shuuri = repairs; 修行 shugyou = training, apprenticeship
顔 2		^95. these scratches at the lower left belong to the 顔 **kao** (face) of a **Cow** wearing this cow bell; **Gan**dalf hopes to restore the face to its head, which is missing from this platform on top of this 貝 (money chest)	顔 kao = face; 笑顔 egao = smiling face; 洗顔 sengan = face washing

役 2	^557. this man with two hats received his second hat from Edward-the-King because he 役に立った **yaku** ni tatta (was useful) in taking care of this π (**Yak**) which is standing on this 又 (table)	兵役 heieki = military service; 役に立つ yaku ni tatsu = to be useful; 区役所 kuyakusho = ward office
投 2	^558. since this guy on the left wants to make **To**ast before taking a **Na**p, he kneels to push this π off this 又 (table) where he keeps his toaster, but he might 投げる **na**geru (throw) the π off instead	投資 toushi = investment; 投げる nageru = to throw
設 3	^1068. **Mo**ses 言 (said) that he will **Se**t-up-a-**Su**per 設備 **setsu**bi (facility) where he will **Se**ll π (yaks) like the one on this 又 (table)	設ける moukeru = to set up; 設備 setsubi = equipment, facility; 設計 sekkei = design or plan; 設定する settei suru = to set up
没 2	^806. this π (yak) looks down at this water from his perch on this 又 (table) and **Bo**asts that, if he jumps in, the people in some nearby **Bo**ats will make sure that he doesn't 没する **bo**ssuru suru (sink)	没頭 bottou = immersing oneself; 没する bossuru = to sink, go down, to set, to pass away, to die, to disappear; 日没 nichibotsu = sunset
殺 3	^838. I read a **Sat**isfying-**Su**perman novel about a **Sa**laryman who saw this drone fly over this 木 (tree) and 殺す **koro**su (kill) this π (yak) on a 又 (table), after which the man suffered a **Coro**nary (heart attack)	殺人 satsujin = murder; 殺到する sattou suru = to rush at or surge; 殺す korosu = to kill
疫 1	^1142. this π (yak) on this 又 (table) was 病 (sick) in this sick bed during an 疫病 **eki**byou (epidemic), but it was healed by Edward-the-King	疫病 ekibyou = a plague or epidemic; 免疫 men'eki = immunity
穀 1	^1172. this 士 (man) stands high on this roof and drinks **Co**ke as he surveys this 禾 (grain plant with a ripe head), and he wonders how much of the 穀物 **koku**motsu (grain) will be eaten by this π (yak) on this 又 (table)	穀倉 kokusou = granary; 穀物 kokumotsu = grain, cereal
般 2	^1050. **Han**sel 一般的に ip**pan**teki ni (usually) keeps a **Pan**da on the top of this 又 (table) in this 舟 (boat), but sometimes he keeps π (yaks) like this on it as well	般若 hannya = prajna, wisdom, insight into the nature of reality (Buddhism); 一般的に ippanteki ni = commonly, generally, usually
盤 1	^1197. **Ban**anas are shipped on this 舟 (boat), and I mash them in this 皿 (bowl) before eating them with this π (yak) at this 又 (table), since they are the 基盤 ki**ban** (foundation) of our diet	吸盤 kyuuban = suction cup, sucker; 基盤 kiban = foundation, basis
包 3	^548. our **Ho**stess will 包む **tsutsu**mu (wrap) this package, which contains this 己 (snake) in addition to **Tsu**its-(suits)-piled-on-**Tsu**its, including **Zoot Su**its-for-our-**Meet**ing	包装 housou = wrapping; 出刃包丁 debabouchou = a knife; 包む tsutsumu = to wrap; 小包 kozutsumi = a package sent by mail
砲 2	^738. a **Ho**bo in **Po**land 包 (wrapped) this 石 (stone) in cloth and used a 大砲 tai**hou** (cannon) to fire it toward me, so I shot at him with a 鉄砲 tep**pou** (gun)	鉄砲 teppou = gun; 大砲 taihou = cannon; 砲火 houka = gunfire
抱 5	^986. this kneeling guy 包 (wraps) a **Bow**ling ball with three **Ho**les as a present for his **Da**ughter, who loves **Eastern-Da**nce, and then he 抱く **da**ku (embraces) her and **Call**s-a-**Ca**b	辛抱 shinbou = endurance, patience; 抱擁する houyou suru = to embrace; 抱く daku = to embrace, hold or hug; 抱きしめる dakishimeru = to hug someone tightly; 抱く idaku = to embrace, hold or entertain (an idea); 抱える kakaeru = to hold or carry under or in the arms, to have (e.g., problems with debt), to employ or hire
沈 2	^835. this guy with this bad haircut and these lopsided legs was wading in this water with some **She**ep-at-the-**Zoo** when one of them struck him on the **Chin**, he injured this right leg, and he 沈めた **shizu**meta (sank)	沈める shizumeru = to sink or submerge; 沈黙 chinmoku = silence

女 6	^235. an **O**ld-**Na**sty taskmaster is forcing some 女の人 **onna** no hito (women) named **Jo**sephine and **O**prah to carry this cross to **Me**xico, but they will **Need-Yo**gurt if they are going to make it to the **Ma**ll	女の人 onna no hito = woman; 女性 josei = woman; 女将 okami = mistress, landlady, hostess; 乙女 otome = maiden; 女房 nyoubou = one's wife; 海女 ama = fisherwoman
安 3	^236. Queen **Anne** is this 女 (female) with this bad haircut who gives us 安心 **an**shin (relief) by showing us the **A**rt of cooking 安い **yasu**i (cheap) **Ya**k-**Sou**p	安心する anshin suru = to feel relieved; 安部 Abe = a surname; 安い yasui = cheap
案 1	^120. Queen **Anne** is a 女 (female) with this bad haircut, and she will 案内する **an**nai suru (show us around) and demonstrate her 案 **an** (proposal) for living in 木 (trees) like this one	案内する annai suru = to show around; 案 an = proposal, idea
好 3	^239. **Su**perman 好き **su**ki (likes) the way that this 女 (female) and this 子 (child) hide their **Cold-No**ses in their **Co**ats	好きです suki desu = I like it; 好き zuki = enthusiast, used as a suffix, e.g., ryokouzuki = travel lover; 好む konomu = to like or favor; 好物 koubutsu = favorite food
姉 3	^241. compared to 妹 (little sister, # 244), this 姉 **ane** (big sister) has wider hips like these, tells more **Ane**cdotes, eats more **Ne**ctarines, and is more **Chic**, since she lives in this 市 (city)	姉 ane = older sister; お姉さん oneesan = honorable older sister; 姉妹 shimai = sisters
妹 2	^244. compared to 姉 (big sister, # 241), 妹 **imouto** (little sister) has these narrow hips, she has **Immo**bile-**To**es, she plays with **Mi**ce, and she is a woman of the 未 (future)	妹 imouto = younger sister; 姉妹 shimai = sisters
娘 1	^316. our 娘 **musume** (daughter) is this 良 (good) 女 (female) who worked at the **Mu**seum-during-the-**Sum**mer	娘 musume = daughter
怒 3	^319. this 女 (female) with this fiery 心 (heart) is an **O**ld-**Co**der, and she 怒った **oko**tta (got angry) when some **Do**ughnuts and some **E**aster-**Ca**ndy disappeared from this 又 (table)	怒る okoru = to get angry; 激怒 gekido = fury, outrage; 怒り ikari = anger, fury
努 2	^519. this 女 (female) rides in **Tsu**ki-(moon)-**To**boggans and 努める **tsuto**meru (makes an effort) for her job on the moon, where she expends 力 (force) making **Do**ughnuts on this 又 (table)	努める tsutomeru = to make an effort; 努力 doryoku = effort
妙 2	^856. this 女 (woman) is a **Tall-E**xpert on cats, but she was 少 (a little) surprised when she heard a **Me**ow from a 奇妙な ki**myou** na (strange) animal	妙なる taenaru = exquisite; 妙 myou = strange, odd, unique
妃 1	^1078. this 女 (female), who is an 王妃 ou**hi** (queen), **He**ars this 己 (snake) in her bedroom	王妃 ouhi = queen
茶 2	^212. King **Charles'** 茶 **cha** (tea) bushes grow in small houses like this and are symmetrical, since he **Sa**ws them back every year	お茶 ocha = honorable tea; 喫茶店 kissaten = cafe
珍 2	^407. when this 王 (king) visited a 珍しい **mezurashii** (unusual) **Me**xican-**Zoo**-to-see-a-**Ra**m, he wore this rocker-bottom shoe, but he fell and hurt his **Chin**	珍しい mezurashii = unusual, rare; 珍味 chinmi = delicacy, dainties
参 2	^406. wobbling on this rocker-bottom shoe, this ム (cow) travels many **Mi**les as she 参ります **ma**irimasu (humbly goes) to **San** Francisco	参る mairu = to humbly come or go; 参加 sanka = participation
未 2	^672. an **E**agle-at-the-**Ma**ll 未だに **ima**da ni (even now) perches on the shorter branches at the top of this tree, but in the 未来 **mi**rai (future), it will leave its perch to seek a **Me**al	未だに imada ni = even now, still, until this very day; 未来 mirai = future
味 3	^245. as I look into this 口 (**M**irror) and contemplate this 未 (future), I see that I am **Ag**ing, but I still have good 味 **aji** (taste) when choosing **E**aster clothes	意味 imi = meaning; 味 aji = taste; 美味しい oishii = delicious (usually written おいしい)

自 4	^55. this 目 (eye) belonging to this tiny self is good, so I can drive my **Jee**p 自分で **ji**bun de (by myself) to transport some **Shee**p, after giving **Mizu**-(water)-to-the-**Cat** with the Orange-Nose	自分 jibun = by oneself, on one's own; 自然 shizen = nature; 自ら mizukara = personally, on one's own initiative; 自ずから onozukara = naturally
息 4	^315. a person close to this 自 (self)'s 心 (heart) is my 息子 **musuko** (son), who is a **Mus**ical-Uber driver with big **Ear**s and **Icky** 息 **iki** (breath), and who is always **Soak**ed with sweat	息子 musuko = son; 息吹 ibuki = breath; 息 iki = breath, respiration; 休息 kyuusoku = rest, relief, relaxation
鼻 2	^795. this **Ha**waiian-**Na**nny has this tiny 鼻 **hana** (nose) resembling a **Bea**k on top of her head which expresses her 自 (self), and she welcomes us to this 田 (rice paddy)	鼻 hana = nose; 耳鼻科 jibika = ear, nose & throat specialty
算 3	^789. **San**ta Claus holds a 竹 (bamboo) cane over his head when he teaches his 算数 **san**suu (arithmetic) class in **Zan**zibar, and his 目 (eyes) watch the students **Sorro**wfully as he assumes a 開 (welcoming) stance	計算 keisan = calculation; 算数 sansuu = arithmetic; 暗算 anzan = mental calculation; 算盤 soroban = abacus
嗅 2	^959. my 自 (self) is in love with this **Cute** 犬 (dog) which 嗅ぐ **ka**gu (sniffs) my **Ca**r for bombs and grabs them in this 口 (mouth)	嗅覚 kyuukaku = sense of smell; 嗅ぐ kagu = to sniff or smell
夕 1	^160. this 夕 (half moon) shines above the **Yu**kon during the 夕方 **yuu**gata (evening)	夕方 yuugata = evening; 夕べ yuube = last night
多 2	^161. 多い **oo**i (many) 夕 (half moons) like these are **Or**biting Jupiter, and I saw them on my **Tab**let computer	多い ooi = a lot; 多分 tabun = probably
移 2	^801. we **U**tilize-**Su**perman to 移動する idou suru (move) 多 (many) stalks of 禾 (grain) like this because it's **Ea**sy for him	移る utsuru = to move (one's lodging), to change or be infected with; 移動する idou suru = to move (an object)
外 5	^163. in order to get these 卜 (tomatoes) during this 夕 (evening), Justice **Soto**mayor has to go 外 **soto** (outside) the **Ho**ckey-Arena near the **Ha**waiian-**Zoo** and find a **Gui**de, who keeps a **Ge**cko	外 soto = outside; 外に hoka ni = besides, in addition; 外す hazusu = to remove; 外人 gaijin = foreigner; 外科 geka = surgery (medical specialty)
舞 3	^584. **Ma** (Mother) is caught in this cage of illness, so I will お見舞いする omi**mai** suru (pay a visit to a sick person) in the 夕 (evening), sit by her bedside, drink **Boo**ze, and listen to **M**ichael **J**ackson music	舞う mau = to dance; 舞台 butai = stage, setting, scene; 舞 mai = a dance
式 1	^249. this woman with a ball above her shoulder, who is participating in a 式 **shiki** (ceremony), leans over this 工 (crafted object), and she sees that it is a **Shift-Key**	結婚式 kekkon shiki = wedding ceremony
試 3	^436. this tall leaning woman with a ball above her shoulder 言 (says) that she prefers **Tall-Men**, she raises **Shee**p and she has a big **Kokoro** (heart), and she 試す **tame**su (tries) to leap over this shift key during a 式 (ceremony) which is a 試験 **shi**ken (test) for her dance class	試す tamesu = to attempt; 試験 shiken = examination; 試みる kokoromiru = to attempt
拭 2	^1114. a **N**eutered-**Goo**se scattered **Foo**d on the floor just before this 式 (ceremony), and this guy on the left had to get down on his knees to 拭く **fu**ku (wipe) it up	拭う nuguu = to wipe; 拭く fuku = to wipe or mop
代 5	^552. this man on the left, who is the president, tilts his hat to examine this face of this tall leaning woman, the vice-president, and he sees that, if he **Dies**, she will start a new 時代 ji**dai** (era) in government; she is **C**alculating that she can 代わる **ka**waru (replace him in) his position, and order people to eat more **Yo**gurt and to wear **Sheepskin-R**obes or **Ti**ger pelts	時代 jidai = era; 代わる kawaru = to take the place of; 千代田 Chiyoda = a ward in Tokyo; 身代金 minoshirokin = ransom; 永代 eitai = permanence, eternity
袋 2	^581. this man at the upper left tilts his hat back to examine this leaning woman with a ball above her shoulder, who uses a fancy 袋 **fukuro** (bag) when she carries **Beer** on **Fuku**oka-**Roa**ds and tries not to spill it on this 衣 (clothing)	足袋 tabi = Japanese-style socks; 袋 fukuro = sack, bag; 手袋 tebukuro = gloves

青 3	^155. an **Ow**l sitting on this perch on top of this 月 (moon) sees an 青い **aoi** (blue) sky and feels **Sa**fe but still makes a **Sour** face		青い aoi = blue; 青年 seinen = young man; 真っ青な massao na = deep blue, ghastly pale
晴 4	^37. in **Ha**waii, when the weather 晴れる **ha**reru (clears up), we see this 日 (sun) next to a 青 (blue) sky, and we can sit in a **Bar** and watch **Sai**ls moving out in the **Har**bor		晴れる hareru = to clear up, to be sunny, to refresh (spirits), to be cleared (of a suspicion); 素晴らしい subarashii = wonderful; 晴天 seiten = fair weather; 晴海通り Harumi Doori = name of a street in Tokyo
情 2	^156. **NASA** sent **Joan**, this astronaut on the left, some 情けない **nasa**kenai (regrettable) instructions, ordering her to repair this owl's perch on this 月 (moon), but she drew herself up to her full height like this and refused		情けない nasakenai = disappointing, regrettable; 愛情 aijou = love
請 2	^1064. a **Sai**lor 言 (speaks) about his love for skies that are 青 (blue) like this, and he 請求する **sei**kyuu suru (demands) an end to air pollution caused by **Co**al		請求 seikyuu = demand, request; 請う kou = to beg or ask
清 2	^1112. this 清い **kiyo**i (pure) water on the left is **Sa**fe to drink, it comes in a bottle that is 青 (blue) like this, and we will use it to make the **King's-Yo**gurt		清掃 seisou = cleaning; 清い kiyoi = clear, pure
背 4	^152. in a **High** place on the 北 (north) side of this 月 (moon), these two **Se**cretaries sit back-to-back, and they are the **Sa**me 背 **sei** (height) which they find **So-Mo**ving		背景 haikei = background, setting; 背が高い se ga takai = the height is tall; 背 sei = height; 背く somuku = to rebel against, disobey
肩 2	^845. during a **Cata**strophe at the **Ken**tucky Derby, this man with this 月 (moon) tattoo on his chest sustained an injury to this 肩 **kata** (shoulder) under this shirt		肩 kata = shoulder; 肩甲骨 kenkoukotsu = shoulder blade or scapula
消 3	^158. **Ke**vin Costner lives on this 月 (moon), where there is this three-pronged switch that can 消す **ke**su (turn off) the flow of this water to his enemies, who live in **Ki**ev, where they have good **Show**s		消す kesu = to erase, turn off, extinguish, wipe out; 消える kieru = to go out (referring to, e.g., a fire); 消化 shouka = digestion (food and information)
化 3	^487. this man on the left has studied 化学 **ka**gaku (chemistry), and he tilts his hat back in order to watch this ヒ (hero) mix **Che**micals and pack them in **Ba**gs and **Carton**s		化粧 keshou = makeup; 化かす bakasu = to bewitch or enchant; 化学 kagaku = chemistry
花 2	^211. this man at the lower left tilts his hat back to examine this ヒ (hero) who is packing **Hannah**'s 花 **hana** (flowers), which come from plants like these, into **Carton**s		お花見 ohanami = honorable flower viewing; 生け花 ikebana = Japanese flower arrangement; 花粉 kafun = pollen
靴 1	^603. this man in the center tilts his hat back to examine this ヒ (hero), who is Superman, who is complaining that some 靴 **kutsu** (shoes) he just purchased are too narrow, so that it feels as though open-top needles like this one on the left are **Cutting-Superman'**s feet		靴 kutsu = shoe; 革靴 kawagutsu = leather shoes
傾 2	^925. this man on the left, who has a hat that 傾く **katamu**ku (tilts), wants to **Cata**pult-this-ヒ-(hero)-to-the-**Moon**, but the hero has lost his head, as indicated by this headless platform on the right, and he will retreat to a **Ca**ve until they find it		傾く katamuku = to tilt or incline, to go down; 傾斜する keisha suru = to tilt or slant
貸 2	^90. this leaning woman with a ball above her right shoulder is trying to **Catch** this man with a slanted hat before he falls off this 貝 (money chest), after which she plans to ask him to 貸す **ka**su (lend) her money to buy food for her **Tiger**		貸す kasu = to lend; 賃貸 chintai = lease, rental
賃 1	^707. this man on the left tilts his hat back as he gazes at this 王 (king) and demands the 家賃 ya**chin** (rent) for a palace that the king is using, but the king socks him on the **Chin**, and he falls off this money chest		家賃 yachin = rent; 電車賃 densha chin = train fare
賀 1	^994. a **Ga**mbler uses this 力 (force) to protect the money in this 貝 (money chest) which he spends on 祝賀会 shuku**ga**kai (celebrations) where he puts food in this 口 (mouth)		祝賀会 shukugakai = celebration; 佐賀県 saga ken = Saga Prefecture

市 2	^242. this lady with these wide hips and this pointy hat spins around the 都市 to**shi** (city) looking for her **Shee**p who are **Itchi**ng to see her	都市 toshi = city; 市長 shichou = mayor; 市場 ichiba = (physical) market
制 1	^1155. this 牛 (cow) on a spinning chair and リ Ri work for **Sa**feway, where they have set up 制度 **sei**do (systems) to control the workers	制度 seido = system or regime; 制服 seifuku = a uniform
製 1	^580. this 牛 (cow) on a spinning chair and this リ Ri manufacture 製品 **seihin** (finished products), such as this 衣 (clothing), to be sold at **Sa**feway stores	製品 seihin = finished product
放 2	^117. this **Hope**ful 方 (honorable person) named **Hannah** wants to 放送する **hou**sou suru (broadcast) information to dancers like this, and she will also work to 放す **hana**su (release) dancers from jail	放送 housou = broadcasting; 奔放 honpou = wild; 放す hanasu = to release; 開けっ放し akeppanashi = left open
惑 2	^624. when I lived in a **Ma**rs-**Do**me and we fought a **War**-against-the-**Koo**l-Aid industry, I had a brave 心 (heart) like this and was assigned to hold this halberd and look out this reinforced 口 (box, or window) for people who caused us 迷惑 mei**waku** (trouble)	惑わす madowasu = to delude or seduce; 迷惑 meiwaku = trouble, annoyance; 当惑 touwaku = embarrassment, bewilderment
減 2	^1148. **Gen**ghis went through **Hell** when he lived in this two-sided lean-to near this water which he could not drink due to this napkin covering this 口 (mouth), and where he was guarded by this halberd, causing him to 減る **heru** (lose) weight	減少 genshou = a decrease; 加減する kagen suru = to moderate, downgrade; 減る heru = to reduce, lose (weight)
感 1	^640. in **Kan**sas, when people are locked up in two-sided lean-tos like this, have their 口 (mouths) covered with napkins like this, and are threatened with halberds like this, their 心 (hearts) beat rapidly, and they 感じる **kan**jiru (feel) anger	感じる kanjiru = to feel; 感動する kandou suru = to be moved; 感じ kanji = impression, perception, feeling
戒 2	^875. since the **Kai**ser's men carry handcuffs like these and halberds like this, and talk to **Im**ages-of-**Shee**p, the public should 警戒する kei**kai** suru (be cautious)	警戒する keikai suru = to be cautious; 戒める imashimeru = to admonish, warn
械 1	^138. the **Kai**ser owned a 機械 ki**kai** (machine) made from this 木 (wood), and it included these handcuffs and this halberd to deal with criminals	機械 kikai = machine
単 1	^636. this 田 (rice paddy) was spinning with these three waves of heat emerging from its top, and it was 簡単 kan**tan** (easy) for it to get a **Tan**	簡単 kantan = easy; 単語 tango = word; 単位 tan'i = credit (school) or unit
戦 3	^933. our **Se**nator says that it's 単 (easy) to fight a 戦争 **sen**sou (war), if you carry **Ear**-**Coo**ties-like-these-in-a-**Sa**ck to cast on your enemies and if a **Tall**-**Ta**xi-driver-**Carries** this halberd for you	戦争 sensou = war; 戦 ikusa = battle; 戦う tatakau = to fight (this can also, less frequently, be written 闘う tatakau)
弾 4	^780. it's 単 (easy) for me to **Hear** the **Dan**ce music at the **Ha**waiian-**Zoo**, where people 引 (pull) strings as they 弾く **hi**ku (play) guitars and eat **Ta**males	弾く hiku = to play a piano or guitar; 爆弾 bakudan = bomb; 弾む hazumu = to become lively, to accelerate; 弾 tama = bullet
使 2	^480. this man on the left 使う **tsuka**u (uses) this servant on the right, who has a dislocated right hip and wears these ordinary glasses (not bifocals), and the man tilts his hat back to watch when the servant goes to the **Tsu**itcase-(suitcase)-in-the-**Car**, where there is a fresh **Sheet**	使う tsukau = to use; 使用 shiyou = use, employment; 大使 taishi = ambassador
便 3	^481. this man on the left is a **Tall**-**Yorkshire** man who tilts his hat back in order to watch this servant named **Ben** who has this dislocated right hip and wears these bifocals, which are 便利 **ben**ri (convenient) when reading small print in **Bin**go instructions	便り tayori = news, letter; 便利 benri = convenient; 郵便 yuubin = mail
更 2	^1000. this Benjamin Franklin, who invented these bifocals and has this dislocated right hip, made a 変更 hen**kou** (change) in his kitchen, stipulating that leftover food should be kept **Col**d and covered with **Sara**n wrap	変更 henkou = a change or alteration; 更に sara ni = again, furthermore
丈 2	^613. to impress **Joan** of Arc, this 大 (big) right-wing guy drinks from a **Tall**-**Keg** and then dislocates this right hip; it looks dangerous, but he is 大丈夫 dai**jou**bu (all right)	丈夫 joubu = healthy, hearty, strong; 大丈夫 daijoubu = all right; 丈 take = size, height
口 4	^426. this square 口 **kuchi** (mouth) drinks **Koo**l-Aid and **Co**la, and it eats **Ku**waiti-**Chee**se that I carry in a **Gucci** handbag	口説く kudoku = to persuade, seduce or make advances; 人口 jinkou = population; 口 kuchi = mouth; 入口 iriguchi = entrance

Chapter 7

育 3	^151. this ム (cow) under a tire stop sits on this 月 (moon), thinking that giving **Soda** is bad when one 育てる **soda**teru (raises) a child, and that a child's 教育 kyou**iku** (education) should be mostly about **Ear-Coo**ties and how to **Hatch-a-Goose-in-a-Coop**	育てる sodateru = to raise; 教育 kyouiku = education; 育む hagukumu = to nourish, nurture
台 2	^538. this ム (cow) rests on a 口 (box) that resembles a 台 **dai** (platform); she is on a **Diet**, and she is **Tired** of it	台 dai = platform; 台風 taifuu = typhoon
治 4	^539. **Naomi** 治した **nao**shita (cured) this ム (cow) on this 口 (platform) **Chea**ply by mixing medicine with this water, but **Osa**ma bin Laden **Jeer**ed her efforts	治す naosu = to heal; 治安 chian = safety; 治める osameru = to govern or reign; 政治 seiji = politics
始 2	^540. this 女 (female) leaves her **Hat-in-her-Jeep** and 始める **haji**meru (begins) removing this ム (cow) from this 口 (box) so that she can replace it with a **Sheep**	始める hajimeru = to begin; 開始する kaishi suru = to begin
苔 1	^957. after drinking from a **Cold-Keg**, this ム (cow) lay down on this 口 (box) and covered itself with this blanket of 苔 **koke** (moss)	苔 koke = moss, lichen
選 2	^352. this snail is a 選挙 **sen**kyo (election) van, carrying these two 己 (backward candidates) for the **Sen**ate, who are campaigning 共 (together), from which one had to 選ぶ **era**bu (choose) during an **Era** of turmoil	選挙 senkyo = election; 選ぶ erabu = to choose
羽 4	^755. at **Hane**da airport, I saw these two **hane** 羽 (feathers) in the **Hat** of a **Warrior** who was driving an **Uber** car	羽 hane = feather, wing; 羽織 haori = short jacket worn over kimono; 一羽 ichiwa = one bird; 羽毛 umou = down, feathers
弱 2	^471. a **Yogi-was-Wandering** when he saw **Jack** Nicholson holding these two feathers with 弱い **yowa**i (weak) shafts	弱い yowai = weak; 弱点 jakuten = weak point, weakness
港 3	^549. at this 港 **minato** (port) in Cologne, which is controlled by **Mighty-NATO**, there is this tower on the upper right that supports cranes used to load ships, and this 己 (snake) on the lower right is swimming in this water and headed for the **Congo**	空港 kuukou = airport; 港 minato = port; 香港 honkon = Hong Kong
記 2	^550. I read a 記事 **ki**ji (article) containing a lot of 言 (words) about this 己 (snake) that **Ki**lled a person and the **Sh**eep-that-escaped-to-the-**Roo**f	記入 ki'nyuu = entry, filling in forms; 記す shirusu = to record or write
己 2	^652. this snake was the h**Onore**e at our awards ceremony, but its 己 **onore** (self) got **Cold**, so it went home	己 onore = self; 利己的な rikoteki na = egotistic, self-centered
改 2	^700. the **Arab-Tax** collector on the right, who is a dancer, has gone out to fly her **Kite**, but 改めて **arata**mete (again) she has encountered this big 己 (snake) on the left	改める aratameru = to change, correct; 改正する kaisei suru = to revise, reform, amend
面 5	^282. this **Old-Mo**torcar is a **Jeep** with this antenna, and this working 目 (eye) on its back panel is an 面白い **omo**shiroi (interesting) innovation that protects it from 面倒な **men**dou na (annoying) **Men** from the **North** who might want to **Tsue-(sue)-the-R**appers who ride in it	面白い omoshiroi = interesting; 真面目な majime na = sincere; 地面 jimen = the surface of the earth, the ground; 箕面市 Minooshi = a city near Osaka; 面 tsura = a face
夏 3	^522. in 夏 **natsu** (summer), this dancer with a ponytail wears a **Nat**ty-**Suit** and is driven in this limousine **Car** with this antenna to **Getty**sburg	夏 natsu = summer; 初夏 shoka = early summer; 夏至 geshi = summer solstice
優 3	^528. this man on the left is 優しい **yasa**shii (kind), he plays a **Yankee-Saxophone**, he tilts his hat back in order to view this 優秀な **yuu**shuu na (excellent) antenna on his limousine, he acts from this 心 (heart), his girlfriend is this **You**thful dancer with a ponytail, and they will **Soon-buy-a-Goo**se	優しい yasashii = kind; 優秀 yuushuu = excellent; 優れる sugureru = to excel
灰 2	^444. if you light this **High** 火 (fire) inside this lean-to, you will generate 灰 **hai** (ash) and make the inside of the lean-to 灰色 **hai**iro (grey), and the **Kai**ser will get mad	灰 hai = ash; 灰色 haiiro = grey; 石灰岩 sekkaigan = limestone

回 2		^4. I wash this **K**ite in **Ma**donna's-**Wa**shing machine and watch it 回る **mawa**ru (rotate) many 回 **kai** (times)	三回 sankai = three times; 回る mawaru = to turn, intransitive
四 3		^6. over **Yo**nder, there are 四件の **yon**ken no (four) houses with four sides and three interior spaces like this, occupied by **Yo**delers and **Shee**p	四 yon = four; 四つ yottsu = four items; 四日 yokka = 4th of the month; 四季 shiki = four seasons
西 4		^464. my **Ni**ece-has-**Shee**p, and she lives in this house with 四 (four) sides and this high balcony in 西 **nishi** (west) **Swe**den, where she feels **Sa**fe and can study **Sci**ence	西 nishi = west; 西瓜 suika = watermelon; 西欧 seiou = Western Europe; 関西 Kansai = southwest part of Japan, including Osaka; 東西 touzai = East and West
国 4		^170. my 国 **kuni** (country) is like this 玉 (jewel) in a box, and it's full of **Cunn**ing people who drink a lot of **Co**ke and Gold-**Koo**l-Aid, and dig up a lot of **Coa**l	国 kuni = country; 韓国 kankoku = South Korea; 中国 chuugoku = China; 国会 kokkai = Diet
困 2		^280. while this 木 (tree) was in a **Co**ma, someone built this box around it, so that it 困っている **koma**tte iru (is in trouble), and some **Co**neheads say that this is a 困難な **kon**nan na (difficult) situation	困る komaru = to be troubled, inconvenienced; 困難 konnan = difficult
図 3		^281. this is a framed 図 **zu** (drawing) of these two people riding on this giraffe, returning from the **Zoo**, where they saw some **Toa**ds, and heading to the 図書館 **to**shokan (library), where there is going to be a **Hacka**thon	図 zu = drawing; 地図 chizu = map; 図書館 toshokan = library; 図る hakaru = to plot or attempt
団 2		^686. this sunny kneeling guy wants to **Dan**ce with **Ton**y Blair and the rest of his 団体 **dan**tai (group), but he has gotten 付 (stuck) to this gum that he dropped in this box	団体 dantai = group of people, an organization; 布団 futon = floor cushion, or Japanese bedding
囲 3		^1202. a **C**arpentry-**C**orporation built this fence to 囲む **kako**mu (surround) this 井 (well), and now it's **Ea**sy to keep **In**truders out	囲む kakomu = to surround or circle; 周囲 shuu'i = surroundings; 雰囲気 fu'inki = atmosphere, ambience, mood
井 3		^983. **J**oan of Arc decided to try to lose some # (pounds) like this on **Ea**ster, so she walked down to an 井戸 **i**do (well) with some **In**nocent kids	天井 tenjou = ceiling; 井戸 ido = water well; 井上 Inoue = a family name
星 2		^48. this 日 (sun) that 生 (lives) is a 星 **hoshi** (star), admired by **H**orses-and-**Shee**p as they eat **Sa**ge grass	星 hoshi = star; 星座 seiza = constellation
性 3		^209. **Sa**gacious researchers stand straight and tall like this as they confidently **Say** that chromosomes like this one on the left determine the 性 **sei** (gender) of this 牛 (cow) on this platform, and they can **Sho**w us these chromosomes under a microscope	性 saga = one's nature, or custom; 男性 dansei = man, male; 女性 josei = woman, female; 相性 aishou = affinity, compatibility
産 4		^210. **San**ta keeps has this bell on the roof of this lean-to, which rings to announce that 牛 (cows) on platforms like this 生 (live) inside, and he supports a 産業 **san**gyou (industry) that creates treatments for **Oo**zing wounds caused by poorly fitting **U**gandan-**Boo**ts, including **Y**am-and-**Ge**kko-based ointments	産業 sangyou = industry; 産む umu = to give birth, produce, lay an egg; 産着 ubugi = baby clothes; お土産 omiyage = souvenir
祝 3		^274. this **Sh**ah **iwa**u 祝う (celebrates) with this 兄 (big brother); they are happy that eels are on the menu and say "Eels-are-Wacky!" as they **Shuck** corn for the feast and **Shoot** off fireworks	祝う iwau = to celebrate; 祝日 shukujitsu = national holiday; 祝儀 shuugi = celebration, wedding, gratuity
兄 4		^420. 兄 **ani** (older brother) has this square 口 (head) and these lopsided legs, and he ate like an **Ani**mal when he visited his **Ni**ece in **Kyou**to, where she offered him some **Ca**ke	兄 ani = my older brother; お兄さん oniisan = your older brother; 兄弟 kyoudai = siblings; 父兄 fukei = parents, guardians
競 4		^935. these two 兄 (older brothers) are **K**iller-**S**oldiers who 立 (stand) as they ride **Se**gways out of **C**aves near **Kyou**to in order to 競争する **kyou**sou suru (compete)	競う kisou = to compete with; 競り seri = auction; 競馬 keiba = horse racing; 競技 kyougi = competition
残 3		^605. a **N**oble-**Co**de allows warriors to drink nightcaps like this and then 残す **noko**su (leave behind) victims of **G**ory attacks with halberds like this, but this is considered cruel and 残念 **zan**nen (regrettable) behavior in **Zan**zibar	残る nokoru = to remain; 名残 nagori = remnants, traces; 残念 zannen = regrettable

山 3		^146. a **Y**ak-with-**M**agic friends, like **San**ta Claus, lives on this 山 **yama** (mountain) in **Zan**zibar	山登り yamanobori = mountain climbing; 富士山 fujisan = Mt. Fuji; 火山 kazan = volcano
岸 2		^500. **Gan**dalf visits a 海岸 kai**gan** (beach) under this 山 (mountain), where he has this telephone pole in this lean-to and also **Kee**ps-**Shee**p	海岸 kaigan = beach; 岸 kishi = beach, shore
端 4		^730. I 立 (stand) below this 山 (mountain) and admire this limousine, which looks as strong as a **Tan**k but is actually patched together with **Hashi** (chopsticks), and I wonder whether 万端 ban**tan** (all) of my friends will be able fit inside of it when we take it to a **P**arty at a **B**arcelona-**T**avern	万端 bantan = all, everything; 端 hashi = end, edge, border; 片つ端 katappashi = one side, one edge; 半端 hanpa = insufficient, incomplete, insincere; 道端 michibata = the roadside
岩 2		^816. while fighting in an **E**astern-**W**ar, **Gan**dalf rolled 石 (stones) like this down this 山 (mountain), and the enemy was buried in 岩 **iwa** (rock)	岩 iwa = rock; 溶岩 yougan = lava
辿 1		^882. a **Tan-Doe** and this snail 辿った **tado**tta (followed) the same path up this 山 (mountain), but the doe arrived at the top first	辿る tadoru = to follow or trace
催 2		^1110. this man on the left tilts his hat back to examine this 山 (mountain) where he will 催す **moyoo**su (hold) a convention of zookeepers, and he will ask a **M**otormouth-**Y**ogi-to-**O**pen the ceremonies and demonstrate this **Sci**entifically designed net	催す moyoosu = to hold an event; 開催する kaisai suru = to hold a meeting or open an exhibition
合 4		^294. this napkin fits neatly on this 口 (box) under this roof, suggesting that our plans to market **I**ce-cold **G**oat milk will 合う **a**u (come together) in **A**frica, if we can buy **Ga**s for our milk trucks	具合 guai = condition, state; 都合 tsugou = circumstances; 合う au = to come together, to match or suit; 合戦 gassen = battle
答 2		^295. when I met with my **Co**lorado-**Ta**x attorney in this little house and asked about my **To**bacco investments, her 答え **kota**e (answer), which 合 (matched) my needs, was to invest in this 竹 (bamboo) instead	答える kotaeru = to reply; 回答 kaitou = answer, response
拾 2		^595. this guy on the left is a **Hero** who crawls toward this enemy storehouse and 拾う **hiro**u (picks up) this 口 (box) of **Sho**es, which 合 (matches) the needs of our army	拾う hirou = to pick up; 拾得する shuutoku suru = to acquire or obtain
給 1		^997. this 糸 (skeet shooter) 合 (matched) up with a produce company and now earns a high 給料 **kyuu**ryou (salary) shooting **Cu**cumbers	給料 kyuuryou = salary; 補給する hokyuu suru = to supply or supplement
覚 4		^54. these three **Old-Boys** on a roof 覚える **obo**eru (memorize) lines for a play; if you 見 (look) up, you can see a **Sa**murai, his **Za**mbian-friend-**Ma**x, and **Ka**rl-the-**Koo**l-Aid vendor	覚える oboeru = to memorize; 目が覚める me ga sameru = to wake up; 目覚める mezameru = to wake up; 目覚しい mezamashii = outstanding, striking, spectacular; 覚悟する kakugo suru = to be prepared for something unwelcome
堂 1		^64. this 口 (hall), which is a 食堂 shoku**dou** (dining hall), is built on this mound of 土 (soil), and these three old boys stand on its roof eating **D**oughnuts	食堂 shokudou = dining hall
員 1		^88. 員 **in** (members) are **In**siders, who have access to three-drawer 貝 (money chests) like this and wear hats like this	社員 shain = company employee
賞 1		^991. these three old boys on a roof, who are 員 (members) of a club, 覚 (memorize) scripts for **Sh**ows and 入賞する nyuu**shou** suru (win prizes)	受賞する jushou suru = to win an award or prize
労 1		^1075. these three old boys go through a lot of 苦労 ku**rou** (hardship) as they train 力 (powerful) **R**obots on this roof	苦労 kurou = hardship
個 1		^395. this man on the left is a 個人 **ko**jin (individual), and he tilts his hat back to examine this box where he keeps 古 (old) food **C**old	卵三個 tamago sanko = three eggs; 個人 kojin = individual
固 2		^731. I keep an 古 (old) **C**odebook and a **Cata**logue in this box, which is made of 固体 **ko**tai (solid) plastic	頑固 ganko = stubborn; 固い katai = hard, firm, upright (this can sometimes be spelled 堅い or 硬い)

刀 3	^102. I bought this 刀 **katana** (sword) from a **Cata**logue-store-in-**Na**rnia in order to cut my **Toe**nails; it was **Cheap**, but it's missing its handle	刀 katana = sword; 短刀 tantou = dagger; 太刀 tachi = long sword
切 3	^103. it takes 七 (seven) people to 切る **ki**ru (cut) with this big 刀 (sword); if you want to buy one, a friend **Sets-yoU** up, but it's very 大切 tai**setsu** (important) to wear a **Ki**mono and **Si**gn a contract	親切 shinsetsu = kind; 切る kiru = to cut; 横切る yokogiru = to cut across; 一切 issai = everything in affirmative sentences, nothing or never in negative sentences
初 3	^104. this **Happy-Ji**mmy, who has a pointy hat and these two lips, kisses this 刀 (sword) before his 初めての **haji**mete no (first) battle and **Sho**ws it to his admirers, after which all of the people remove their **Hats**	初めて hajimete = for the first time; 最初 saisho = the beginning; 初恋 hatsukoi = first love
分 6	^105. when Daniel **Boone** lived in the **Pun**jab, after drinking **Boo**ze, he tried to 分かる **wa**karu (understand) an **Ita**lian magnet, using this 刀 (sword) to cut it into 八 (eight) parts, which then 分かれた **wa**kareta (separated) from one another; this was **Fun** to **Wa**tch	十分 juubun = enough (this can also be read as juppun, or jippun, = 10 minutes); 五分 gobu = half; 大分 ooita = Oita, a prefecture in Kyushu; 五分 gofun = 5 minutes; 分かる wakaru = to understand; 分かれる wakareru = to separate or branch off
辺 4	^362. I keep this 刀 (sword) on the back of this snail when guarding the **Hen**s in this **hen** 辺 (area) from **Att**ack; **Be**tty is my favorite, and then there is **Na**sty-**Be**cky	この辺 kono hen = around here; その辺り sono atari = around there; 水辺 mizube = waterside; 田辺 Tanabe = a family name
勝 3	^149. in order to achieve a 優勝 yuu**shou** (victory), this 月 (moon) **Sho**ne its light with this 力 (force) to ignite this bonfire, and it 勝った **ka**tta (won) a **Ca**lendar and a **Ma**ssage	優勝 yuushou = victory, championship; 勝つ katsu = to win; 勝る masaru = to outclass, to outdo
楽 6	^520. this 白 (white) oven is a **Ga**dget which some **Gaku**sei (students) and a **Tall-Norwegian** have mounted on this 木 (tree), and it is 楽しい **tano**shii (pleasant) to stare at when **Ra**bbits, **Racco**ons and **Goo**fy-**Ra**dicals are playing	楽器 gakki = musical instrument; 音楽 ongaku = music; 楽しい tanoshii = pleasant; 楽観 rakkan = optimism; 楽 raku = comfort, pleasure, relief; 神楽 kagura = sacred Shinto music and dance
薬 3	^521. 薬 **kusuri** (medicines), which a doctor will prescribe after a **Cursory** exam and which come from **Ya**ms and other plants like these, sometimes have 楽 (pleasant) side-effects, such as causing people to **Yak** (talk) too much	薬 kusuri = medicine; 眠り薬 nemurigusuri = sleeping medicine; 薬局 yakkyoku = pharmacy; 薬品 yakuhin = medicine, drug
集 3	^202. this net has been placed in this 木 (tree) to 集める **atsu**meru (collect) **Atsu**i (hot) flying travelers, who travel without **Sho**es and carry **Tsui**tcases-(suitcases)-full-of-**Dough** (money)	集まる atsumaru = to congregate, intransitive; 集合 shuugou = an assembly; 集う tsudou = to gather or meet
葉 4	^543. in **Ha**waii, a **Yo**gi came out of a **Bar** and saw these 葉 **ha** (leaves) hanging over this bucket on this 木 (tree) next to his **Jeep**	葉 ha = leaf; 紅葉 kouyou = autumn colors; 言葉 kotoba = word; 紅葉 momiji = Japanese maple, autumn colors
梨 1	^1184. リ Ri climbed into this 木 (tree) belonging to his enemy, saw that its 梨 **nashi** (pears) were 禾 (ripe), and started **Gnashi**ng his teeth in anger	梨 nashi = pear tree, or a pear
元 3	^421. a **Motor**cycle gang led by these 二 (two) leaders, **Gen**ghis and **Gan**dalf, rests on lopsided legs like these and has a solid 元 **moto** (base) for a 元気な **gen**ki na (healthy) lifestyle	元 moto = base, origin, source; 元気 genki = cheerful, healthy; 元日 ganjitsu = January 1
完 1	^759. in **Kan**sas, a man with a bad haircut like this operates from a strong 元 (base) like this and 完了する **kan**ryou suru (finishes) his projects	完了する kanryou suru = to finish; 完全な kanzen na = perfect, entire
院 1	^424. a ß (Greek) doctor with a bad haircut like this built a 病院 byou**in** (hospital) on this 元 (base) with lopsided legs for people with **In**fections	病院 byouin = hospital

7-41

統 1	^1125. our 大統領 dai**tou**ryou (president) saw this 糸 (skeet shooter) shooting **To**ads at this ム (cow) under this tire stop which was standing on these lopsided legs	統計 toukei = statistics; 大統領 daitouryou = president of a country
流 4	^654. when this ム (cow) under a tire stop encounters **Naga**ina (a snake from a Kipling story) in a **Roo**m in **Ha**waii, it climbs onto this three-legged stool, empties its **Reu**sable water bottles onto her head, and watches this water 流れる **naga**reru (flow)	流す nagasu = to flush; 流布 rufu = circulation, dissemination; 流行る hayaru = to become popular or successful (usually spelled はやる); 流行 ryuukou = vogue, fashion
荒 3	^968. this three-legged man named **Ara**fat engages in **A**griculture, as suggested by this plant radical, and he grows **C**orn, but when he invites people to sit on this shaky stool, he is being 荒い **ara**i (rude)	荒い arai = violent, rough, rude; 荒れる areru = to be stormy or rough, to fall into ruin; 荒野 kouya = wilderness, the wild
慌 2	^710. on a **C**old morning, this man on the left was **A**wakened by this guy with three legs who threw these plants and this shaky stool at him, and first he drew himself up to his full height like this, but then he 慌てた **awa**teta (panicked)	恐慌 kyoukou = a panic; 慌てる awateru = to be confused or panic, to hurry
係 3	^492. this man on the left is a 係員 **kakari** in (person in charge), he tilts his hat back to examine this **Cape** on this 糸 (skeet shooter), and he shows that he **Can-Carry** his weight in their 関係 kan**kei** (relationship) by giving the shooter some **Caca**o beans	関係 kankei = relationship; 係員 kakari'in = person in charge; 係り kakari = duty (this can also be spelled 係)
孫 2	^1072. this 子 (child) is the 孫 **mago** (grandchild) of this 糸 (skeet shooter), with whom he has a good 係 (relationship), and the skeet shooter waves this cape and sings a **Song** when the child scores a **Magnificent-Goal**	子孫 shison = descendant; 孫 mago = grandchild; 孫娘 magomusume = granddaughter
県 1	^572. **Ken** and Barbie like to move around in their 県 **ken** (prefecture), and they keep their maps in this three-drawer cabinet on this three-legged self-propelled shelf	県 ken = prefecture; 広島県 hiroshima ken = Hiroshima prefecture
以 2	^601. 以前に **izen ni** (a long time ago), after digging a trap with this hoe and producing this drop of sweat, **Mo**ses caught this giraffe, and it was **Easy**	前以て maemotte = beforehand, in advance; 以前に izen ni = a long time ago
似 3	^824. this man on the left tilts his hat back to examine this hoe which my **Nie**ce used, while emitting this drop of sweat, to dig a trap for this giraffe, which had a 類似 rui**ji** (resemblance) to one that he caught, but he would ride on the giraffe's **Neck**, while she rode in a **Jee**p	似ている nite iru = resembling; 真似 mane = imitation, mimicry; 類似 ruiji = a resemblance
工 2	^246. this 工 **kou** (crafted object) resembles an I-beam, seen on end, which is used inside **Coal** mines and in **Coo**ling towers	工場 koujou = factory, 大工 daiku = carpenter
紅 3	^247. this 糸 (skeet shooter) shoots 紅茶 **kou**cha (black tea) at this 工 (crafted object), which is a tube of 口紅 kuchi**beni** (lipstick), but its owner, who works in a **Coal** mine, just cleans her **M**otorcycle-**M**irrors and leaves for **Beni**hana (a chain of teppanyaki restaurants)	紅茶 koucha = black tea; 紅葉 momiji = Japanese maple, autumn colors; 紅 beni = red, rouge, lipstick; 口紅 kuchibeni = lipstick
差 1	^631. I 差し上げた **sa**shiageta (humbly gave) our king this エ (egg) to rub in his eyes because he was suffering from 時差ボケ ji**sa**boke (jet lag), but the エ was **Salty**	時差ボケ jisaboke = jet lag; 交差点 kousaten = traffic intersection; 眼差し manazashi = a look or gaze
功 1	^634. if you want to 成功する sei**kou** suru (succeed) in the **Coal** business, you need to use 工 (crafted objects) like this and expend a lot of 力 (force)	成功 seikou = success; 功績 kouseki = achievement
恐 2	^869. an **Old-Soldier** was buying エ (eggs) like this in **Kyou**to when he saw this desk that had been slashed, and he felt 恐れ **oso**re (fear) in this 心 (heart)	恐れ osore = fear; 恐ろしい osoroshii = frightening, terrible; 恐慌 kyoukou = panic
江 2	^1026. Excellent craftsmen carved precious 工 (crafted objects) like this from **Coral**, found in water like this, during the 江戸 **e**do (ancient Tokyo) period	江戸 edo = old name for Tokyo; 長江 choukou = Yangtze River in China
死 2	^164. if this ヒ (hero) 死ぬ **shi**nu (dies) during this 夕 (evening), they will put his body under this **Sheet** and carry it off in a **Jee**p	死ぬ shinu = to die; 死亡 shibou = death; 早死に hayajini = early death, dying young
列 2	^1124. after this リ Ri put on a **Re**tro-**Su**it and stood in 列 **retsu** (line) at a **Re**staurant, he drank this nightcap	列 retsu = line; 配列 hairetsu = arrangement, disposition; 列車 ressha = train

懐 3	^928. this man on the right is a **Kai**ser with this cross on his crown and these three eyes, and this man on the left, who is wearing this 衣 (clothing) which is a **Natty-Su**it and holds himself tall and proud, reminds the kaiser of a time when they slept on a **Futon**-in-a-**Coro**lla, which elicits 懐かしい **natsu**kashii (nostalgic) feelings		懐中電灯 kaichuu dentou = flashlight; 懐かしい natsukashii = nostalgic, evoca-tive of times past; 懐 futokoro = bosom, heart
聴 1	^934. Margaret **Cho** wears this cross on her head and has these three eyes, and she tells her 聴衆 **chou**shuu (audiences) that she has big 耳 (ears) like this and this good 心 (heart)		聴衆 choushuu = audience; 聴解力 choukairyoku = listening comprehension
徳 1	^1159. this man with two hats thinks that this woman, who resembles 聴 (Margaret Cho) without her 耳 (ears), is a paragon of 美徳 bi**toku** (virtue) and that she is **To**tally-**Cool**, and he will offer her one of his hats		美徳 bitoku = virtue
用 2	^364. we will 利用する ri**you** suru (use) this fence to enclose a cow, so that we can make our own **Yo**gurt and stop **MooChi**ng from the neighbors		用事 youji = errand; 利用する riyou suru = to use; 用いる mochiiru = to use
備 2	^367. this man on the left tilts his hat back to examine the **Sonar** equipment that he uses to monitor the **Beer** that is kept in a 設備 setsu**bi** (facility), which is this lean-to under this roof garden, with this 用 (fence) protecting it		備える sonaeru = to prepare, have, equip with; 準備 junbi = preparation
角 3	^81. this fish-head guy with bifocals and straight legs got caught in a **Car-Door** at a 角 **kado** (corner) near a **Ca**ctus farm, where he kept a **Tsu**itcase-(suitcase)-full-of-Notebooks		角 kado = outside corner; 四角い shikakui = square, rectangular; 角 tsuno = horn, antler, feeler
触 3	^475. this **Fool**ish 角 (fish-head guy with bifocals) is sidling up to 触る **sawa**ru (touch) this 虫 (insect) which he **Saw-Wa**lking down the road, but he will get **Shock**ed by its stinger		触れる fureru = to touch (usually unintentional); 触る sawaru = to touch (usually intentional); (手)触(り) tezawari = touch or feel; 接触する sesshoku suru = to touch or contact
解 4	^618. this 角 (fish-head guy with glasses) is a **Kai**ser who has found that the 解決 **kai**ketsu (solution) to his financial problems is to sell 刀 (weapons) like this and 牛 (beef) like this, as well as **To**matoes and **Ge**ckos, and he **Hopes-to-buy-a-Do**lphin with the proceeds		解決 kaiketsu = solution; 解く toku = to solve or undo, transitive; 解熱 ge'netsu = lowering a fever; 解ける hodokeru = to unravel, to come untied
眩 2	^937. this 目 (eye) belongs to a museum **Cura**tor who was drinking **Ma**ssachusetts **Boo**ze and didn't see that this tire stop was about to fall on this truncated 糸 (skeet shooter); moreover, a sudden 眩しい **mabu**shii (dazzling) light distracted him		眩む kuramu = to be blinded or dazzled; 眩しい mabushii = dazzling, blinding
幻 2	^1129. **Gen**ghis saw this truncated 糸 (skeet shooter) holding this フ (oar), and he thought it was a **Ma**riner-using-a-**Bo**at-to-**Ro**w-**Sheep** across a lake, but this turned out to be a 幻想 **gen**sou (illusion)		幻想 gensou = fantasy, illusion; 幻覚 genkaku = hallucination; 幻 maboroshi = illusion, vision
深 3	^694. a **Fool**ish-**Cashier** from **Buch**arest installed this platform with lopsided legs at the top of this 木 (tree) and dove into this water below, but the water was 深い **fuka**i (deep), and a **Shin**to priest had to rescue him		深い fukai = deep; 興味深い kyoumi-bukai = very interesting; 深夜 shinya = dead of night; 深刻 shinkoku = serious
探 3	^699. this guy on the left has **Saga**ciously set up this platform with lopsided legs in this 木 (tree), where he kneels as he uses binoculars to 探す **saga**su (look for) his **Sad-Goo**se and where he also works on his **Tan**		探す sagasu = to search or look for; 探る saguru = to grope, look for, probe; 探険 tanken = exploration, expedition (this can also written 探検 tanken)
過 4	^361. **Su**perman placed these two **Cartons** into the center of these larger boxes for transport on this snail, but he やり過ぎた yari**sugi**ta (overdid it), such that this carton in the center of the upper box slipped out of place, and the **Aya**tollah-got-**Mad**, but later he gave Superman some **Superior-Golf** clubs		過ぎる sugiru = to exceed; 過去 kako = the past; 過ち ayamachi = fault, error; 過す sugosu = to spend or to pass time (this can also be spelled 過ごす)

Chapter 8

訳 2	^437. the 訳 **wake** (reason) that this 尺 (**Wake**ful eye) is watching these 言 (words) is to check the accuracy of the 通訳 tsuu**yaku** (interpretation) being done for a **Yaku**za (gangster)	訳 wake = reason, interpretation; 言い訳 iiwake = excuse; 通訳 tsuuyaku = interpreter, interpretation
駅 1	^380. this reminds us of the old custom of changing 馬 (horses) like this at the royal 駅 **eki** (station) under this 尺 (wakeful eye) belonging to Edward-the-**Ki**ng	駅 eki = station
沢 2	^1100. this 尺 (wakeful eye) **Saw-this-Water**, and it reminded him of the 沢山 **taku**san (many) 訳 (reasons) that he likes to use **Tap-water-to-make-Kool**-Aid	沢村 Sawamura = a family name; 金沢 Kanazawa = a city in Honshu; 光沢 koutaku = luster
寺 2	^213. this 寺 **tera** (temple), which is built into the side of a hill, features a **Terra**ce and a **Jee**p, but it is covered in this 土 (soil)	寺 tera = temple; 清水寺 Kiyomizudera = a temple in Kyoto; 寺院 jiin = temple
時 3	^215. this 日 (sun) shines on this 寺 (temple), and the temple's sundial says the 時 **toki** (time) is 一時 ichi**ji** (1:00), when **To**lstoy comes in his **Jee**p and we go eat **To**mato-**Qui**che	時計 tokei = clock, or watch; 時間 jikan = time; 時 toki = time; 開花時 kaikadoki = blossoming time
持 2	^216. this guy on the left crawls up to this 寺 (temple) in the **Mo**rning, since his feet hurt from walking all night, asking whether they 持つ **mo**tsu (have) a **Jee**p that he can use	持つ motsu = to hold or have; 支持する shiji suru = to support
待 2	^217. this man with two hats 待つ **ma**tsu (waits) at this 寺 (temple) and says that he just bought his second hat at the **Ma**ll and is **Ti**red of shopping	待つ matsu = to wait; 招待 shoutai = invitation
特 2	^218. this 特別な **toku**-betsu na (special) 牛 (cow) on the left was given to this 寺 (temple) by **To**lstoy, and it is **To**tally-**Coo**l	特急 tokkyuu = limited express train; 特別な tokubetsu na = special
侍 1	^1118. this man on the left tilts his hat back to gaze at this 寺 (temple), where he has come to pray because he is **Sad-that-a-Moo**nie-took-his-**Ri**ce and gave it to a 侍 **samurai** (Japanese warrior)	侍 samurai = Japanese warrior
等 5	^1132. these two 竹 (bamboo) clamps at the top of this 寺 (temple) indicate that it has earned a ranking of 二等 ni**tou** (2nd place) for the bamboo toys it sells, including small statues of **To**ads, **Do**es, **Ra**bbits and **Hito** (people), but it also sells **Nasty-Dough**nuts, and overall it is about 等しい **hito**shii (equal) to other temples	上等 joutou = excellent, very good; 平等 byoudou = equal; これ等 korera = these (usually written これら); 等しい hitoshii = same, equal; 等々 nadonado = etc.
及 2	^883. this graph of a **Cu**te baby's breathing patterns 及ぶ **oyo**bu (extends) to occasions when she was fed **Old-Yo**gurt	普及する fukyuu suru = to become popular or widespread; 及ぶ oyobu = to reach or extend to
吸 2	^427. this 口 (mouth) on the left and this graph of breathing patterns on the right remind us of a baby named **Su**e who cannot 吸う **su**u (suck) properly but is very **Cu**te	タバコを吸う tabako wo suu = to smoke tobacco; 吸収する kyuushuu suru = to digest
携 2	^1011. this guy on the left is a **Tall-Zoo**keeper-from-**Sa**pporo, and he is so tall that he has to kneel to show us this graph that he 携帯する **kei**tai suru (carries) depicting escape attempts by animals from this net and from **Ca**ges at the zoo	携わる tazusawaru = to engage (in); 携帯する keitai suru = to carry; 携帯電話 keitai denwa = cellular phone
級 1	^1131. this 糸 (skeet shooter) is examining these breathing patterns of a **Cu**te baby, which it thinks will grow up to be a 高級な kou**kyu**u na (high class) person who shoots skeets	高級 koukyuu = high class or quality; 同級生 doukyuusei = classmate
夜 3	^489. a **Yo**semite-**Roo**ster tripped on this tire stop and scratched this dancer on the cheek one 夜 **yoru** (night), and this man on the left tilted his hat back to examine the wound and advised her to put **Yo**gurt and **Ya**m extract on it	夜 yoru = night; 夜中 yonaka = middle of the night; 今夜 konya = tonight
丸 2	^866. **Ga**ndalf was **Ma**rooned on a 丸い **maru**i (round) island after pirates slashed his boat 九 (nine) times	弾丸 dangan = bullet; 丸 maru = circle

五₂		^179. 五 **go** (five) **Go**lfers **Eat-Su**shi as they stare like this down a fairway	五人 gonin = five people; 五つ itsutsu = five items
語₃		^435. these 五 (five) **Go**lfers stand on this 口 (box), they stare because they have **Cata**racts, they know only a little 英語 ei**go** (English), and they mix up 言 (words) like this, saying **Gatari**de instead of Gatorade	英語 eigo = English; 語る kataru = to talk; 物語る monogataru = to tell or indicate; 物語 monogatari = story
互₂		^1207. these two コ (youths) have discovered a **Go**ld mine in the Philippines, and they speak **Taga**log 互いに **tagai** ni (with each other)	相互 sougo = each other, one another, mutuality; 互いに tagai ni = with each other, mutually, reciprocally
虫₂		^9. I heard a **Mushy** story about a 虫 **mushi** (insect) that lies on the ground like this and goes 中 (inside) a house to **Chew** up the furniture	虫 mushi = worm, insect, bug; 害虫 gaichuu = harmful insects
強₄		^478. since I practice archery with this bow and work out with this barbell, I am 強い **tsuyo**i (strong) and can carry **Tsui**tcases-(suitcases)-of-**Yo**gurt made from **Goat** and **Shee**p milk to sell in my business in **Kyou**to	強い tsuyoi = strong; 根強い nezuyoi = firmly rooted, persistent; 強引 gouin = coercive, high-handed; 強いる shiiru = to force; 勉強 benkyou = study
独₁		^724. I saw a **Docu**mentary about this woman who lives in 孤独 ko**doku** (isolation) because she is fond of 虫 (insects) like this and contorts herself for them	孤独 kodoku = solitude, isolation; 独立 dokuritsu = independence
騒₂		^826. this 馬 (horse) 騒いだ **sawa**ida (made a fuss) when it **Saw-a-Warlord** listening to **Soul** music at this 又 (table) with this buzzing 虫 (insect) nearby	騒ぐ sawagu = to make noise, to make a fuss; 騒々しい souzoushii = noisy
置₂		^569. Oprah combines this thick handle with this thin handle when she lifts heavy items like **Chee**se that she stores in this three-drawer cabinet and 置く **o**ku (places) them on shelves like this	置く oku = to place something; 位置 ichi = position
直₇		^570. **Nao**mi and **Su**perman say that if we use this three-drawer shelf cabinet with this thin handle to store lighter items, like **Jeep-Keys** for our **Jeep-Car**, and Margaret **Cho**'s-**Kool**-Aid packets, we can 直す **nao**su (correct) our storage problems and simplify our **Cho**res, and we think that they are **Tada**shii (correct)	直す naosu = to correct or repair something; 真っ直ぐ massugu = straight; 正直 shoujiki = honest; 直に jika ni = directly; 直面 chokumen = confrontation; 直行便 chokkoubin = nonstop flight; 直ちに tadachi ni = immediately
値₃		^571. this man on the left, who is **A-Thai** person, tilts his hat back to examine this three-drawer cabinet with a thin handle on this shelf, where we keep lightweight items like **N**ecklaces, and he would like to 直 (repair) the cabinet for a **Chea**p 値段 **ne**dan (price)	値 atai = value, price; 価値 kachi = value; 値段 nedan = price
電₁		^263. this wire is emerging from this 田 (transformer) under this 雨 (rain), suggesting that 電気 **den**ki (electricity) is being generated from lightning strikes in **Den**mark	電気 denki = electricity
奄₁		^1095. an **Ama**teur engineer built this 大 (big) 電 (electric transformer) on 奄美大島 **Ama**mi Ooshima (an island)	奄美大島 Amami Ooshima = an island between Kyushu and Okinawa
俺₁		^956. 俺 **ore** (I) am this man on the left, and I tilt my hat back in order to examine this 大 (big) 電 (electric) transformer in **Ore**gon	俺 ore = I, me; 俺たち oretachi = we, us
滝₁		^1179. we were 立 (standing) and **Talki**ng about a scheme to make 電 (electricity) like this using hydropower from this water that flows over a 滝 **taki** (waterfall)	滝 taki = waterfall, cascade
亀₂		^908. this resembles a 亀 **kame** (turtle) that I photographed with my **Came**ra in **K**iev, since it has a head like a fish, a shell that resembles two linked 田 (rice paddies) and a tail	亀 kame = turtle, tortoise; 海亀 umigame = sea turtle; 亀裂 kiretsu = crack, crevice, fissure
縄₂		^1003. this skeet shooter fires at these 田 (rice paddies) that are joined by this 縄 **nawa** (rope) that **Narco-Wa**rlords made from straw, and **Joa**n of Arc is impressed	縄 nawa = rope; 沖縄 Okinawa; 縄文時代 joumon jidai = the Jomon period (14,000 - 300 BC)

小 5		^253. a 小さい **chii**sai (small) **Ch**impanzee registered and then **Show**ed up wearing a **Coat** at a 小学校 **shou**gakkou (elementary school) in **O**saka, where it majored in **Art**	小さい chiisai = small; 小学校 shougakkou = elementary school; 小鳥 kotori = little bird; 小川 ogawa = brook; 小豆 azuki = red bean
少 3		^254. our **Succu**lent plants are 少ない **suku**nai (few), and **S**uperman-and-his-**Co**-workers got 少し **suko**shi (a little) pleasure from them at our 小 (small) plant **Show**, but ノ (no) one was satisfied	少ない sukunai = a little; 少し sukoshi = a little; 少々 shoushou = a little
歩 4		^408. wearing shoes with rounded soles like this in **Aru**ba, I will 歩く **aru**ku (walk) for the Clean Air Trust fundraiser, together with **A-You**th I know, in order to help 止 (stop) **P**ollution 少 (a little), near my **Ho**me	歩く aruku = to walk; 歩み ayumi = walking, step, history, record; 散歩する sanpo suru = to walk; 歩道 hodou = sidewalk
省 3		^1010. a **Shou**gun drank 少 (a little) **Ha**waiian-**Boo**ze and felt that it was pushing down on this 目 (eye), causing him to worry about his **Sa**fety, so he did some 反省 han**sei** (self-scrutiny) and decided to 省く **habu**ku (cut down) on his drinking	省略 shouryaku = abbreviation, omission; 省く habuku = to omit, to cut down (cost); 反省 hansei = scrutiny, self-scrutiny, regret
砂 4		^782. a **Ja**panese person uses a **Sharp** tool to turn 少 (a few) 石 (stones) like this into 砂 **suna** (sand) for a **Sa**lary, but his **S**upervisor-**Na**gs him endlessly	砂利道 jarimichi = gravel path; 土砂降り doshaburi = pouring rain; 砂漠 sabaku = desert; 砂糖 satou = sugar; 砂 suna = sand
秒 1		^1137. a **Bee-O**wner has only 少 (a little) of this 禾 (ripe grain), but he enjoys seeing one or more of his bees fly through it every 秒 **byou** (second)	一秒 ichibyou = a second (1/60 minute); 秒針 byoushin = the second hand on a clock
出 5		^147. these two volcanoes 出す **dasu** (put out) lava, which 出る **de**ru (emerges), **Shoots** up into the air, **Da**shes down the slopes and burns a **Sweet Debutante's Shoes**	外出する gaishutsu suru = to go out; 出す dasu = to put out; 出納 suitou = accounts; 出る deru = to leave or go out; 出席 shusseki = attendance
秋 2		^445. **Achi**lles visited us in 秋 **aki** (autumn) to admire this 禾 (ripe grain) and our 火 (fire)-like leaves, and also to show us his new **Shoe**s	秋 aki = autumn; 晩秋 banshuu = late fall
科 1		^511. a 科学者 **ka**gakusha (scientist) extracts **Ca**lcium from this 禾 (ripe grain) and uses it to fill these two containers on this slanted shelf	科学 kagaku = science; 科学者 kagakusha = scientist
和 6		^513. when this 禾 (grain plant) gets ripe, we use 口 (mouths) like this to eat 和食 **wa**shoku (Japanese food) served from a **Wa**gon, experience 平和 hei**wa** (peace), **Yawn-and-Wa**sh the dishes, but sometimes there are **Nagging-Gho**sts from **O**ld times, like **T**olstoy, and **Y**ogis-who-have-**Re**tired	温和 onwa = mild, calm, gentle; 和らぐ yawaragu = to soften; 和む nagomu = to be softened, to calm down; 和尚 oshou = Buddhist priest; 大和 yamato = ancient Japan; 日和 hiyori = weather, climatic conditions
利 2		^564. this リ **Ri** 利用する **ri**you suru (uses) this 禾 (ripe grain) to make **Q**uiche	利用する riyou suru = to use; 利く kiku = to be effective (this is usually spelled 効く)
香 4		^681. this grain plant with a ripe head in **Co**lombia stands in this 日 (sun), enjoying the 香り **kao**ri (fragrance) of some **Cows** from **Hon**duras which are part of a **Ca**rnival	線香 senkou = incense stick; 香り kaori = fragrance, aroma; 香港 honkon = Hong Kong; 香川県 kagawa ken = Kagawa Prefecture
季 1		^1047. the **Key** to remembering the 季節 **ki**setsu (seasons), is to associate this 禾 (ripe grain) with autumn and this 子 (child) with spring	季節 kisetsu = season; 四季 shiki = the four seasons
種 2		^1098. in order to grow 重 (heavy) 禾 (ripe grain) like this, I store 種 **tane** (seeds) in **Tan-Eggshells** and **Shoot** them over my fields	種 tane = seed; 種類 shurui = variety, type;
失 4		^206. this 大 (big) 牛 (cow) is an **Ushi-**(cow)-from-**Na**rnia, and she is **U**ber in some ways, but she steps on our **Sheets**, and she is 失礼 **shitsu**rei (rude) to our **Sheep**	失う ushinau = to lose; 失せる useru = to disappear; 失礼 shitsurei = discourtesy; 失敗する shippai suru = to fail

私 3	^510. 私 **watakushi** (I) feed this 禾 (ripe grain) to my **Shee**p and to ム (cows) like this, and I am a **W**ashington-**Takushi**i (taxi) driver who uses a lawyer named **W**allace-**to**-create-**Tax-Shields**		私 watakushi = I; 私 watashi = I; 私用の shiyou no = private
払 1	^591. this guy is kneeling to examine this ム (cow), which is being **Hara**ssed, and he is willing to 払う **hara**u (pay) for it		払う harau = to pay; 支払い shiharai = payment
仏 3	^678. this man on the left tilts his hat back to examine this ム (cow), which he would never eat since he is a 仏教 **bu**kkyou (Buddhism) teacher who wears nice **Boo**ts, drinks **Boo**ze and eats **Hottoke**eki (pancakes)		仏壇 butsudan = Buddhist altar found in Japanese homes; 仏教 bukkyou = Buddhism; 仏 hotoke = Buddha
宗 3	^676. our 宗教 **shuu**kyou (religion) encourages 祭 (festivals) with spinning 丁 (nails) like this, and it attracts **Moon-E**xperts with bad haircuts like this who promise to stay **So**ber and wear nice **Sho**es		宗 mune = religion, sect; 宗家 souke = head of family; 宗教 shuukyou = religion
奈 1	^1006. in 奈良 **Na**ra, a 大 (big) **Na**zi who is 宗 (religious) rides on flying carpets above spinning nails like this		奈良 Nara = ancient capital of Japan; 神奈川県 Kanagawa ken = a prefecture in Japan
甘 2	^541. **Ama**nda bought this half-full bucket of 甘い **ama**i (sweet) molasses and made **Ca**ndy		甘い amai = sweet; 甘味所 kanmidokoro = a cafe featuring Japanese-style sweets
期 2	^711. when this 月 (moon) is full, it's the 時期 ji**ki** (season) for our **Go**ats to play by moonlight, and this woman on the left, who has this bucket with compartments and a wide skirt, makes 甘 (sweet) **Qui**che from their milk		末期 matsugo = the hour of death (this can also be pronounced makki); 時期 jiki = time, season; 学期 gakki = semester
箕 1	^1178. I had a **Mea**l in 箕面市 **Mi**noushi with this woman with this wide skirt and this bucket with several compartments, and we ate these 竹 (bamboo) shoots		箕面市 Minooshi = a city north of Osaka
焼 2	^446. using this 火 (fire) on the left, we 焼く yaku (grill) these three **Ya**ms on these skewers above this base with lopsided legs and eat them during movie **Show**s		焼く yaku = to grill, toast, etc.; 焼却 shoukyaku = incineration
灯 1	^626. when I place this 丁 (nail) in this 火 (fire), it glows like a **To**rch (flashlight), but it can't replace a 電灯 den**tou** (electric light)		街灯 gaitou = street light; 電灯 dentou = electric light
炎 2	^788. an **En**tertainer piled 火 (fire) upon 火 (fire) until a large 火炎 ka**en** (fire) was blazing at my **Home-in-Northern-Oregon**		火炎 kaen = fire; 炎 honoo = blaze, flame
談 1	^790. a **Dan**cer 言 (spoke) to her neighbors about 炎 (fire) prevention, and their conversation turned into a general 相談 sou**dan** (consultation)		相談 soudan = consultation; 冗談 joudan = a joke
焚 1	^1183. **Ta**rzan started this 火 (fire) in this 林 (grove) in order to make a 焚き火 **ta**kibi (bonfire)		焚き火 takibi = bonfire; 焚く taku = to burn (wood)
滅 3	^1193. when I **Met-Su**perman in this lean-to in **Me**xico, he told me that, according to his **Horo**scope, we were threatened with 絶滅 zetsu**metsu** (extinction) from a combination of this water, this napkin-covered 火 (fire) and halberds like this one		絶滅 zetsumetsu = extinction; 滅入る meiru = to feel depressed; 滅ぼす horobosu = to ruin or destroy
言 4	^430. **Gen**ghis used this 口 (mouth) to 言う **i**u (speak) 言葉 **koto**ba (words) about his favorite instruments, the **Koto** (Japanese harp) and the **Gon**g, which sound good to his **Ea**rs		言語 gengo = language; 言葉 kotoba = words; 伝言 dengon = message; 言う iu = to speak or tell
信 1	^431. this man on the left 信じる **shin**jiru (believes) in **Shin**tou, and he tilts his hat back to show his sincerity before he 言 (speaks) about his 信念 **shin**nen (beliefs)		信じる shinjiru = to believe; 信号 shingou = stoplight; 信念 shinnen = belief
目 3	^51. among **Me**chanics with big 目 **me** (eyes) who work on refrigerators like this, the one who came to our house is the **Most-Coo**l, and he takes his annual **B**onus-as-**Ko**ol-Aid		目 me = eye; 目的 mokuteki = purpose; 面目ない menbokunai = ashamed
見 2	^53. this 目 (eye) on lopsided legs 見る **mi**ru (looks) in a **Mi**rror and 見る **mi**ru (sees) **Ke**n and Barbie		見る miru = to look at or see; 拝見する haiken suru = to humbly look at or see
耳 2	^57. **Mi**mi sits in her **Jee**p, showing off this 耳 **mimi** (ear) which **Mimi**cs, or resembles, an 目 (eye)		耳 mimi = ear; 耳鼻科 jibika = ear, nose & throat specialist

行 6	^334. this man with two hats works with this hammer and nail, and then he likes to **Eat**, and he 行く **iku** (goes) to see an **Old-Coder-who-is-his-Nanny** and trades one of his two hats for some **Corn** to put in **Gyo**za for the **Yu**le celebration to be held in his **Yard**	行く iku = to go; 行う okonau = to conduct; 銀行 ginkou = bank; 行事 gyouji = event; 東京行き toukyou yuki = bound for Tokyo; 流行る hayaru = to become popular (usually spelled はやる)
達 4	^347. this snail carries this 羊 (sheep) which is covered by this 土 (soil), and it attracts many 人達 hito**tachi** (people), who are at**Tach**ing signs with **Dark-Cheese** and **Ta**ffy to this snail, complaining about the sheep's condition; this is titsu for **Tatsu**, since the sheep's owner is attaching his signs as well	人達 hitotachi = people; 友達 tomodachi = friend; 達成 tassei = achievement; 速達 sokutatsu = express mail
辛 3	^384. while singing **Kara**oke and eating 辛い **kara**i (spicy) food on a **Shin**gle at a dude ranch, I found this needle in the food, so I **Tsu**ed-(sued)-the-**Ranch**	辛い karai = spicy, hot; 香辛料 koushinryou = spices; 辛い tsurai = painful, tormenting
幸 4	^385. I live in this four-level tower in a **Shia**-country-torn-by-**War**, and there are some **Sad-Chil**dren here, and a lot of 辛 (spicy) food, but if I can take **Silent-Walks** and fight off **Col**ds, that means 幸せ **shiawa**se (happiness) for me	幸せ shiawase = happiness; 幸子 Sachiko = a girl's given name; 幸い saiwai = lucky, happy; 幸福 koufuku = happiness
申 3	^10. **Mo**ses 申す **mou**su (speaks humbly) after these lips are stitched together with thread on a **Mormon-Ship** by a **Shin**to priest	申す mousu = to humbly speak; 申込書 moushikomisho = application form; 申請する shinsei suru = to apply or request
神 7	^273. this Shah, who is feeling **Cold**, 申 (speaks humbly) as he stands on a roof **Shin**gle in his skinny **Jean**s praying to the 神道 **shin**tou (a Japanese religion) 神 **kami** (gods), but a **Commie** (Communist) from **Kan**sas is waiting to **Ca**ll him to a **Mee**ting	神戸 Koube = a city in Japan; 神道 Shintou = a Japanese religion; 神社 jinja = Shintou shrine; 神 kami = god; 女神 megami = goddess; 神田 Kanda = an area in Tokyo; 神奈川 Kanagawa = a prefecture in Japan; お神酒 omiki = sake offered to the gods
伸 2	^697. this man on the left emerges from a **Shin**to shrine, tilts his hat back, sees that these lips are stitched together, suggesting that **No** one wants to tell him that his ride has gone, and he 申 (humbly says) that he must 伸ばす **no**basu (extend) his visit	追伸 tsuishin = postscript; 伸ばす nobasu, transitive = to lengthen, stretch, develop, expand
由 3	^73. there is a **Unit** of rice at the top of this 田 (rice paddy), and the 理由 ri**yuu** (reason) is that a **You**th will be taking the rice to some **Yukon-Eagles**	経由で keiyu de = via, by way of; 理由 riyuu = reason; 由緒 yuisho = a history or lineage
宙 1	^898. I put this bad haircut on this unit of rice near this rice paddy to make it less attractive to 宇宙人 u**chuu**jin (space aliens) who might want to **Chew** on it	宇宙 uchuu = universe, cosmos, space
油 2	^942. the 由 (reason) that I have this water plus this 由 (Unit of rice) is to provision my **Abu-Dhabi-Ram** that lives near an 油 **abura** (oil) field	石油 sekiyu = petroleum; 油断 yudan = negligence, inattentiveness; 油 abura = oil
甲 1	^1157. I can **Cope** with stress by grabbing this shaky sign and using it to break 甲羅 **kou**ra (shells)	甲羅 koura = shell
押 3	^592. this **Old** guy on the left gets onto his knees to 押す **o**su (push) on this shaky sign in **Ohio**, causing it to fall onto some **Old-Sheep**	押す osu = to push; 押収 oushuu = seizure, confiscation; 押入れ oshiire = closet, which can also be written 押し入れ
求 2	^810. this 水 (water) 犬 (dog) from **Cu**ba belongs to a 球 (baseball) player who 求む **moto**mu (seeks) a **Motor**cycle	要求 youkyuu = a request or demand; 求む motomu = to seek or demand
球 2	^606. this 王 (king) and this 水 (water) 犬 (dog) from **Cu**ba are watching a 野球 ya**kyuu** (baseball) game while eating **Tamales**	野球 yakyuu = baseball; 電気の球 denki no tama = lightbulb
救 2	^977. this dancer on the right gets energy from **Superior-Kool**-Aid and uses this 水 (water) 犬 (dog) from **Cu**ba to help her 救う **suku**u (rescue) drowning people	救う sukuu = to rescue; 救済 kyuusai = help, rescue, relief

又₁	^24. a **Mata**dor liked this table so much that he bought it 又 **mata** (again)	又 mata = again
取₃	^58. someone 取った **to**tta (took) a **To**rpedo from this 又 (table) and used it to **Shoot** a **To**ry in this 耳 (ear)	取る toru = to take or get; 気取る kido-ru = to put on airs; 取得する shutoku suru = to acquire; 取引 torihiki = business deal
恥₂	^309. when Prince **Ha**rry heard the beating of this 心 (heart) in this 耳 (ear), he felt 恥ずかしい **ha**zukashii (embarrassed) and consulted a **Ha**rvard-**Ge**nius	恥ずかしい hazukashii = embarrassed, shy; 恥 haji = shame, dishonor
餌₂	^843. a dog's 耳 (ears) prick up when an **E**xpert dog handler serves it an **E**gg-**Sa**ndwich as 餌 **esa** (animal food), and it 食 (eats) the sandwich	餌食 ejiki = prey or victim; 餌 esa = animal food or bait
極₃	^610. at the **Kyo**to-**Kool**-Aid club, on a cold night, this kangaroo sits on this 口 (chair) on this carpet near this 又 (table) next to this 木 (tree) and drinks **Gold-Kool**-Aid through his 口 (mouth) while pondering 極力 **kyoku**ryoku (as much as possible) how to **Keep-Wa**rm, which is 極めて **kiwa**mete (extremely) difficult	南極 nankyoku = the antarctic, South Pole; 至極 shigoku = extremely; 極める kiwameru = to attain or master; 極めて kiwamete = extremely
寂₂	^864. **Ja**ck Nicholson, who has a bad haircut like this, is seated at this 又 (table), eating **Sa**lty-**Be**ans with only this taser on this 小 (small) hill for company, and he feels 寂しい **sabi**shii (lonely)	静寂 seijaku = silence, stillness; 寂しい sabishii = lonely
茂₁	^1186. the **Sheep**-at-**Ge**ttysburg feed on these plants which 茂る **shige**ru (grow thickly), and then they sleep in lean-tos supported by halberds like this	茂る shigeru = to grow thickly; this can also, less commonly, be spelled as 繁る shigeru
震₂	^265. this 雨 (rain) is falling during a 地震 ji**shin** (earthquake), and since only this L and Y are supporting this lean-to and arrow that make up this **Shin**to shrine, it will 震える **furu**eru (tremble) and collapse into **Fu**ll-blown-**Ru**in	地震 jishin = earthquake; 震える furueru = to tremble
振₃	^823. when this guy on the left 振り返った **furi**katta (looked back) at this lean-to and saw these two **Shin**to priests named L and Y **Foo**lishly pointing this arrow at him, he got **Fur**ious, but he fell to his knees in order to become a smaller target	振動数 shindousuu = frequency; 振り返る furikaeru = to turn the head, look back, think back; 銀行振込み ginkou furikomi = bank transfer
農₁	^1105. L and Y are 農家 **nou**ka (farmers) who work in this lean-to, and they sing 曲 (songs) as they use arrows like this to scratch N**o**tes about their crops in the dirt	農業 nougyou = agriculture; 農家 nouka = farmer, farmhouse; 農夫 noufu = farmer
濃₂	^1106. after this 農 (farmer) added this water to his **Co**rn field, L and Y used this arrow to scratch a N**o**te in the dirt, stating that the field had become 濃い **ko**i (dark)	濃い koi = dark, thick, strong, dense; 濃度 noudo = concentration
社₃	^271. this **Sha**h and a **Ja**panese partner are looking at this 土 (soil), on which **Ya**ks-and-**Sheep-Ro**am, where they plan to build a 会社 kai**sha** (company)	会社 kaisha = company; 神社 jinja = a Shinto shrine; 社 yashiro = a Shinto shrine
礼₁	^275. this Shah feels お礼 o**rei** (gratitude) to this **La**dy, who helped him after he was 失礼 shitsu**rei** (rude) to her	お礼 orei = gratitude, thanks; 失礼 shitsurei = discourtesy
視₁	^844. this Shah 見 (watches) his **Sheep**, using his good 視力 **shi**ryoku (eyesight)	視力 shiryoku = eyesight
祉₁	^1066. this Shah tries to 止 (stop) **Sheep** rustling in order to ensure the 福祉 fuku**shi** (welfare) of his wool business	福祉 fukushi = welfare
祥₁	^1160. this Shah traces the 発祥 has**shou** (origin) of his wool business to a **Show** about 羊 (sheep) like this that he watched in his youth	発祥 hasshou = origin
今₅	^292. **Ima**gine that 今 **ima** (now) it is 7 o'clock, and it's time for the **Co**nductor to step under this roof, turn the **Ke**y, start the **Co**mmuter train and settle back to drink a **Ke**g of beer	今 ima = now; 今度 kondo = this time, next time; 今日 kyou = today; 今年 kotoshi = this year; 今朝 kesa = this morning
念₁	^314. 今 (now), this 心 (heart) belonging to my **Ne**gative-**Ne**phew is driving him to the right of the political spectrum, and that's 残念 zan**nen** (too bad)	残念 zannen = too bad; 信念 shinnen = belief

Chapter 9

倉 2		^1170. since **So**ldiers value 口 **Kuura**as (coolers) like this highly, they store them in secure 倉庫 **sou**ko (warehouses) like this, with several layers of roofing above them	倉庫 souko = warehouse; 穀倉 kokusou = granary; 倉 kura = storehouse (this can also be written 蔵)
創 1		^1171. this guy リ Ri is a **So**ldier who helped to 創立する **sou**ritsu suru (establish) this army 倉 (warehouse) containing this 口 (box)	創造 souzou = creation; 創立する souritsu suru = to establish
別 3		^561. **Bets**y with this square head doesn't like this リ Ri with this pointy toe 別に **betsu** ni (particularly), and they 別れる **waka**reru (break up) after リ Ri **Wa**lks-on-the-**Ca**t and destroys its **Be**d, causing Betsy to reach for this 刀 (sword)	別に betsu ni = particularly; 別れる wakareru = to separate; 別居 bekkyo = separation of family members
両 1		^579. 両方 **ryo**hou (both) Pope **Leo** and his friend rode on this chairlift seat	両方 ryouhou = both
満 2		^1153. since I consumed 両 (both) this water and this plant material at a **Me**al in **Man**hattan, I had 満腹 **man**puku (a full stomach)	満ちる michiru = to become full; 満員 mannin = full house, no vacancy
綱 1		^1200. this 糸 (skeet shooter) was shooting at this 岡 (hill), which resembles a two-sided lean-to containing this chairlift seat hanging from two frayed 綱 **tsuna** (cables), when a **Tsuna**mi swept him away	綱 tsuna = a rope, cord, cable; 綱引き tsunahiki = tug of war; 命綱 inochizuna = lifeline
石 5		^458. this guy with a flat hat is leaning over this 口 (box) looking for an 石 **ishi** (stone) that was delivered by an Indonesian-**Sh**ip on orders from a **Se**lfish-**K**ing to be placed in a **Sh**ack for a **Se**cretary to sit on while she drinks a **Co**ke	小石 koishi = pebble; 一石 isseki = one stone; 磁石 jishaku = magnet; 石けん sekken = soap; 石 koku = approx. 278 liters of rice
磨 3		^126. **Su**perman will **Mee**t-the-**Ga**mbler who installed this 林 (grove) and this 石 (stone) inside this lean-to, and his **Ma** (mother) told him to 磨く **miga**ku (brush) his shoes before entering	磨る suru = to grind; 磨く migaku = to brush; 研磨 kenma = grinding, abrading, polishing
確 2		^619. **Ka**rl-the-**Ko**ol-Aid vendor hides behind this 石 (stone) and watches this swooping bird try to attack the **Ta**lented-**Shee**p that he keeps inside this net, but he thinks that 確かに **tashi**ka ni (certainly) the net will protect them and that his Kool-Aid will provide energy for a counterattack	正確 seikaku = precise; 確かに tashika ni = for sure, certainly; 確かめる tashikameru = to confirm
拝 2		^593. before this person named **Oprah**-**Ga**mbles, she kneels and 拝む **oga**mu (prays humbly), and since she is holding these flowers **Hi**gh, we can 拝見する **hai**ken suru (humbly see) them	拝む ogamu = to assume the posture of prayer with hands held together, to revere; 拝見する haiken suru = to humbly read or see
千 3		^22. a **Se**nator keeps 千 **sen** (1,000) blocks of チ (**Chee**se) like this at the **Zen** center	千 sen = 1,000; 千葉 Chiba = name of a prefecture in Japan; 三千 sanzen = 3,000
汗 2		^629. **Asses** (donkeys) 汗をかく **ase** wo kaku (sweat) water like this when we make them carry telephone poles like this to **Kan**sas	汗をかく ase wo kaku = to sweat; 発汗 hakkan = perspiration
軒 2		^1146. **Ken** and Barbie parked this 車 (car) next to this telephone pole while they were visiting 一軒 ik**ken** (one house), but they had **No-Key**	一軒 ikken = one house; 軒 noki = eaves
幹 2		^1062. **Mi**ckey Mouse lives in this Disney wagon in **Kan**sas next to this sheltered telephone pole made from a 幹 **miki** (tree trunk)	幹 miki = tree trunk; 幹部 kanbu = an executive; 新幹線 shinkansen = bullet train
刊 1		^990. in **Kan**sas, リ Ri has an office next to this telephone pole, where he 刊行する **kan**kou suru (publishes) books	週刊誌 shuukanshi = weekly magazine; 刊行する kankou suru = to publish
加 2		^714. a **Ca**rpenter exerted a lot of 力 (force) to swallow **Coo**l-**Wa**ter through this big 口 (mouth) when he 参加した sa**nka** shita (cooperated) with some research on water intoxication	参加 sanka = participation; 加える kuwaeru = to add or include

重 5		^284. this 車 (car) is 重い **omo**i (heavy) because **Old-Mo**ses added these extra hubcaps to each wheel, and **Casa**nova and Margaret **Cho** 重ねた **kasa**neta (piled up) even more weight by adding **Juice** and **Eggs** to the trunk	重い omoi = heavy; 重ねる kasaneru = to pile up; 慎重な shinchou na = cautious, prudent; 体重 taijuu = a person's weight; 紙一重 kamihito'e = paper-thin (difference)
動 2		^286. a 重 (heavy) 自動車 jidousha (car) which 動く **ugo**ku (moves) under its own 力 (force) can escape **Do**berman dogs and **Uber-Go**phers	自動車 jidousha = car; 動く ugoku = to move, intransitive
働 2		^287. this man with a slanted hat 働く **hatara**ku (labors) making **Hat**s-for-**Ara**bs, using this 力 (force) to 動 (move) 重 (heavy) hats from one place to another, and he gets paid good **Dough** (money) for doing so	働く hataraku = to labor; 労働者 roudousha = laborer
各 2		^1033. after this dancer jumps over this box, she breaks up with **Karl-the-Kool**-Aid vendor, and they drive away in 各自の **kaku**ji no (their own) **Cars**	各駅 kakueki = each station; 各国 kakkoku = each country
客 3		^524. this dancer with a ponytail, who has this bad haircut, leaps over this box in order to win a **Kia** from a 客 **kyaku** (customer) who is a **Kayak**er named **Karl-the-Kool**-Aid vendor	客観 kyakkan = object (vs. subject); お客 okyaku = honorable guest; 旅客 ryokaku = passenger, traveler
落 2		^526. when this water flowed in from the left, this dancer jumped over this 口 (box) to escape, and her head struck these leaves, causing some **Oranges** and a **Raccoon** to 落ちる **o**chiru (fall) from the tree above	落ちる ochiru = to fall; 落とす otosu = to knock down or drop; 落語 rakugo = Japanese comic story telling
絡 2		^230. this 糸 (skeet shooter) shoots at this dancer as a way to 連絡する ren**raku** suru (contact) her about the approach of a **Raccoon** with a bad **Chara**cter, and she leaps over this box to escape the beast	連絡する renraku suru = to contact; 絡まる karamaru = to become entangled in
格 3		^762. when this dancer visited a **Court**house, she saw **Karl-the-Kool**-Aid vendor hiding in this 木 (tree), and she expressed her dislike for his 性格 sei**kaku** (personality) by jumping over this box and driving off in her **Car**	格子 koushi = lattice work or grill; 性格 seikaku = personality, disposition; 格好 kakkou = form, appearance, suitability
枚 1		^129. this dancer is a **Miser** who might give you some of the paper that she makes from this 木 (tree); if you ask for some, she says, "何枚 nan**mai** (how many sheets) do you need?"	紙二枚 kami nimai = two sheets of paper
内 3		^396. this 家内 ka**nai** (wife) with a **Knife** and some **Uber-Cheese**, who is 内 **uchi** (inside) a dwelling, puts her head through a hole in the roof of this two-sided lean-to and complains about her **Diet**	家内 kanai = my wife; その内に sono uchi ni = before long; 境内 keidai = grounds (of a temple)
肉 1		^397. this is an x-ray of some 肉 **niku** (meat) that was sent to us by my **Niece-in-Ku**wait	肉 niku = meat
納 4		^705. this 糸 (skeet shooter) thinks that he sees either the **Nose** or a **Toe** of **Osa**ma, who is a **Na**sty man, protruding from 内 (inside) this two-sided lean-to on the right, and he will 納める **osa**meru (conclude) his mission by shooting him with a skeet	納入 nounyuu = payment of taxes, etc, supply (of goods, etc.), delivery; 出納 suitou = receipts & expenditures; 納める osameru = to pay a bill, to put away, to conclude; this can also be written 収める; 納得する nattoku suru = to acquiesce, agree
召 2		^106. a **Shou**gun is **Merry** as he 召し上がる **me**shiagaru (honorably eats) with this 口 (mouth), after cutting his food with this 刀 (sword)	召喚する shoukan suru = to summon; 召し上がる meshiagaru = to honorably eat
招 2		^560. this guy on the left wants to write a letter to 招く **mane**ku (invite) a **Manne**quin to a Broadway **Show**, but first he has to kneel in order to remove this 刀 (sword) from this writing 口 (box)	招く maneku = to invite; 招待 shoutai = invitation
紹 1		^658. a **Shou**gun asks this 糸 (skeet shooter) for a 紹介 **shou**kai (introduction) to the skeetshooter's daughter, and he places this 刀 (sword) on this 口 (box) to indicate that he is serious about this	紹介 shoukai = introduction; 紹介状 shoukaijou = letter of introduction

紙 2		^221. this 糸 (skeet shooter) is firing skeets onto the flat 紙 **kami** (paper) roof of this pavilion, since it is occupied by **Commie**s (Communists) who are using **Shie**lds for protection	紙 kami = paper; 折り紙 origami = paper-folding art; 紙幣 shihei = paper money
低 2		^222. this guy on the left has **Hiccup**s that are knocking his hat off kilter, and he is too 低い **hiku**i (low) to see over this 紙 (paper) pavilion which has been **Tape**d to this flat rock	低い hikui = low; 最低 saitei = the worst
氏 2		^709. 中村氏 nakamura**shi** (Mr. Nakamura) keeps **Sheep** in this 紙 (paper pavilion) and he uses an Uber-**Jeep** to haul them around	中村氏 nakamura shi = Mr. Nakamura; 彼氏 kareshi = boyfriend; 氏 uji = clan
昏 1		^1074. this 氏 (mister) from the **Con**go stood in this 日 (sun) too long and fell into a 昏睡 **kon**sui (stupor)	昏睡 konsui = coma, stupor
婚 1		^240. this 女 (female) from the **Con**go will 結婚する kek**kon** suru (marry) this 氏 (mister), and she is writing wedding invitations in this 日 (sun)	結婚 kekkon = marriage
底 2		^1096. after he **Sold-his-Coal**, this 氏 (mister) hit 底 **soko** (bottom), and now he lives in this paper pavilion **Tape**d to a rock inside this lean-to with a chimney	底 soko = bottom; 靴底 kutsuzoko = shoe sole; 海底 kaitei = bottom of the sea
抵 1		^1195. this guy is kneeling in order to try to move this 紙 (paper) pavilion, but the **Tape** attaching it to this flat rock produces too much 抵抗 **tei**kou (resistance)	抵抗 teikou = resistance, opposition; 抵当 teitou = mortgage
林 2		^125. **Hay-is-growing-in-Ash**land near this 林 **hayashi** (grove) of 木 (trees) with **Wrink**led bark	林 hayashi = grove; 小林 Kobayashi = a family name; 森林 shinrin = forest
森 2		^127. **Maure**en likes to visit these three 木 (trees) in this 森 **mori** (forest) and worship the **Shin**tou spirits there	森 mori = forest; 森林 shinrin = forest
禁 1		^943. our **King** 禁じる **kin**jiru (prohibits) spinning of 林 (groves) like these, since it isn't good for the trees	禁じる kinjiru = to prohibit; 禁物 kinmotsu = a forbidden thing
主 4		^166. since this 主人 **shu**jin (master) is not a 王 (king), he wears this tiny cap instead of a crown, but he has good **Shoe**s, he uses an **Old-Mo**bile phone, and he likes to visit **New-Shee**p at the **Zoo**	主人 shujin = husband, master, landlord, landlady, proprietor, host or hostess; 主な omo na = main, chief; 地主 jinushi = land owner; 坊主 bouzu = Buddhist monk
住 2		^167. this man on the left, who drinks a lot of **Ju**ice and graduated **Su**mma cum laude, tilts his hat back to gaze at this 主 (master) outside a house where they both 住む **su**mu (reside)	住所 juusho = address; 住む sumu = to reside
注 2		^168. while **Che**wing gum, this 主 (master) 注ぐ **soso**gu (pours) this water and often spills it, which is why the carpet's condition is only **So-So**, and therefore 注意してください **chuu**i shite kudasai (please be careful)	注文する chuumon suru = to order; 注意する chuui suru = to warn; 注ぐ sosogu = to pour
駐 1		^381. this 主 (master) 駐車する **chuu**sha suru (parks) this 馬 (horse), while the horse **Chew**s hay	駐車する chuusha suru = to park a vehicle
鹿 2		^895. these three eyes in this lean-to observe 鹿 **shika** (deer) and **Sheep-in-California**, as they 比 (compare) shelters and **Ca**lculate the available space for bedding down	鹿 shika = deer; 小鹿 kojika = fawn; 馬鹿 baka = fool, idiot, usually written バカ
薦 2		^1030. the three eyes in this lean-to saw the lower half of this 鳥 (bird), which was eating these plants, and **Soon**-called-**Superman**, who 推薦した sui**sen** shita (recommended) that the **Sen**ate pass a law to protect the bird	薦める susumeru = to advise (this is usually written 勧める susumeru); 推薦する suisen suru = to recommend
片 3		^181. this person, who is kneeling on one knee, holds out this tray with this **Cata**logue of **Pen**s on it, but a **Hen** that is watching can only see 片方 **kata**hou (one side) of it	片方 katahou = one side, the other side, one of a pair; 一片 ippen = a slice or piece; 破片 hahen = shard, fragment
版 1		^1086. **Han**sel is kneeling on the left, showing Gretel a 版画 **han**ga (woodblock print) on this tray, but she gives it this F and marks it with this X	版画 hanga = woodblock print; 出版 shuppan = publication

Kanji	Mnemonic	Vocabulary
飲₂	^399. the oil **In**dustry in **Nor**way uses 欠 (oil derricks) like this to make money so that its employees can 食 (eat) and 飲む **no**mu (drink	飲食 inshoku = drinking and eating; 飲む nomu = to drink or swallow
歌₂	^534. this 欠 (oil derrick) belongs to a 歌手 **ka**shu (singer) who sings **Ca**tholic music and reads from a music stand with these two song sheets when she 歌う **uta**u (sings) at an Ugandan-**Ta**vern	歌手 kashu = singer; 歌う utau = to sing
次₄	^536. this 欠 (oil derrick) has **Tsu**perior-(superior)-**Gea**rs, and we used it to pump this water for our **Shee**p, but 次に **tsugi** ni (next) it broke down, and we had to get some spare parts from a **Tsu**itcase (suitcase) in the **Jee**p	次に tsugi ni = next; 次第に shidai ni = gradually; 取り次ぐ toritsugu = to convey or transmit; 次回に jikai ni = next time
資₁	^91. I save 資金 **shi**kin (funds) in this three-drawer 貝 (money chest), and 欠 (next) I intend to buy some **Shee**p	資料 shiryou = literature, documents; 資金 shikin = funds, capital
吹₂	^537. this 欠 (oil derrick) drinks oil as **Foo**d and then 吹く **fu**ku (blows) it out through this 口 (mouth) because it's too **Swee**t	吹く fuku = to blow, breathe, whistle; 吹奏楽 suisougaku = wind instrument music
羨₂	^662. this 王 (king) put on these rabbit ears and gave a **Sen**ator an estate, and 次 (next) the senator found **Ur**anium-in-the-**Ya**rd, which made other politicians feel 羨ましい **uraya**mashii (envious)	羨望 senbou = envy; 羨ましい urayamashii = envious
茨₁	^1007. at **Easter-Bara**ch Obama bought these plants, and 次 (next) he took them to 茨城県 **ibara**ki ken (Ibaraki Prefecture)	茨城県 Ibaraki ken = Ibaraki prefecture
名₃	^162. Napoleon's **Mai**d went into a **Mee**ting-in-**Yo**semite, wrote her 名前 **na**mae (name) on this 口 (card) and hung it from this 有名 yuu**mei** (famous) 夕 (half moon)	名前 namae = name; 有名 yuumei = famous; 名字 myouji = family name
迷₃	^623. **Mighty M**ouse helps a **Mai**d on this snail which transports **May**onnaise and this 米 (uncooked rice), but he often 迷う **mayo**u (loses direction), becomes a 迷子 **mai**go (lost person) and causes 迷惑 **mei**waku (inconvenience)	迷子 maigo = lost person; 迷信 meishin = superstition; 迷惑 meiwaku = trouble, annoyance; 迷う mayou = to lose direction
理₁	^78. this 王 (king) and this 里 (sincere guy) are **Rea**sonable and have their 理由 **ri**yuu (reasons) for their actions	理由 riyuu = reason; 料理 ryouri = cooking
裏₂	^887. this sincere guy, エ, and Y have a **Ur**anium mine, and they've installed this tire stop at the 裏 **ura** (back) of the mine to keep cars from driving in from the **Rea**r	裏 ura = back, rear, hidden aspect; 表裏 hyouri = two sides, inside and out
里₂	^1060. this sincere guy admires a **Sa**tellite-**To**wer that is covered in Christmas **Wrea**ths, located in a 里 **sato** (village)	里 sato = hometown, village; 人里 hitozato = human habitation; 郷里 kyouri = hometown
悪₄	^313. **War-Ru**ined the health of this 心 (heart), and it was feeling 悪い **waru**i (bad), but it got help from this 亜 (Red Cross) and also some **Acu**puncture treatments from its **A**unt in O**saka**	悪い warui = bad; 悪 aku = evil; 悪しからず ashikarazu = don't take it badly; 嫌悪 ken'o = hatred, disgust
負₃	^87. a **Foo**lish guy keeps this **Ol**d fish head, which he plans to give to his **Ma** (mother), on this 貝 (money chest), after he accepted it as payment for a 負債 **fu**sai (debt), on which he 負けた **ma**keta (lost) money	負債 fusai = debt; 負う ou = to be indebted to, or to bear responsibility, to be injured; 負ける makeru = to lose
危₃	^547. this fish head, who has been **Abu**sed, sits on this lean-to and tries to escape this 危ない **abu**nai (dangerous) uncoiling snake lurking inside, which has already **Ki**lled an **Aya**tollah	危ない abunai = dangerous; 危険 kiken = danger; 危うい ayaui = dangerous, risky
換₂	^554. this guy on the left, who is a **Ca**ptain from **Kan**sas, kneels in order to 換える **ka**eru (exchange) this decoration on the right side of this 大 (big) fish-headed general's chest for the one on the left	換える kaeru = to replace or exchange (this can also be spelled 替える); 交換する koukan suru = to exchange
療₁	^1069. Pope **Leo** is a 大 (big) man, and when he's 病 (sick), he lies in this bed with his arms propped up like this and undergoes chi**ryou** 治療 (medical treatment), consisting of heat therapy that is produced by this spinning 日 (oven)	治療 chiryou = medical treatment

者 2		^276. this 者 <u>mono</u> (person) is playing a **Mono**tonous game with this 土 (soil) and these **Sha**rp scissors that he keeps in this 日 (cabinet)	悪者 warumono = villain; 学者 gakusha = scholar; 金の亡者 kane no mouja = a money-grubbing person
緒 3		^232. this 糸 (skeet shooter) fires skeets toward this **Older** 者 (person) whom he has **Cho**sen, and she **Sho**ws up, and they are 一緒に is<u>sho</u> ni (together) at last	鼻緒 hanao = straps of geta (wooden clogs); 情緒 joucho = emotion; 一緒に issho ni = together
都 3		^277. this ß (Greek) 者 (person) carries a **Tsu**itcase (suitcase) of **To**matoes to a 都市 <u>to</u>shi (city) known as Athens, where 都合がいい <u>tsu</u>gou ga ii (it will be convenient) to **Meet-Yak-O**wners	都合 tsugou = circumstances, convenience; 都市 toshi = city; 都 miyako = capital
暑 2		^278. this 者 (person) stands under this 日 (sun) **At-Su**perman's house, feels too 暑い <u>atsu</u>i (hot), and decides to go to the **Sho**re	暑い日 atsui hi = hot day; 暑中 shochuu = mid-summer, hot season
著 3		^1088. Margaret **Cho** is this 者 (person) who is the 著者 <u>cho</u>sha (writer) of a book which she was scheduled to discuss on TV, but her pants came into contact with this poison ivy plant and, although her **Ara**b-friend-**Wa**shed them, the **Itchy-Jeans-Ru**ined her TV appearance	著者 chosha = a writer; 著す arawasu = to write or publish; 著しい ichijirushii = remarkable, conspicuous
箸 1		^1144. this 者 (person) carrying a knife under his right shoulder uses 竹 (bamboo) 箸 <u>hashi</u> (chopsticks) to **Harm-Sheep**	箸 hashi = chopsticks; 割り箸 waribashi = splittable (disposable) chopsticks
品 3		^5. these three **Pin**k boxes contain **Shi**ny-**A**rtistic 品物 <u>shina</u>mono (goods) for **Hin**dus	返品 henpin = returned goods; 品物 shinamono = merchandise; 品質 hinshitsu = quality
器 2		^853. this 大 (big) family has these four 口 (mouths) to feed, and they **U**tilize-**Su**permarket-**Wa**lnuts, as well as **Qui**che, which they store in 器 <u>utsuwa</u> (containers)	器 utsuwa = container or receptacle, ability; 食器 shokki = tableware; 便器 benki = toilet bowl, urinal
繰 1		^1034. this 糸 (skeet shooter) sees this 品 (merchandise), which is three packages of **Koo**l-Aid, stuck at the top of this 木 (tree), tries to shoot it down and then 繰り返す <u>ku</u>rikaesu (does it again)	繰り返す kurikaesu = to repeat, to do something over again
操 2		^1192. an **Aya**tollah-**Tsue**d (sued) the skeet shooter who was 繰 (repeatedly) unable to dislodge these Kool-Aid 品 (packages) from this 木 (tree) and then told this guy on the left, who is a **So**ldier, to kneel in order to 操作する <u>sou</u>sa suru (operate) a machine to do the job	操る ayatsuru = to control, manipulate, handle; 操作 sousa = operation (of a machine); 体操 taisou = gymnastics, exercise
指 4		^691. this guy on the left is kneeling to consult with this 旨 (uber Marine) on the right, who controls the **Yukon-Bee**f industry with one 指 <u>yubi</u> (finger); during the day, they kneel and watch their **Shee**p, but at night they sleep on **Satin-Shee**ts and dream of **Sa**skatchewan	指 yubi = finger; 指定席 shiteiseki = reserved seat; 指図 sashizu = direction, command; 指す sasu = to point; 目指す mezasu = to aim at
脂 2		^1180. this 旨 (uber Marine) works under this 月 (moon) caring for his **Shee**p, including **Abu**-Dhabi-**Ra**ms, and they have a high 脂 <u>abura</u> (fat) content	脂肪 shibou = fat; 脂 abura = fat
詣 3		^1204. this 旨 (uber Marine) is thinking about **Mo**wing the lawn, but he puts his 指 (finger) in the air and 言 (says), "This isn't a **Mow-Day**. Let's do a 詣で <u>mou</u>de (temple visit) instead and then get some **Cake**."	詣で moude = a temple or shrine visit; 初詣 hatsumoude = first shrine visit of the year (this can also be written 初詣で); 造詣 zoukei = knowledge, mastery
最 3		^42. 最近 <u>sai</u>kin (recently), when this **Sign** is turned on, I sit at this 又 (table), and this 耳 (ear) can hear a lawn **Mo**wer from behind the sign and also the traffic on the **Motor**way	最近 saikin = recently; 最高 saikou = the best; 最早 mohaya = by now, no longer; 最も mottomo = the most
向 3		^340. the **Moor** is **Co**ld on the 向こう <u>mu</u>kou (opposite) side of this roof, where the **National-Ta**lent contest is held	向こう mukou = the other side; 向く muku = to face toward; 方向 houkou = direction; 日向 hinata = sunny place

普 1	^576. this is just a 普通 **fu**tsuu (ordinary) stove, with these four burners and this 日 (stove body), for cooking **Food**	普通 futsuu = ordinarily, usually, generally
並 4	^575. since there is no 日 (stove body), as seen in 普(通) futsuu (ordinarily, # 576), these are just lines that 並ぶ **nara**bu (line up) on the wall of a temple in **Nara**, spelling a **Ha**teful message, and the authorities will soon be **Nami**ng the culprit, who must be **Nasty**	並ぶ narabu = to line up, intransitive; 並列 heiretsu = arrangement, parallel, abreast; 並の nami no = ordinary, usual; 町並み machinami = a townscape
円 3	^39. 千円 sen'en (1,000-yen) coins are 円い **maru**i (round) like this reclining 日 (sun), and since they have legs like these, they are able to dance and **En**tertain people who are **Maroo**ned in **Mars-Orbit**	千円 sen'en = 1,000 yen; 円い marui = round; 円やか maroyaka = round, mellow
映 3	^36. by **U**tilizing-this- 日 -(**Sun**) on the left, we can 映す **utsu**su (project) 映画 **ei**ga (movies) about **A**pes in **Ha**waii onto this screen on the right	映す utsusu = to project on a screen; 映画 eiga = movie; 映える haeru = to shine
声 2	^40. this 士 (man)'s girlfriend is a **Co-Ed** who wears this mask when they go **Sa**iling; the mask doesn't block these two eyes or her mouth, nor does it affect her 声 **koe** (voice)	声 koe = voice; 歌声 utagoe = a singing voice; 声援 seien = cheering, support
英 1	^43. this movie screen shows an 英語の **ei**go no (English language) 映 (movie) about **A**pes, and the plant radical above it reminds us of the plants they eat	英語 eigo = the English language; 英雄 eiyuu = hero
央 1	^1063. I like to watch movies starring **O**prah on this 映 (movie) screen, and I sit in the 中央 chuu**ou** (middle) of the theater	中央 chuu'ou = center, middle
免 2	^1140. this fish-head guy with glasses knows that success is all **Men**tal and that he has to stand on these two lopsided legs, and he will **Manage-a-New-Ga**s station after getting his 免状 **men**jou (diploma)	免許 menkyo = a license; 免れる manugareru = to be exempted from, to avoid
色 3	^473. this snake with these two eyes and this fish head has an 色 **iro** (color) like **Iron**; it is sitting up high and has a good 景色 ke**shiki** (view) of a **Shiite-King**, who lives by the **Shore-in-Ku**wait	茶色 cha'iro = brown; 景色 keshiki = view; 血色 kesshoku = complexion
絶 3	^673. this 糸 (skeet shooter) is a **Z**ealous meditator who 絶対に **zettai** ni (absolutely) wants to wear a **Zen-Tsu**it (suit), but the tsuits they are selling are the wrong 色 (color) and don't fit him because he is too **T**all	絶対に zettai ni = absolutely, by any means; 絶望 zetsubou = despair; 絶える taeru = to discontinue or cease
晩 1	^35. this fish-head guy with glasses and lopsided legs wants to go to the **Ban**k while this 日 (sun) is still shining, since it will be closed 今晩 kon**ban** (this evening)	今晩 konban = this evening
勉 1	^474. this fish-head guy with glasses **Ben**ds this tentacle and kneels, using his 力 (power) of concentration to 勉強する **ben**kyou suru (study)	勉強 benkyou = study
力 3	^107. in **Chica**go-**Rambo**, who leans a little to the right like this, controlled his motorcycle's 力 **chikara** (force) with this handle attached to this 刀 (sword), before **Ricky** and Pope **Leo-Cu**t him off with a popemobile	力 chikara = force; 力作 rikisaku = masterpiece; 努力 doryoku = effort
九 3	^111. this **Cu**ban guy with 九 **kyuu** (nine) **Koo**ky kids eats **Coconuts-with-No**mads and, compared to 力 (force), doesn't lean right	九 kyuu = nine; 九月 kugatsu = September; 九つ kokonotsu = nine objects
万 2	^113. **Ban**kers in **Man**ila use this swiveling flat top on 万 **man** to count 一万円 ichi**man**'en (10,000 yen) bills	万事 banji = everything; 二万 niman = 20,000
方 3	^114. this nice feather hat that this 方 **kata** (honorable person) is wearing is his 方 **kata** (method) of impressing people; during a **Q**uest, if there is a **Cata**strophe you can count on him to **H**old you tightly	行方 yukue = whereabouts; 方 kata = honorable person; 夕方 yuugata = evening; 方がいい hou ga ii = it would be better; 一方 ippou = one side
心 4	^306. don't throw **Coconuts-at-Roy's Shin**gles, since you may damage his 心 **kokoro** (heart); instead eat your **Coconuts** over on the **Gold-Coa**st	心 kokoro = heart; 心配する shinpai suru = to worry; 肝心 kanjin = essential; 心地 kokochi = feeling, sensation, mood; 居心地 igokochi = the way one feels in a particular ambience

Chapter 10

車 2		^283. this **C**urvy-**Roo**my-**Ma**gnificent 車 <u>**kuru**ma</u> (car) belongs to the **Sh**ah	車 kuruma = car, wheel; 自転車 jitensha = bicycle
連 3		^353. this **Ren**tal 車 (car) broke down, and after I 連絡した <u>**ren**raku shita</u> (contacted) the agency, they sent this snail to pick up the car, after which they 連れて行った <u>**tsu**rete itta</u> (took me along) to my destination, but I left my **Tsu**it (suit) and my **Tsu**itcase-(suitcase)-of-**Ra**men in the trunk	連絡する renraku suru = to contact; 連れて行く tsurete iku = to bring a person along; 連なる tsuranaru = to stand in a row
軍 1		^725. 軍人 <u>**gun**jin</u> (soldiers) 運 (carry) **Gun**s, and they ride in 車 (cars) covered with armor like this one	軍人 gunjin = soldier; 海軍 kaigun = navy; 陸軍 rikugun = army; 将軍 shougun = Shogun
運 2		^354. this snail 運ぶ <u>**hako**bu</u> (carries) this 軍 (soldier), and the soldier 運ぶ <u>**hako**bu</u> (carries) a **H**at-on-**Co**ld days; **U**ndoubtedly the hat helps to keep him warm	運ぶ hakobu = to carry or transport; 運動 undou = exercise, 運 un = luck, fortune
陣 1		^638. this ß (Greek) guy puts on his **Jean**s, gets in this 車 (car) and drives to his 陣地 <u>**jin**chi</u> (encampment) in Athens	陣地 jinchi = encampment, position
庫 2		^919. when it's **C**old, I keep this 車 (car) in this 車庫 sha<u>**ko**</u> (garage), except when I take it to the **Go**lf course	車庫 shako = garage; 兵庫県 hyougoken = Hyogo prefecture
輝 2		^979. this 光 (light) on the left 輝く <u>**kagaya**ku</u> (shines), and it is being used in a signal lamp in **Ki**ev by this 軍 (soldier) to **C**all-a-**G**allant-**Y**achtsman	光輝 kouki = brightness, splendor; 輝く kagayaku = to shine, glitter, sparkle
載 2		^1175. a **N**orwegian who is a **S**cientist is guarding this 車 (car) with this halberd, but he notices this 土 (soil) on the car and checks his 記載 ki<u>**sai**</u> (records) to determine when it was last washed	載る noru = to be printed or placed on; 載せる noseru = to put on top of, to publish; 記載 kisai = record, listing, entry
表 4		^582. in this **O**mote**l** (honorable motel), there are many 表 <u>**omote**</u> (surfaces), such as the ones in this owl's perch supported by the owners エ (Eric) and Y (Yolanda), who welcome **H**ealers-from-**O**regon, guests from **Pyo**ngyang, and **Ara**b-guests-like-**Wali**	表 omote = surface, front, outside; 表 hyou = a surface, chart or diagram; 裏表紙 urabyoushi = back cover; 発表する happyou suru = to announce, publish, reveal, make a presentation; 表す arawasu = to signify, represent or express
麦 3		^1103. this dancer is a **Bar**maid-who-drinks-**Koo**l-Aid, as well as beer made from 麦 <u>**mugi**</u> (barley), and when she carries this owl's perch into our **Bar**, we have to **M**ove-our-**Gear**	麦芽 bakuga = malt; 蕎麦屋 sobaya = a soba restaurant; 麦 mugi = barley, wheat
旦 2		^668. since my 旦那 <u>**dan**na</u> (husband) spends time in this 日 (sun), he has a nice **Tan**, and he likes to **Dan**ce on this floor	一旦 ittan = for a moment, once; 旦那 danna = master, husband
担 3		^729. this **K**neeling-**N**ancy on the left has this 旦 (husband), who has a nice **Tan** and 担当する <u>**tan**tou suru</u> (takes charge of) their **C**ats	担う ninau = to carry or bear; 担当 tantou = charge (duty); 担ぐ katsugu = to carry on one's shoulder
垣 2		^777. my neighbor put this window in our 垣根 <u>**kaki**ne</u> (fence) so he could watch me hunt for my **C**ar-**K**eys and fly my **K**ite, but I covered it up with this 土 (soil)	垣根 kakine = hedge, fence; 垣間見る kaimamiru = to take a peep at, to catch a glimpse of
壇 1		^679. I sit in this **Dan**k 土 (soil) to watch this TV set with an antenna, on a cabinet above a carpet, which is next to the 仏壇 butsu<u>**dan**</u> (Buddhist altar) in my home	壇 dan = stage; 仏壇 butsudan = Buddhist altar found in Japanese homes
昔 3		^33. nowadays old people fund **M**useums-with-**C**ash, but in 昔 <u>**mukashi**</u> (the olden days), all they had was this 日 (sun), these plants, and a **S**elfish-**K**ing named **J**ack	昔 mukashi = olden times; 昔日 sekijitsu = old times; 今昔 konjaku = past and present
借 3		^485. in 昔 (the olden days), this man went to this 昔 (bank teller's window), tilted his hat back so that the teller could identify him, 借りた <u>**ka**rita</u> (borrowed) **C**ash and took it to his **Sh**abby **Sh**ack	借金 shakkin = debt; 借家 shakuya = rented house; 借りる kariru = to borrow or rent
赤 3		^447. 十 (ten) headless four-legged hens like this wore 赤い <u>**akai**</u> (red) jackets and managed to get into the **Aca**demy Awards in **Ca**lifornia, but a **S**elfish-**Ki**ng sat in front of them at the show	赤い akai = red; 赤ちゃん akachan = baby; 真っ赤 makka = bright red; 赤道 sekidou = equator

中 ₃	^8. 中村さん **Naka**mura-san (Mr. Nakamura) **Chew**s on this yakitori 中 **naka** (inside) his car parked outside the **N**ational-**Ca**thedral and drinks **J**ui**ce**	散歩中 sanpo chuu = in the middle of a walk; 真ん中 mannaka = middle; 一日中 ichinichijuu = all day long
仲 ₂	^657. this man on the left tilts his hat back to view this 中 (chicken on a stick) that he is **Chew**ing with a 仲良し **naka**yoshi (close friend) who works with him at the **N**ational-**Ca**thedral	仲 naka = relationship; 仲良し nakayoshi = close friend; 仲介 chuukai = mediation
遣 ₂	^765. **Ken** 遣わす **tsuka**wasu (dispatches) Barbie on a trip aboard this snail, where she will sleep in the bottom bunk and keep her **Tsui**tcase-(suitcase)-**Carry**-on above this platform 中 (inside) the top bunk	派遣する haken suru = to send (a person), to dispatch; 遣わす tsukawasu = to dispatch; 気遣う kizukau = to care for, worry, pay attention
沖 ₁	^1002. an **O**ld-**Ki**ng who lived in 沖縄 **Oki**nawa used to get 中 (inside) this water	沖 oki = open sea, off the coast; 沖縄 Okinawa
非 ₁	^682. this bird is a **He**ro with two wings who can fly in a 非常 **hi**jou (emergency)	非常 hijou = emergency, extreme, great
悲 ₂	^851. this 非 (**He**ro) with two wings lives in **Cana**da, and sometimes his 心 (heart) feels 悲しい **kana**shii (sad) during the long winters	悲鳴 himei = scream, shriek, cry of distress; 悲しい kanashii = sad
兆 ₂	^849. we were sitting on these two benches, looking at 一兆 ic**chou** (one trillion) stars, and I was getting ready to **Kiss-Za**ch when he started talking about Margaret **Cho**, and I took that as a bad 兆し **kiza**shi (omen)	兆し kizashi = sign, omen; 前兆 zenchou = premonition, omen; 一兆円 icchouen = one trillion yen
逃 ₃	^850. my **N**iece was on a **T**oll road when she spotted this snail carrying 兆 (a trillion) bacteria that were trying to 逃げる **ni**geru (escape) from a hurricane, and she thought about following them, but her car had **No-Ga**s	逃げる nigeru = to escape or run away; 逃亡 toubou = escape, flight; 逃れる nogareru = to escape
挑 ₂	^1001. this kneeling guy has to clean the floor and do a 兆 (trillion) other **Cho**res that 挑む **ido**mu (challenge) him, but he has to wait until his **E**agle-is-**Do**zing	挑戦する chousen suru = to challenge; 挑む idomu = to challenge
眺 ₂	^1136. this is the 目 (eye) of **Naga**ina (a snake from a Kipling story), which she uses to survey the 眺め **naga**me (view) in front of her, as she imagines that there are 兆 (a trillion) mice out there and that her primary **Cho**re is to catch them	眺める nagameru = to gaze or look at; 眺め nagame = a view; 眺望 choubou = a view
菜 ₂	^121. during the Vietnam war, people installed barbecue grates like this in 木 (trees) like this in **Sai**gon and cooked **N**atural 野菜 ya**sai** (vegetables), represented by this plant radical at the top	野菜 yasai = vegetable; 菜っ葉 nappa = green leafy vegetables
立 ₈	^11. this **Tax** collector, who acts **D**affy and is at**Tach**ing **D**amp-**Chee**se to his head, carries a **D**amp-**Te**ddy bear as he 立つ **ta**tsu (stands) on these shaky legs and faces his critics, who **Ri**dicule him for wearing **Reu**sed **Ritz**y clothes	立つ tatsu = to stand; 目立つ medatsu = to stand out; 立場 tachiba = position; 夕立 yuudachi = evening rain shower; 天橋立 amanohashidate = a sandbar in Kyoto Prefecture; 立派 rippa = splendid; 建立 konryuu = the act of building (a temple or monument); 起立する kiritsu suru = to stand up
泣 ₂	^12. when I **Nag** my children, they 立 (stand) and 泣く **na**ku (cry) tears like this, and they look **Cute**	泣く naku = to cry; 号泣 goukyuu = lamentations, wailing
位 ₂	^270. this man tilts this hat back in order to examine this 立 (Easter bell), and he uses it to win 第一位 dai ichi **i** (first place) in a bell-ringing competition, for which he receives a prize of **Ku**waiti-**Ri**ce and a high 位 **kurai** (rank)	第一位 dai ichi i = first place; 位 kurai = rank; どれ位 doregurai = how far (or long, many, much)
気 ₅	^321. when I stayed at this spot marked with an X in this lean-to in **Ki**ev, I played with **Ge**ese, I wore **Ke**ds (a brand of shoes) like the other **Gue**sts, I drank **Kool**-Aid, and the 天気 ten**ki** (weather) was good	天気 tenki = weather; 風邪気味 kazegimi = a bit of a cold (upper respiratory infection); 寒気 samuke = a chill; 何気ない nanigenai = casual; 意気地 ikuji = self-respect

竹 2		^134. these two cowboys, viewed from the side, each with his hat pushed back on his head, are **Tall-Kennedys** admiring some 竹 **take** (bamboo); the cowboy in front is kneeling, and they are both drinking **Cheap-Kool-Aid**	竹の子 takenoko = bamboo shoot; 竹林 chikurin = bamboo grove
笑 3		^199. there was a **Warra**nt for my arrest, but I went out under this 天 (sky) and watched this 竹 (bamboo) blow in the wind, and it made such an **Excellent Show** that I had to 笑う **wara**u (laugh)	笑う warau = to laugh; 笑顔 egao = smiling face; 爆笑 bakushou = burst of laughter
簡 1		^648. in **Kan**sas, it's 簡単 **kan**tan (easy) to hang hammocks between 竹 (bamboo) gate posts like these and lie in them for a long 間 (time) under a 日 (sun) like this	簡単 kantan = simple and easy
門 2		^409. a **Mon**k watches this 門 **mon** (gate), through which he can see a **Cathedral-Dome**	門 mon = gate; 門出 kadode = leaving one's home, starting in life
問 3		^410. **Ton**y Blair hung this **Mon**et 口 (painting) in this 門 (gate) and charged people a **To**ll to walk past it, but this created some 問題 **mon**dai (problems)	問屋 tonya = wholesaler; 問題 mondai = a problem; 問う tou = to ask, question, inquire, to charge (with a crime)
間 5		^411. standing near this 門 (gate), Ken, his **Ma** (mother), Barbie's friend **Ida**, and **Gengh**is **Khan** measure the 間 **aida** (duration) of time by watching the shadows that this 日 (sun) casts on the ground	世間 seken = society, other people; 間違える machigaeru = to make a mistake; 間 aida = duration, between; 人間 ningen = human being; 時間 jikan = time, hour
聞 3		^412. Daniel **Boon**e had big 耳 (ears) like this, and he used to sit in this 門 (gate) reading a 新聞 shin**bun** (newspaper) while wearing a **Ki**mono and feeding **Gee**se, while he 聞いた **ki**ita (listened) to gossip	新聞 shinbun = newspaper; 聞く kiku = to hear or ask; 人聞き hitogiki = reputation
開 3		^413. my **A**unt stands in this 門 (gate) with this welcoming stance, signaling that she will 開ける **a**keru (open) the gate so that people may bring their **Ki**tes inside, where they can **Hear-Ra**p music	開ける akeru = to open, transitive; 開発 kaihatsu = development; 開く hiraku = to open or unfold, transitive
閉 3		^414. **To**lstoy stands in this 門 (gate) and extends this left hip to create a **Shi**eld to block passage, signifying that the gate 閉まっている **shi**matte iru (is closed) to people who want to harvest **Hay**	閉じる tojiru = to close; 閉める shimeru = to close, transitive; 閉鎖する heisa suru = to close down
闘 2		^728. these 豆 (beans) in this 門 (gate) 付 (stick) to the **To**es of this 寸 (sunny kneeling guy), and a **Tall-Taxi-driver-with-a-Car** will go through a 奮闘 fun**tou** (hard struggle) to clean them up	奮闘 funtou = hard struggle, strenuous effort; 闘う tatakau = to fight, make war (usually written 戦う)
悶 2		^807. **Moses-and-his-Dad** have their 心 (hearts) set on this new 門 (gate), but they 悶える **moda**eru (worry) and **Moan** about the expense	悶える modaeru = to be in agony, to worry; 悶々 monmon = worry, agony
襲 2		^941. an **Old-Soldier** once 立 (stood) on this 月 (moon) and used to **Shoot** at the enemy and 襲う **oso**u (attack) them, but now he wears this civilian 衣 (clothing) and combs his hair with this comb	襲う osou = to attack; 襲撃 shuugeki = an attack
着 4		^52. this 目 (eye) belonging to a 王 (king) is full of fun when he 着く **tsuku** (arrives) at his palace in **Ki**ev with some **Gee**se while 着ている **ki**te iru (wearing) this trailing gown and these rabbit ears, while carrying his **Tsu**itcase (suitcase), after drinking a lot of **Cha**mpagne-and-**Kool-Aid**	着る kiru = to wear clothes; 水着 mizugi = swimsuit; 着く tsuku = to arrive; 着席 chakuseki = taking a seat
美 4		^771. this 美しい **utsuku**shii (beautiful) truncated 羊 (sheep) rests on a 大 (big) **Uber-Tsu**itcase-(suitcase)-full-of-**Kool-Aid**, and it admires its **Bea**uty when it looks into a **Mi**rror although it is starting to get **Old**	美しい utsukushii = beautiful; 美術 bijutsu = fine arts; 夏美 Natsumi = a woman's given name; 美味しい oishii = delicious (usually written おいしい)
認 2		^1036. when a **Ninja** goes to **Meet-To**lstoy to get 是認 ze**nin** (approval) for an undercover project, he 言 (speaks) from this 心 (heart) and shows Tolstoy this 刀 (sword), which was slashed during one of his missions	是認 zenin = approval; 確認 kakunin = confirmation; 認める mitomeru = to recognize, admit or allow

上 7		^171. when we saw that this stick 上っていた **nobo**tte ita (was rising) asymmetrically from the surface, we **A**sked some **Commies** (communists) if **Jo**an of **Arc** might have inserted it in the ground, but **Nobo**dy thought so, since she is just an **U**gandan **U**eitaa (waiter) who lives in an **U**ber-**Wag**on	上げる ageru = to give, or to raise something up; 川上 kawakami = upriver; 上手 jouzu = skillful; 上る noboru = to go up; 上手い umai = skillful, delicious (usually written うまい); 上 ue = up; 上着 uwagi = outer garment
下 9		^172. this tool for digging **C**abbages from the ground 下 **shita** (below) was designed by a **Cool-Dad** who works at the **Getty** Museum, flies a **H**elicopter, rides a **Motor**cycle, swims in the **O**cean, plays the **Sa**xophone, eats **Sheet**s-of-**Mo**lasses and is good at **Sheep-Ta**lk	地下鉄 chikatetsu = subway; 下る kudaru = to descend; 下品な gehin na = vulgar; 下手 heta = unskillful; 足下 ashimoto = underfoot; 下ろす orosu = to withdraw money; 下げる sageru = to lower or to hang down (transitive); 川下 kawashimo = downstream; 下着 shitagi = undergarment
不 2		^176. digging in soil with my **Boo**t, I encounter this symmetrical three-part carrot, but it's 不足 **fu**soku (insufficient) as a **Foo**d source	運動不足 undoubusoku = not enough exercise; 不足 fusoku = insufficiency; 不便 fuben = inconvenient
杯 4		^848. **Heidi Buy**s a **Pie** and goes to play **Sakka**a-(soccer)-with-a-**Zoo-Kee**per, but this 木 (tree) in the middle of the field serves to 不 (negate) that idea, so she shares 一杯 ip**pai** (one cup) of sake with him instead	二杯 nihai = two cups, glasses, spoons or bowls; 三杯 sanbai = three cups; 一杯 ippai = one cup, or full of; 杯をする sakazuki wo suru = to share a cup of sake
価 2		^484. this man is tilting his hat back in order to examine the 物価 buk**ka** (price) of this **Carry**-on suitcase that **A-Thai** guy wants to buy	物価 bukka = price; 価 atai = value, price
進 3		^203. this net on this snail 進む **susu**mu (advances) slowly and collects **Su**perior-**Sou**venirs to benefit **Su**perman's-**Su**mmer-**Mu**sic program at a **Shin**tou shrine	進む susumu = to advance; 進 Susumu = a boy's given name; 進出する shinshutsu suru = to advance or expand; 精進料理 shoujinryouri = vegetarian cuisine, as eaten by Buddhist monks
準 1		^204. 十 (ten) fishermen are placing this fish trap in this water as 準備 **jun**bi (preparation) for **Jun**gle fishing	準備 junbi = preparation
誰 1		^440. 誰 **dare** (who) **Dare**s to 言 (speak) from this net?	誰 dare = who
離 2		^666. **Hannah** fishes with this net on a **Reef** and catches these X's and ム's, which she 離れる **hana**reru (separates) into these two cans	離れる hanareru = to part; 離婚 rikon = divorce; 距離 kyori = distance
推 2		^1029. this guy on the left is **Swe**dish, and he kneels in front of this net in which I am confined and 推薦する **sui**sen suru (recommends) that my jailer **O**pen it	推薦する suisen suru = to recommend; 推す osu = to recommend or endorse
羅 1		^1158. these three eyes observe this 糸 (skeet shooter), who is a **R**ascal, shooting at the 甲羅 kou**ra** (shell) of a turtle that is being held in this net	甲羅 koura = shell
棒 1		^820. these 三 (three) 人 (people) used a **Boa**t to bring us a telephone 棒 **bou** (pole) like this made from this 木 (tree)	棒 bou = a stick or pole; 相棒 aibou = a buddy or partner; 泥棒 dorobou = thief
春 2		^506. during the first 春 **haru** (spring) when King **Harol**d-**Ru**led, some 三 (three) 人 (people) combinations (i.e., triplets) were born, but even though they had 日 (sun)-like (i.e., sunny) dispositions, the king **Shun**ned those babies	春 haru = spring; 晩春 banshun = late spring
奏 2		^757. these 三 (three) 人 (people) gave 演奏 en**sou** (musical performances) under this open 天 (sky) in **Can**ada, featuring **Sou**l music	奏でる kanaderu = to play a stringed instrument; 演奏 ensou = musical performance

Kanji	Mnemonic	Vocabulary
犬 2	^190. this 犬 **inu** (dog), which is 大 (big) and belongs to the **Inu**it tribe, chases this ball that **Ken** threw to Barbie	犬 inu = dog; 番犬 banken = watchdog
吠 2	^944. this 犬 (dog) on the right uses this 口 (mouth) to 吠える **ho**eru (bark), as he protects his master's **Ho**me and **Bo**at	吠える hoeru = to bark, howl, roar, cry; 遠吠え tooboe = howling
伏 3	^945. this man from **Fuku**oka tilts his hat back to serve as a pillow before he 伏せる **fu**seru (lies down), but first he gives **Food** to this 犬 (dog) and drinks some **Booze**	降伏する koufuku suru = to surrender; 伏せる fuseru = to lay an object upside down or face down, to lie down; うつ伏せに utsubuse ni = face down
状 1	^998. **Joan** of Arc thought that the 状態 **jou**tai (circumstances) were right to bring this 犬 (dog) to a park, and she sat on this bench while the dog ran around	状態 joutai = condition, circumstances, state
才 1	^617. this kneeling guy is a left-wing **Sci**entist whose left hip has slipped out of its socket, and since he is a 天才 ten**sai** (genius), he can put it back by himself	才能 sainou = talent; 天才 tensai = genius
胃 1	^153. during the **E**vening, a man in this 田 (rice paddy) rubs his 胃 **i** (stomach) while gazing at this 月 (moon)	胃 i = stomach; 胃癌 igan = stomach cancer
歳 3	^322. 歳 **sai** (age) is a number, and it is divisible like this, but I remain **Si**lent about my age and 止 (stop) before I **Say** it, lest people **Cheat** me	十六歳 juurokusai = 16 years old; 万歳 banzai = "10,000 years," i.e., "long live!"; お歳暮 oseibo = year-end gift; 二十歳 hatachi = 20 years old
何 4	^338. **Nancy** and her **Nanny** see this **Carton** in the **Garden**, and ask this man, who tilts his hat back so that they can see his face, 何ですか **nan** desu ka (what is it?)	何人 nannin = how many people; 何 nani = what; 幾何学 kikagaku = geometry; 如何 ikaga = how? (deferential)
荷 3	^342. Customs officer: "何 (what) is this plant material that your **Nie**ce is carrying in her 荷物 **ni**motsu (luggage)?" Answer: "It's a **Carton** of Christmas **Wreaths**."	荷物 nimotsu = luggage; 出荷する shukka suru = to ship or send; お稲荷さん o'inarisan = the god of harvests & wealth
可 1	^615. this **Carton** inside this lean-to contains some 可愛い **ka**waii (cute) clothing	許可 kyoka = permission; 可能 kanou = possible; 可愛い kawaii = cute
阿 1	^1176. this ß (Greek) **Artist** looked 可 (cute) when she danced in the 阿波踊り **a**wa'odori (an Obon dance festival)	阿波踊り Awa Odori = a dance festival held in Tokushima City during Obon
河 3	^1182. I took this **Carton** of cleaning supplies to my **Garage**, which is this one-sided lean-to, and I used this water from a 河 **kawa** (river) to do a **Car-Wash**	河口 kakou = mouth of a river; 運河 unga = canal; 河 kawa = river (usually written 川)
句 1	^872. our 可 (cute) customer submitted a 文句 mon**ku** (complaint) to the effect that this awning we installed didn't keep her house **Cool** enough	文句 monku = complaint, phrase, words; 俳句 haiku = poem
寄 2	^604. we have **Qui**che and **Yo**gurt in this box in this lean-to, which also contains 寄付 **ki**fu (donations), so if you don't mind this 大 (big) bird with a bad haircut, please 寄る **yo**ru (stop by)	寄付 kifu = donation; 寄る yoru = to drop in at, to gather, to go closer; 年寄り toshiyori = elderly person
奇 1	^854. this reminds us of a 可 (cute) person wearing a **Ki**mono that is too 大 (big) for her, which is a 奇妙な **ki**myou na (strange) sight	奇妙な kimyou na = strange, unique; 好奇心 koukishin = curiosity
椅 1	^855. at **Easter** the Pope sat in a 奇 (strange) 椅子 **i**su (chair) made from this 木 (tree)	椅子 isu = chair
崎 2	^1081. I ate some **Salty-Qui**che on this 山 (mountain) overlooking 長崎 Naga**saki**, and then I felt 奇 (strange)	長崎 Nagasaki = a city in Japan; 宮崎県 miyazaki ken = Miyazaki Prefecture

司 2	^608. after my 上司 jou**shi** (superior) removed this napkin from the top of this box inside this lean-to, we found that the box contained **Shee**p food, in addition to some **Tsou**p-(soup)-that-**Casa**nova-left-by-the-**Door**	寿司 sushi = raw fish slices on rice; 上司 joushi = one's superior (in a company); 健司 kenji = a boy's given name; 司る tsukasadoru = to rule, administer
伺 1	^341. this man on the left, who is an Uber-**Ca**lifornia-**Ga**mbler, 伺う **ukaga**u (humbly visits) this lean-to and tilts his hat back in order to examine the napkin covering this box, and he 伺う **ukaga**u (humbly inquires) about the contents of the box before betting on them	伺う ukagau = to ask humbly, to visit humbly
飼 3	^830. a 飼主 **kai**nushi (shepherd) in **Ca**lifornia who is **Ki**nd removes this napkin from this 口 (box) in this lean-to and allows his animals to 食 (eat) the **Shee**p food found within	飼う kau = to keep a pet or raise livestock; 飼主 kainushi = shepherd, pet owner (also written 飼い主); 飼育 shiiku = breeding, raising, rearing
覗 1	^982. when I wanted to 見 (see) what was under the napkin on this box in this lean-to, I parked in a **No-Zo**ne and ran over to 覗く **nozo**ku (snoop)	覗く nozoku = to snoop, often spelled のぞく
痛 2	^368. since this マ (mammoth) damaged my **Tsu**it (suit) from **Ita**ly, I'm making it sleep on this 用 (fence) pressed against the headboard of this sick bed, which 痛い **ita**i (hurts)	頭痛 zutsuu = headache; 痛い itai = painful
病 3	^369. this 内 (chest x-ray) of a **Ya**nkee in this sick bed suggests a 病気 **byou**ki (illness) which could be a disorder in the **Ya**nkee's-**Mi**nd, or maybe it's **B.O.** (bacterial overgrowth)	病む yamu = to fall sick; 病 yamai = illness; 病気 byouki = illness
左 2	^456. when I play this 工 (crafted object), which is a **Sa**xophone, I usually hug it like this using this 左 **hidari** (left) arm, but that's difficult now, since I was injured by a **Hide**A**way**-bed's-**Re**coil	左折 sasetsu = left turn; 左手 hidari te = left hand
佐 1	^993. this man on the left had some **Sa**gging on the 左 (left) side of his face, so he tilted his hat to show a plastic surgeon, who was able to offer 補佐 ho**sa** (help)	佐賀県 saga ken = Saga Prefecture; 大佐 taisa = colonel; 補佐 hosa = aid, help
区 1	^320. this 区役所 **ku**yakusho (ward office) in **Ku**wait is a storefront, and this X marks the spot where citizens from the ward are served	区役所 kuyakusho = ward office
駆 2	^776. this 馬 (horse) 駆ける **ka**keru (runs) after a **Car** in this 区 (ward) in **Ku**wait	駆ける kakeru = to run; 先駆者 senkusha = originator, pioneer
爽 1	^798. this 大 (big) guy likes to listen to **Sou**l music, and these X's represent four songs that he finds especially 爽快 **sou**kai (refreshing)	爽快 soukai = refreshing, exhilarating
館 3	^305. this is a 旅館 ryo**kan** (Japanese inn), where these 食 (meals) are prepared on the left, and these bunk beds on the right, under a roof that looks like this bad haircut, are lighted by **Can**dles to discourage **Yak-Atta**cks during the night when the **Darkness-is-Terrifying**	旅館 ryokan = Japanese inn; 館 yakata = mansion, palace; 田舎館 Inakadate = a village in Aomori
追 2	^821. this snail is carrying these **Tsui**theart (sweetheart) bunk beds to Osaka and trying to 追いかける **o**ikakeru (chase) a rival snail, but progress is slow	追求する tsuikyuu suru = to pursue a goal, to chase; 追う ou = to chase
官 1	^880. a guy from **Kan**sas, who is a 警官 kei**kan** (policeman), retreated to the top of this bunk bed after he got this bad haircut	警官 keikan = policeman; 仕官 shikan = military officer
呂 1	^7. when I **Row**, these stacked vertebrae stick out; afterwards I walk to the 風呂 fu**ro** (bath)	風呂 furo = bath, bathhouse, bathtub
宮 3	^1079. a **Goo**fy **Cu**ban dictator with a bad haircut like this built a 宮殿 **kyuu**den (palace) with this 呂 (bath), where he planned to **Meet-Ya**nkees	神宮 jinguu = high-status Shinto shrine; 宮殿 kyuuden = palace; お宮参り omiyamairi = shrine visit
営 2	^684. honest **Abe** used to sit in a 呂 (bath) under this roof where these three old boys stood, and they would invent instruments with **Eerie-Tona**l qualities to sell in their 営業 **ei**gyou (business)	経営 keiei = management; 営業 eigyou = business; 営む itonamu = to run a business

Chapter 11

Kanji		Mnemonic	Vocabulary
子	4	^182. this thin 子 **ko** (child) from **Su**dan loves this マ (mother), and when he gets **C**old at night, he sleeps under a **Shee**pskin in a **Jee**p	様子 yousu = condition; 子供 kodomo = child; 迷子 maigo = a lost person; 男子 danshi = boy; 王子 ouji = prince
字	1	^183. this 子 (child) has this bad haircut, but he writes excellent 字 **ji** (characters), and we are giving him a **Jee**p	漢字 kanji = kanji
学	3	^184. this 子 (child) attends a 学校 **ga**kkou (school) with a **Ga**rden, and these three old boys on this roof **Mana**ge his education, allotting him a **Ga**llon-of-**Ko**ol-Aid every week	学校 gakkou = school; 学ぶ manabu = to learn; 学のある人 gaku no aru hito = a learned person
厚	2	^185. this poor 子 (child) is getting crushed under this heavy 日 (weight) in this lean-to **At-Su**perman's house, and he will likely become somewhat 厚い **atsu**i (thick, i.e., wide) as a result, but he will just have to **C**ope with that	厚い atsui = thick; 濃厚 noukou = density, concentration
古	3	^392. a **Foolish-Roo**ster often sits on this **Go**ld cross above this 古い **furu**i (old) tomb, where my **Coa**ch was buried	古い furui = old; 名古屋 Nagoya = city in Japan; 古代 kodai = ancient times
苦	3	^393. my **Niece-Ga**thers flowers in a cemetery in **Ku**wait, and it's 苦い **niga**i (bitter) for her to see these 古 (old) tombs overgrown with plants like these, with **Ku**waiti-**Roo**sters perched on them	苦い nigai = bitter; 苦労 kurou = hardship; 苦しい kurushii = hard, painful; 見苦し migurushi = unsightly
故	3	^394. due to a **Foolish-Roo**ster, this 古 (old) dancer from **Co**lombia was involved in a 事故 ji**ko** (accident), and now she has to fly home by **U.A.** (United Airlines)	故郷 furusato = hometown (usually written ふるさと); 事故 jiko = accident; 故に yue ni = therefore
湖	2	^716. this water in a 湖 **mizuumi** (lake) is connected by a river to the **Mizu**-(water)-in-the-**Umi** (ocean), and on **C**old nights when this 月 (moon) is out, I can see reflections of 古 (old) buildings on its surface	湖 mizuumi = lake; 湖水 kosui = lake water
去	3	^343. a **Sa**laryman purchased this ム (cow) in **Kyo**to 去年 **kyo**nen (last year), but now it's covered in this 土 (soil), so he's sending it down to **Ko**be	去る saru = to leave; 去年 kyonen = last year; 過去 kako = the past
法	3	^344. this 土 (soiled) ム (cow) 去 (leaves), but since there's a **Ho**le in the bridge, it falls into this water, and we decide to pass a 法律 **hou**ritsu (law) telling the **Po**lice to prohibit cows on the bridge, which we **Ho**pe will solve the problem	法律 houritsu = law; 文法 bunpou = grammar, syntax; 法華経 hokekyou = the Lotus Sutra
果	3	^587. my **Cool-Da**d saw these four 果物 **kuda**mono (fruits) growing on this 木 (tree), so he **Ha**rvested them and **Ca**rved them up	果物 kudamono = fruit; 果たす hatasu = to accomplish, realize; 結果 kekka = result
課	1	^588. when our 課長 **ka**chou (section manager) saw these four fruits at the top of this 木 (tree), he 言 (said) that he wanted to **Ca**rve them up	課長 kachou = section manager; 第一課 dai ikka = section # 1
菓	2	^589. in our **Ga**rden there is a 果 (fruit)-bearing 木 (tree) like this under plants like these, and we **Ca**rve up the fruit to make 菓子 **ka**shi (candy)	和菓子 wagashi = Japanese sweets; お菓子 okashi = pastry, confectionery, candy
巣	2	^972. a **So**ldier asked **Su**perman to check on these three old boys who were making a 巣 **su** (nest) at the top of this 果 (fruit) 木 (tree)	卵巣 ransou = ovary; 巣 su = nest, animal habitat, cobweb, honeycomb, den
母	5	^50. this is a 母 **haha** (mother) who frequently says "Ha-Ha" and comes from a **Bo**ring town in **C**alifornia with only one **Ba**r and an **Old-Mo**ron	母 haha = mother; 祖母 sobo = grandmother; お母さん okaasan = honorable mother; 伯母さん obasan = aunt, middle-aged woman; 母屋 omoya = main building or main room
境	3	^719. if you cross this 土 (soil) 境 **sakai** (boundary) in **Kyo**uto, a 兄 (big brother) with a scowl like this who is 立 (standing) guard may **Sock-you-in-the-Eye** and put you in a **Ca**ge	環境 kankyou = environment, surroundings; 境 sakai = boundary, border; 境内 keidai = the grounds of a temple

降 4	^178. after a trip across the **Ocean**, this ß (Greek) guy and this dancer with a ponytail rush to 降りる oriru (get off) their ship, such that she leaps over this knee belonging to a seated person on the dock; they both buy **Food**, the dancer buys some **Co**la, and the Greek guy buys **Boo**ze	降りる oriru = to get off a train, etc.; 降る furu = to rain or snow; 下降 kakou = descent; 小降り koburi = light rain
限 2	^642. this ß (Greek) guy named **Gen**ghis is a 良 (good) hunter who can **Call-Gee**se, and there is no 限界 **gen**kai (limit) on his activities	限界 genkai = limit; 限る kagiru = to be limited to
防 2	^920. this 方 (honorable person) is a **Food-Seller** from ß (Greece) who **Boa**sts about his record in the 予防 yo**bou** (prevention) of food-borne illness	防ぐ fusegu = to prevent or defend; 予防 yobou = prevention
陸 1	^1015. this ß (Greek) guy lives on an island where 土 (soil) like this walks on more 土 (soil), and he will have to swim to the 大陸 tai**riku** (mainland) in order to get some **Rea**l-**Koo**l-Aid	大陸 tairiku = continent, mainland (China); 陸軍 rikugun = army
町 2	^70. this 田 (rice paddy) and this nail can be seen near a rice-producing 町 **machi** (town), where workers wear **Matchi**ng outfits and buy nails like this from Margaret **Cho**	町 machi = town; 町名 choumei = town name or street name
打 3	^590. this guy on the left is an Uber gangster who sometimes kneels like this in order to 打つ **u**tsu (strike) his fallen enemies with this **Cheap** 丁 (**Dagger**)	打つ utsu = to hit or strike; 博打 bakuchi = gambling; 打撃 dageki = shock, impact
貯 2	^667. Margaret **Cho**, who has a bad haircut like this one, has a business which uses nails like this to nail **Tar** paper onto roofs, and she 貯める **ta**meru (saves) her 貯金 **cho**kin (savings) in this 貝 (money chest)	貯金 chokin = savings; 貯める tameru = to save (money)
丁 2	^702. Margaret **Cho** sold this nail to a 丁寧な **tei**nei na (polite) **Tai**lor	丁目 choume = city block, district of a town; 丁寧 teinei = polite, courteous
寧 1	^703. I know a 丁寧 tei**nei** (polite) guy with a bad haircut like this one, a good 心 (heart) like this and three eyes like these who tries to live with a small footprint, and therefore he balances his house on this **Nail**	丁寧 teinei = polite, courteous
半 2	^331. **Han**sel noticed that this 羊 (sheep) painting at the National-Cathedral only depicts 半分 **han**bun (half) of the animal and adds this nose to its head	一時半 ichijihan = half past 1:00; 半ば nakaba = half, the middle
判 3	^1054. **Han**sel says that when he went to a **Ban**quet, he only received 半 (half) a serving of **Pan** (bread), and he 判断した **han**dan shita (judged) that this guy リ Ri was responsible	判断する handan suru = to judge; 評判 hyouban = reputation, popularity, rumor; 審判 shinpan = referee
平 4	^885. a **Beer**hall-**Ow**ner said that a **Hero-Ran** to fight this fire in this flat-topped telephone pole, which was disturbing the 平和 **hei**wa (peace) and creating a **Ha**ze, but after awhile the hero got **Tired**	平等 byoudou = equality; 平たい hiratai = flat, simple; 平和 heiwa = peace, tranquility; 平らな taira na = flat, level
評 1	^1053. the Lone Ranger has a good 評判 **hyou**ban (reputation) in these parts, and when he heard that this telephone pole was on fire, he stopped by to 言 (say) "Hi-Yo Silver"	評判 hyouban = reputation, popularity, rumor; 評価 hyouka = assessment, evaluation
鳥 3	^555. this 鳥 **tori** (bird) with this 白 (white) tuft on its head, this feather and these five **Toes** belongs to a **Tory** who was **Cho**sen to serve in Parliament	鳥取県 tottori ken = Tottori Prefecture; 小鳥 kotori = small bird; 雄鳥 ondori = rooster; 白鳥 hakuchou = swan
島 2	^556. this 鳥 (bird) that lives on this 山 (mountain) on a 島 **shima** (island) near Hiro**Shima** lost its **Toes** to a predator	島 shima = island; 桜島 Sakurajima = a volcano in Kyushu; 半島 hantou = peninsula
鳩 1	^736. these 九 (nine) 鳥 (birds) are 鳩 **hato** (pigeons), and they eat **Ham-and-Toast**	鳩 hato = pigeon, dove
鳴 2	^751. this 鳥 (bird) serves as a lookout for some **Narcos**, and it uses this 口 (mouth) to 鳴く **na**ku (chirp) when their **Mail** arrives	鳴る naru = to chime, ring, sound; 鳴く naku = to chirp, bark, cry (animal sounds); 悲鳴 himei = scream, shriek, cry of distress

友 2	^459. my **You**thful 友達 **tomo**dachi (friend) is hugging this 又 (table) that he made; **Tomo**rrow he will make another	友人 yuujin = friend; 友達 tomodachi = friend
抜 3	^749. this guy on the left is on his knees acting **Batty**, and he and this 友 (friend) run around in **Bat-Sui**ts, threatening people with **Noo**ses, so it might be best to 抜く **nu**ku (extract) our citizens from their vicinity	抜てきする batteki suru = to select; 人気抜群 ninkibatsugun = very popular; 抜きに nuki ni = without (omitting)
愛 5	^523. this dancer with a ponytail is an **Excellent Ice** dancer from **Mexico** who studies **Mana**gement and barbecues **E**els-and-**To**matoes on this grate, putting a lot of this 心 (heart) and 愛情 **ai**jou (love) into her cooking	愛媛県 ehime ken = Ehime Prefecture; 愛情 aijou = love; 愛でる mederu = to love or admire; 愛弟子 manadeshi = favorite student; 愛しい itoshii = lovely, beloved
暖 2	^38. **Ataturk-with-a-Tan** is this 友 (friend) who **Dan**ces in this 日 (sun) until it gets 暖かい **atata**kai (warm), after which he turns his attention to this barbecue grate	暖かい atatakai = warm (atmosphere); 暖房 danbou = heating, heater
援 1	^1177. when this guy on the left is kneeling to put food on this grate, the house gets 暖 (warm), but the kneeling guy gets 応援 ou**en** (support) and **En**couragement from this 友 (friend)	応援 ouen = support; 援助 enjo = assistance, support; 救援 kyuuen = rescue; 声援 seien = support, cheering
髪 3	^501. this 友 (friend), who is a **Cam**bodian-**Immigrant**, owns this 一 (one) ム (cow), and she has these two kinds of 髪 **kami** (hair) flowing right, which she covers with **Hats** that she bought in **Ga**za	髪 kami = hair; 白髪 hakuhatsu = white or grey hair; 先発 senpatsu = washing one's hair; 白髪 shiraga = white or grey hair
水 2	^251. outside the cafeteria at a **Miniature-Zoo**, 水 **mizu** (water) was flowing between these two cliffs, and we ordered **Swe**et drinks	水 mizu = water; 水曜日 suiyoubi = Wednesday; 洪水 kouzui = flood
泳 2	^255. **Oprah-eats-Yogurt** and drinks this water on the left, and honest **Abe** drinks this 水 (water) on the right while wearing a hat with these two feathers, before they 泳ぐ **oyo**gu (swim)	泳ぐ oyogu = to swim; 水泳 suiei = swimming
氷 3	^814. when the Lone Ranger visited **Corinth**, they served him a drink of this **Cold** 水 (water) containing one crystal like this that turned out to be 氷 **koori** (ice), and he said "**Hi-Yo** Silver"	氷 koori = ice; 氷る kooru = to freeze; 氷山 hyouzan = iceberg
永 2	^870. when Honest **Abe** drank this 水 (water), he would wear a hat with these two feathers in it and tell stories for what seemed like an 永遠 **ei**en (eternity) while **Naga**ina (a snake) lurked outside	永遠 eien = eternity; 永眠 eimin = death; 永久 eikyuu = eternity; 永田町 Nagatachou = a district in Tokyo
引 3	^476. since this **Hide**ous tree was twisted, I 引いた **hi**ita (pulled) it down with this rope, but I **In**jured my skin, and now I have a **Hickey**	引く hiku = to pull; 引力 inryoku = attraction, gravitational pull, magnetism; 取引 torihiki = business deal; 割引 waribiki = discount
機 2	^137. we made this 機械 **ki**kai (machine) from four components: this 木 (tree), these two truncated 糸 (skeet shooters), this **Halberd-sent-by-Ta**rzan, and this 人 (person) under a platform, who operates it using a **Key**	機織り hataori = weaving, weaver; 機械 kikai = machine; 飛行機 hikouki = airplane
散 2	^159. as this **Cheer**ful dancer takes a 散歩 **san**po (walk) in the **Sand**, she imagines growing these plants on this 月 (moon)	散る chiru = to disperse or scatter; 散歩 sanpo = a walk
敬 2	^873. this dancer, who lives in this **Cave** in the **Ugandan-Yama** (mountains), wrote a 句 (poem) about these plants around her, which she 敬う **uyama**u (respects)	尊敬する sonkei suru = to respect; 敬う uyamau = to respect or venerate
警 1	^874. this dancer with a ponytail 敬 (respects) the 警察 **kei**satsu (police), and she 言 (says) that they are welcome to attend parties in this **Cave**	警察 keisatsu = the police; 警戒する keikai suru = to be cautious or watch out
驚 2	^971. I 敬 (respect) 馬 (horses) like this that I see in **Kyou**to, but I 驚く **odoro**ku (get astonished) at the **Odoro**us drinks served at the riding academies there	驚異 kyoui = miracle, marvel; 驚く odoroku = to be astonished
垢 2	^665. in Colombia, I attended an **Aca**demy constructed on 土 (soil) like this, and I learned that excessive 垢 **aka** (dirt) on my homework would cause me to get F's like this and that 歯垢 shi**kou** (dental plaque) is caused by poor 口 (oral) hygiene	歯垢 shikou = dental plaque; 垢 aka = dirt

匹 2	^818. I kicked a wall out of this house, 四匹 yon**hiki** (four) of my cats escaped, and now I have a **Hickey** on my **Heel**	二匹 nihiki = two small animals or bolts of cloth; 一匹 ippiki = one small animal or bolt of cloth; 三匹 sanbiki = three small animals or bolts of cloth; 匹敵 hitteki suru = to equal or match
勘 1	^1161. my lunch was served in this bucket with three compartments carried by this 匹 (small animal), which is known in **Kan**sas for exerting a lot of 力 (force) like this, and I was happy until I saw the 勘定 **kan**jou (check)	勘弁 kanben = pardon, forgiveness; 勘定 kanjou = bill, check, calculation
詰 2	^781. this 士 (man) 言 (says) that he has 詰めた tsumeta (stuffed) this 口 (**Tsu**itcase) with **Kit**tens-from-**Su**dan, and he is offering them for adoption	詰める tsumeru = to stuff, fill or pack into; 詰問 kitsumon = cross-examination
結 4	^231. this 糸 (skeet shooter) will 結婚する ke**kkon** suru (marry) this 士 (man) standing on this 口 (box) of wedding clothes, who wears **Ke**ds (a brand of shoes), likes to put **Ke**tchup-in-his-**Sou**p, sells **Mo**vie-**Sou**venirs and lives in the **Yu**kon	結婚 kekkon = marriage; 団結 danketsu = unity, combination; 結ぶ musubu = bind, connect, e.g., 手を結ぶ te wo musubu = to join hands; 髪を結う kami wo yuu = to put up the hair;
前 2	^157. this 月 (moon) and this リ Ri, who is a **Mae**stro, are carrying this bench to a **Zen** temple, but the 月 is standing 前 **mae** (in front of) リ and will get to the temple 前 **mae** (before) リ	二年前 ninen mae = two years ago; 駅前 eki mae = in front of the station; 午前九時 gozen kuji = 9:00 a.m.
揃 1	^644. this guy on the left fell to his knees and expressed **Sorro**w when he learned that he had left town 前 (before) the circus came, and he 揃う **soro**u (assembles) with other non-attendees to commiserate	揃う sorou = to be complete, to be equal, to be the same, to assemble
輸 1	^288. 前 (before) I moved to this house in the **Yu**kon, I 輸入した **yu**nyuu shita (imported) 車 (cars) like this one	輸入する yu'nyuu suru = to import; 輸出する yushutsu suru = to export
愉 1	^733. this man owned this 愉快 **yu**kai (pleasant) house in the **Yu**kon 前 (before), but the place where he lives now is 不愉快 fu**yu**kai (unpleasant), and he raises himself to his full height to show disapproval	愉快 yukai = pleasant, cheerful; 不愉快 fuyukai = unpleasant
論 1	^813. **Ron**ald Reagan got into a 口論 kou**ron** (argument) at this 冊 (library) and 言 (said) some angry words	口論 kouron = argument, quarrel
輪 2	^690. **Rin**go wanted to go to this 冊 (library), but a 車輪 sha**rin** (wheel) fell off this 車 (car), and he had to **Walk**	車輪 sharin = wheel; 輪 wa = round shape (ring, circle etc.); 指輪 yubiwa = ring
業 3	^332. when I went to **Watch-Za**chary teach a 授業 ju**gyou** (class), he had decorated the room with this Christmas tree, and he served the students **Gyo**za made with **Goat** meat	仕業 shiwaza = deeds; 卒業 sotsugyou = graduation; 授業 jugyou = class; 自業自得 jigoujitoku = paying for one's mistakes
僕 2	^333. 僕 **boku** (I) am this **Bony-Koo**l-Aid salesman on the left, and ever since I cut the central trunk from this 業 (Christmas tree), making it resemble a husband with an extra pair of arms who is decorated with lights, I stay in bed, tilting my hat back like this to watch TV and wishing that my **Sh**eets-had-**M**ore-**B**ells on them	僕 boku = I (male); 僕 shimobe = manservant, menial
長 2	^502. this 社長 sha**chou** (president) with this long hair flowing to the right is Light Years ahead of his peers, and he owns **Naga**ina, a 長い **naga**i (long) cobra who was **Cho**sen to represent her tribe	長い nagai = long; 社長 shachou = company president
張 3	^477. 長 (long) 弓 (twisted) stories are often heard on 出張 shuc**chou** (business trips), where businessmen who are **Cho**sen by their managers sit around the **Har**bor, beg each other's **Par**don, and 引っ張る hip**par**u (pull) their noses	出張 shucchou = business trip; 張り合う hariau = to compete or contend with; 引っ張る hipparu = to pull; 頑張る ganbaru = to do one's best
訪 3	^713. this 方 (honorable person) on the right, who is a **Tall-Zoo**keeper, 言 (speaks) about an **Oto**scope-that-I-left-at-the-**Zoo** when he 訪ねる **tazu**neru (visits) my **Ho**me	訪ねる tazuneru = to visit; 訪れる otozureru = to visit or arrive; 訪問する houmon suru = to visit

弟 4	^529. 弟 **otouto** (younger brother), who wears these rabbit ears and eats only Organic-TomaToes, which is a strange **Di**et, stands with his left hip extended behind this twisted tree, which he wants to make into a **Ta**ble for a **De**butante	弟 otouto = younger brother; 兄弟 kyoudai = sibling; 子弟 shitei = younger people; 弟子 deshi = disciple, apprentice
第 1	^530. this 弟 (younger brother) has these two 竹 (bamboo) clamps in his hair, indicating that he is 第二 **dai** ni (Number Two) in line at Weight Watchers, since he wants to go on a **Di**et	次第に shidai ni = gradually; 次第で shidai de = depending on
沸 2	^531. this **Wa**ter enters these twisted pipes, 沸く **wa**ku (boils) and cooks our **Foo**d	沸く waku = to boil, intransitive; 沸騰する futtou suru = to boil
費 2	^656. in order to make **Tsu**ites (sweets), I 費やす **tsui**yasu (spend) money to buy this 沸 (boiler) for the top of this 貝 (money chest) and **Hea**t up the ingredients; therefore my 費用 **hi**you (costs) are high	費やす tsuiyasu = to spend time or money; 費用 hiyou = cost; 出費 shuppi = expenditures
北 3	^373. this ヒ (hero) next to this bench is a **Ki**ng-checking-his-**Ta**x code, with his head pointing 北 **kita** (north), where he keeps a **Ho**me at the North Pole, and the **Ho**me-is-**Coo**l even during the summer	北 kita = north; 北海道 hokkaidou = Hokkaido; 北部 hokubu = the northern part; 敗北 haiboku = defeat
壮 1	^769. this 士 (man) sits on this bench admiring a 壮観 **sou**kan (magnificent view) while listening to **Sou**l music	壮大な soudai na = magnificent, imposing; 壮観 soukan = magnificent view
装 3	^1043. this 士 (man) likes **Sou**l music, and he can **Yo**del-when-he's-**So**ber; he leans this bench up against a wall in order to clear a space for a **Sho**w and examines this 衣 (clothing) which will be his 服装 fuku**sou** (outfit) during the performance	装置 souchi = equipment, device; 装備 soubi = equipment; 装う yosou = to serve or dish up; 衣装 ishou = clothing, costume
休 2	^122. this man tilts his hat back so that he can use it as a pillow when he 休む **yasu**mu (rests) against this **Cu**ban 木 (tree), but first he plans to drink some **Ya**k-**Sou**p	休む yasumu = to rest; 休暇 kyuuka = vacation
本 4	^123. this 本 **hon** (book) near the bottom of this 木 (tree) in **Ho**nduras tells the story of a **Mo**torcycle that ran into a **Po**ny and broke its **Bo**nes	本屋 honya = bookstore; 山本 Yamamoto = a family name; 一本 ippon = one bottle; 何本 nanbon = how many bottles
体 3	^124. this man on the left was on a plane, and he tilted his hat back to examine this 本 (book) about **Ca**racas'-**Da**rk underworld, but his 体 **karada** (body) got **Ti**red, and he fell asleep during **Ta**ke-off	体 karada = body; 身体 shintai = the human body; 体裁 teisai = appearance, looks
呆 4	^828. **A**chilles saw a man with this big 口 (mouth) **Boa**sting from the top of this 木 (tree), and he 呆れた **aki**reta (got astonished) and went **Ho**me to tell his **A**unt	呆れる akireru = to be disgusted or astonished,; 呆け boke = fool; 阿呆 aho = a fool, usually written アホ; 呆気にとられる akke ni torareru = to be taken aback
褒 2	^829. this man in the center left tilted his hat back and saw that cars were colliding with **Ho**tels, as well as the **Ho**me of this エ and Y, so he invented this tire stop, and people were 呆 (astonished) and 褒めた **ho**meta (praised) him	褒める homeru = to praise, admire or speak well of (this can also be spelled 誉める); 褒美 houbi = reward
悩 2	^1181. when this man on the left took a **Na**p-in-the-**Ya**rd, these three buzzing bees, out of the X (unknown number) in this hive, stung him on the **No**se, causing him to jump up to his full height like this and experience 悩み **naya**mi (distress)	悩み nayami = distress, worry; 苦悩 kunou = agony, anguish
画 2	^77. a **Ga**mbler is making an 映画 ei**ga** (movie) which is set in a rice paddy, and when he shows us this model of this 田 (paddy) with this handle, which he keeps in this box, he **Cac**kles about his 計画 kei**kaku** (plans)	映画 eiga = movie; 漫画 manga = comics; 計画 keikaku = plan
胸 3	^775. when this 月 (moon) shines in **Kyou**to, this hook sometimes snags a person whose 胸 **mune** (chest), represented by this open box, is filled with X's like this, representing dreams of **Moo**n-**E**ncounters with **Moo**n-**A**nimals	度胸 dokyou = courage or audacity; 胸 mune = chest; 胸毛 munage = chest hair

命 3	^961. **Inno**cent-**Chil**dren live with a **Ma**id in this house with this 口 (box) under this napkin on the left and this wobbly table on the right, and their 命 **inochi** (most precious possession) is a cat that lives in the box and **Meow**s too much	命 inochi = life, most precious possession or person; 命じる meijiru = to command or appoint; 寿命 jumyou = life span
令 1	^962. this person under this roof is about to run a **Ra**ce and is waiting for the 命令 mei**rei** (command) to start	命令 meirei = a command or order; 号令 gourei = a command or order
冷 4	^299. this table in Melvin's house is wobbly because one of its legs is too long, and when it **Rain**s, the floors are 冷たい **tsume**tai (cold), so we will **Tsue**-(sue)-Melvin to get him to **Heat** the house, and use a **Sa**w to shorten this table leg	冷蔵庫 reizouko = refrigerator; 冷たい tsumetai = cold object; 冷やす hiyasu = to chill; 冷める sameru = to cool off
齢 1	^989. during the **Ra**ce of life, our 年齢 nen**rei** (age) increases, and we develop problems with 歯 (teeth) like this, but we also get to give more 令 (orders) to younger people	年齢 nenrei = age
机 2	^140. if we put a tsuitcase (suitcase) containing **Key**s under this 机 t**sukue** (desk) made from this 木 (wood), the desk will be **Tsui**t**Case-no-U**e (above the suitcase)	机上 kijou = on the desk, theoretical, academic; 机 tsukue = desk
飢 2	^924. when I 飢えていた **u**ete ita (was starving) in Uganda, I found some old **Qui**che in this tall 机 (desk) and 食 (ate) it	飢える ueru = to starve, to be thirsty or hungry; 飢きん kikin = famine
肌 1	^980. my **Ha**waiian-**D**aughter hides under this 机 (desk) during the day and only exposes her 肌 **hada** (skin) to the sky when this 月 (moon) shines	肌 hada = skin, personality; 肌着 hadagi = underwear; 木肌 kihada = bark of a tree
処 2	^1149. a **Doorman's-Coro**lla hit this desk, causing it to land on this dancer's right leg, but he 処理した **sho**ri shita (dealt with) the situation and later attended her **Show**	お食事処 oshokujidokoro = restaurant (Japanese style); 処理する shori suru = to deal with, handle, eliminate
拠 2	^1151. this kneeling guy crawled from **Ko**be to **Kyo**to to give 証拠 shou**ko** (testimony) to support this dancer whose leg had been injured by this 机 (desk)	証拠 shouko = evidence, proof, testimony; 拠点 kyoten = position, location, base, point
抗 1	^1196. this guy doesn't like this tire stop which was installed on this desk at a **Court**house, and he kneels to ask for its removal before organizing a 抗議 **kou**gi (protest) against it	抵抗 teikou = resistance, opposition; 抗議 kougi = protest
鉛 2	^1092. a **Narco-named-Mari**o uses this 金 (money) to buy 鉛 **namari** (lead) for the bullets that he uses to **En**force discipline on the 八 (eight) guys who are working on this 口 (dock)	鉛 namari = lead; 鉛筆 enpitsu = lead pencil
船 3	^602. this 船 **fune** (boat), which is owned by some **Fo**olish-**Na**rcos, is carrying **Fo**od-from-the-Netherlands, and it's wide open at the rear, but there are 八 (eight) **Sen**sible guys on this 口 (dock) who are working on the problem	船便 funabin = ship mail; 船 fune = ship, boat; 釣り船 tsuribune = fishing boat; 船長 senchou = captain of a ship
豆 4	^721. some **Mad-Men** (i.e., those who work on Madison Avenue as advertisers) watch this TV set with a napkin draped across the top, at a **Zoo** with a **Zookee**per, supporting it with these **To**es and watching the advertisements that they have created for 豆 **mame** (bean) products	豆 mame = bean; 大豆 daizu = soybean; 小豆 azuki = red bean; 豆腐 toufu = bean curd
守 4	^214. while the monks were 留守 r**usu** (absent), **Super**man and **Maureen** removed the 土 (soil) from this 寺 (temple), added this roof which resembles a bad haircut, in order to 守る **mamo**ru (protect) it from falling **Mamm**oths, and tied it down with **Shoe**laces	留守 rusu = absence from a house; 子守 komori = nanny, baby sitter; 守る mamoru = to protect; 守備 shubi = defense, garrisoning
狩 4	^923. this woman on the left is a **Ga**dfly who contorts her body in order to try to 守 (protect) animals threatened by 狩り **ka**ri (hunting), and she **Carries** a **Cat** and **Shoo**s hunters away	キノコ狩り kinokogari = mushroom gathering; 石狩 Ishikari = a city in Hokkaido; 狩る karu = to hunt (animals), to gather (mushrooms, etc.); 狩猟 shuryou = hunting

Chapter 12

世 3		^542. since the 世界 **se**kai (world) is hanging in this bucket supported by this stand and might fall any **Se**cond, people are consulting **Yo**gis to find out how to stay **Sa**fe	世界 sekai = the world; 世の中 yo no naka = life, society, world; 世紀 seiki = century
度 3		^498. 毎度 mai**do** (every time) that **Do**lores prepares this bucket of food in this lean-to, she also feeds it to her **Ta**bby cat at this 又 (table), together with **Ta**p-water-and-**Ko**ol-Aid	今度 kondo = this time or next time; 転勤の度 tenkin no tabi = transfer's occasion; 支度 shitaku = preparation
渡 2		^499. every 度 (time) that we 渡る **wata**ru (cross) this water, we **Wa**lk-**Ta**ll and 渡す **wata**su (hand) money to a **To**ll collector	渡る wataru = to cross; 渡米 tobei = going to America
一 5		^1. I met 一人 **hito**ri (one person), and **He-To**ld me that, when he is **I**tchy, he **E**ats **Tsui**te (sweet) **O**ranges	一人 hitori = one person; 一 ichi = one; 唯一の yuiitsu no = only, exclusive; 一日 tsuitachi = 1st of the month; 一昨日 ototoi = the day before yesterday
二 4		^2. when my **Ni**ece squeezed into a **Full-Ta**xi, she injured her 二つの **futatsu** no (two) **Foo**ts (feet) and smashed her **Ha**t	二 ni = two; 二つ futatsu = two items; 二日 futsuka = the 2nd of the month, two days; 二十歳 hatachi = 20 years old
三 4		^3. when my family **Mee**ts **San**ta, we feed him a **Mea**l, and he gives us 三つ **mi**ttsu no (three) presents to **Sha**re	三越 Mitsukoshi = name of a department store; 三 san = three; 三つ mittsu = three items; 三味線 shamisen = three-stringed Japanese lute
土 4		^59. this kanji points up to the moon, where **Tsu**ki-**Chee**se (moon cheese) is as common as 土 **tsuchi** (soil), and **To**ads conduct **Mee**tings under **Do**mes	土田 Tsuchida = family name; 土地 tochi = land; お土産 omiyage = souvenir; 土曜日 doyoubi = Saturday
士 2		^66. this 兵士 hei**shi** (soldier) needs these long arms in order to catch **Sh**eep for **S**ettlers	紳士 shinshi = gentleman; 富士山 fujisan = Mt. Fuji; 博士 hakase = a Ph.D.
仕 3		^67. this man on the left tilts his hat back in order to gaze at this 士 (man) on the right, for whom he does 仕事 **shi**goto (work), carrying an extra **Sh**eet in a **Tsui**tcase-(suitcase)-in-his-**Ca**r, which is a **Jee**p	仕事 shigoto = work; 仕える tsukaeru = to serve; 給仕 kyuuji = service, waiter
物 4		^401. when we sit by the castle **Mo**ats, this 牛 (cow), old **Bo**ots, empty **Bo**oze bottles and other assorted 物 **mono** (things) like these streamers make **Mono**tonous noise in the wind	荷物 nimotsu = luggage; 動物 doubutsu = animal; 物価 bukka = price of goods; 物 mono = tangible thing
件 1		^488. this man named **Ken** tilts his hat back to investigate a 事件 ji**ken** (incident) involving this 牛 (cow) belonging to Barbie	その件 sono ken = the matter being discussed; 事件 jiken = incident
六 4		^17. after tripping over this tire stop while **Ro**aming along a **Ro**ad-in-**Ku**wait, this mother hen gathers 六 **roku** (six) chicks under this 八 (skirt) to keep them away from **Mo**onies and **Moo**dy-**Ea**gles	六本木 Roppongi = a district in Tokyo; 六人 rokunin = six people; 六つ muttsu = six objects; 六日 muika = the 6th of the month, six days
穴 2		^964. 八 (eight) students in an **Ana**tomy class have bad haircuts like this, they put **Ke**tchup-in-their-**So**up, and they are studying the major 穴 **ana** (holes) in a dog's head	穴 ana = hole; 洞穴 horaana = cave, den; **Note:** 洞穴 can also be read as douketsu = cave, den
慣 2		^92. when we asked about this string of coins on this 貝 (money chest), this man on the left was **Na**sty, pulling himself up to his full height and saying that it was his 習慣 shuu**kan** (custom) to keep them there until he uses them to buy **Ca**ndy	慣れる nareru = to get used to; 習慣 shuukan = customs, habits
買 3		^89. this three-drawer 貝 (money chest) has these three eyes and can see the future, which allows me to 買う **kau** (buy) **Ca**rs, **Ka**yaks and **Bi**kes at bargain prices	買う kau = to buy; 買取 kaitori = a purchase or sale; 売買 baibai = buying and selling

増 3	^61. this 田 (rice paddy) grows **Foo**d in an agricultural **Z**one and produces these two units of rice annually, thanks to this 日 (sun) and this 土 (soil); after new **Ma**chines were introduced, its production 増えた **fu**eta (increased) further	増える fueru = to increase; 倍増する baizou suru = to double; 増す masu = to increase or grow
贈 2	^84. I will take money from this **Oak** 貝 (money chest) on the left and take it to the agricultural **Z**one where this 田 (rice paddy) above this 日 (sun) produces these two units of rice in order to 贈る **oku**ru (give) a bonus to the workers	贈る okuru = to give a present; 贈り物 okurimono = a present; 贈呈 zoutei = a presentation (of a gift, etc.)
黄 3	^976. this model of a rice paddy with a handle and plants on top, which is symmetrical like the Y in **Y**ellow, 横 (crossed) the **O**cean on a **Co**al ship and can be accessed with a 黄色 **kii**ro (yellow) **Key**	黄金 ougon = gold; 黄砂 kousa = yellow dust from the Yellow River region, which blows to Japan; 黄色 kiiro = yellow
横 2	^135. **Yoko** Ono keeps this 黄 (yellow) model of a rice paddy with a handle, with plants above it and legs below, 横 **yoko** (beside) this 木 (tree) in **O**hio	横 yoko = side or width; 横断する oudan suru = to cross (a street, etc.)
演 1	^756. actors with bad haircuts like this 演じる **en**jiru (perform) and **En**tertain us on sets which include water like this and models of 田 (rice paddies) that are connected to handles like this and attached to legs like these	演奏 ensou = musical performance; 演じる enjiru = to perform or act
猫 1	^72. this woman on the left came to this 田 (rice paddy) to look for her 猫 **neko** (cat) among these plants, and she recoiled like this when she discovered a **N**est-of-**Co**bras	猫 neko = cat
描 3	^758. this guy on the left kneels to make raw eggs into paint next to this 田 (rice paddy) under these plants, and he will 描く **ka**ku (paint) the scene using a technique called **E**gg-**A**rt and sell his work to a **Be**erhall-**Ow**ner in **Ca**lifornia	描く egaku = to draw, paint, depict, describe; 描写する byousha suru = to describe; 描く kaku = to draw, paint, depict, describe
父 5	^143. this 父 **chichi** (father) has these thick eyebrows, sits with these crossed legs exposing his **To**es, cooks good **Foo**d, drinks **Boo**ze, eats **Ch**eap-**Chee**se and drives a **Jee**p	お父さん otousan = honorable father; 祖父 sofu = grandfather; 秩父 Chichibu = a city in Saitama Prefecture; 父 chichi = father; 伯父さん ojisan = uncle
月 4	^148. this 日 (sun) with two legs runs to pack a **Tsu**itcase-(suitcase)-of-**Qui**che for a **Gu**est, who will take it to the 月 **tsuki** (moon), where he hopes to **Get-Su**per rich by **Ga**thering-**Soo**t from moon volcanoes	毎月 maitsuki = every month; 月給 gekkyuu = monthly salary; 月曜日 getsuyoubi = Monday; 二月 nigatsu = February
服 1	^150. I will try on some 洋服 you**fuku** (Western clothes) by the light of this 月 (moon) in **Fuku**oka, near this 又 (table), in this dressing room with this clothes hook	洋服 youfuku = Western clothes; 屈服する kuppuku suru = to surrender
報 2	^386. we received a 報告 **hou**koku (report) about a **Ho**rnet with this 幸 (needle)-like stinger near this hook in this dressing room, but a **Moo**nie-drinking-too-much-**Koo**l-Aid had reported it	報告 houkoku = report; 報いる mukuiru = to reward or repay
玉 3	^169. 王 (kings) like this one from **Da**mascus who like **Tama**les like this one on the lower right sometimes pay for them with 玉 **tama** (jewels), but other Syrians prefer to eat **Gyo**za-with-**Koo**l-Aid	10 円玉 juuen dama = ten-yen coin; 玉 tama = ball, jewel; 玉座 gyokuza = throne
床 3	^946. a **Y**outhful-**C**arpenter works in this lean-to with a chimney, in which he **Shows** 木 (wooden) items that he has created, including a 床 **yuka** (floor) and a **To**y-**Co**bra	床 yuka = floor; 起床 kishou = rising, getting out of bed; 床 toko = bed, floor
太 3	^191. this 大 (big) person 太る **futo**ru (gets fat) to the point that he has to sleep on a **Fu**ton, he can only chase balls like this near the floor, he **Ti**res easily, and he worries about the **Tar** in his cigarettes	太る futoru = to get fat; 小太り kobutori = plump; 太陽 taiyou = the sun; 太郎 tarou = a boy's given name
駄 2	^628. **Tar**zan told his **Da**ughter to exercise this 太 (fat) 馬 (horse), since to do otherwise would be 無駄 mu**da** (useless and wasteful)	下駄 geta = Japanese clogs; 無駄 muda = useless, wasteful

狭 ₃		^194. inside a 狭い **sema**i (narrow) aisle in a **S**ecluded-**Ma**rket in **Kyou**to, this lady on the left contorts her body to squeeze past this 夫 (husband) on the right, who **S**ells-**Ba**rbed wire and is surrounded by these flames	狭い semai = narrow, cramped; 狭小 kyoushou = cramped, narrow, confined; 狭める sebameru = to narrow or reduce
挟 ₁		^1009. this guy kneels to try to help this 夫 (husband), a **H**andsome-**Sa**laryman who 挟まった **hasa**matta (got caught between) two walls of flame	挟まる hasamaru = to get between, to get caught in
糸 ₂		^219. this skeet shooter with three legs has been repaired with 糸 **ito** (thread), and we use it to fire at the mosqu**Ito**s that sting our **Shee**p	糸 ito = thread, yarn; 金糸 kinshi = golden thread
後 ₆		^335. this dancer guards her Uber-**Shee**p with this gun that she is pointing towards the 後ろ **ushi**ro (rear), but the man on the left offers to take them in exchange for an **A**tomic clock, some **Co**la, some **Go**ld, some g**No**cchi, a **Sa**xophone, and one of his hats	後ろ ushiro = behind; 後で ato de = later; 後悔 koukai = regret; 午後 gogo = afternoon; 後ほど nochihodo = afterward, later; 明後日 asatte = the day after tomorrow, usually written あさって
曜 ₁		^200. every 曜日 **you**bi (day of the week) in **Yo**semite, this 日 (sun) shines on this bird in this net	日曜日 nichiyoubi = Sunday
濯 ₁		^201. using this **Ta**p-water-and-**Ko**ol-Aid, we wash this bird in this net whenever we do the 洗濯 sen**taku** (laundry)	洗濯 sentaku = laundry
躍 ₁		^992. this 止 (hesitant) squarehead fights against the **Yaku**za (gangsters), and he 活躍する katsu**yaku** suru (is active) every 曜 (day of the week)	躍進 yakushin = progress; 活躍する katsuyaku suru = to be active
田 ₄		^68. **Tar**zan and his **Den**tist went to this 田んぼ **tan**bo (rice paddy) on a **Da**rk night, but this was considered **Ina**ppropriate behavior	田んぼ tanbo = rice paddy; 田園 den'en = pastoral, rural; 上田 Ueda = family name; 田舎 inaka = countryside, home town
奮 ₁		^727. a 大 (big) guy dropped this net into this 田 (rice paddy), causing some 興奮 kou**fun** (excitement), and we had **Fun** trying to fish it out	興奮 koufun = excitement; 奮闘 funtou = hard struggle, strenuous effort
異 ₂		^970. I attended a **Ko**to (Japanese harp) concert on **Ea**ster at this 田 (rice paddy), 共 (together) with some friends, and I found that it 異なった **koto**natta (differed) from the one I attended last year	異なる kotonaru = to differ; 驚異 kyoui = miracle, marvel; 異議 igi = objection
翼 ₂		^912. I left this 田 (rice paddy) and 羽 (flew) with my **Tsui**tcase-(suitcase)-to-**Ba**rcelona's-**Sa**ndy beaches, 共 (together) with some friends, where I ate some **Yo**gurt-and-**Coo**kies, and saw a bird with powerful 翼 **tsubasa** (wings)	翼 tsubasa = wing; 右翼 uyoku = right wing (politics); 左翼 sayoku = left wing (politics)
冬 ₂		^234. this dancer with a ponytail escapes from **To**lstoy by taking a big leap over these two reflections on a patch of ice in 冬 **fuyu** (winter); "I **F**ooled-**You**," she cries	冬期 touki = winter; 冬 fuyu = winter
終 ₃		^233. this 糸 (skeet shooter)'s contract 終わる **o**waru (finishes) when this 冬 (winter arrives), and he remembers his **O**ld-**Wa**rs and goes back to **O**hio and starts **Shoo**ting	終る owaru = to finish, intransitive (this can also be spelled 終わる); 終える oeru = to finish, transitive; 最終電車 saishuu densha = last train
恵 ₃		^720. after gathering 十 (ten) **E**ggs, a **M**exican-**Goo**se and a **Ca**ke for our meal, we 思 (think) that we 恵まれている **megu**marete iru (are being blessed)	知恵 chie = wisdom, intelligence, idea; 恵む megumu = to bless, show mercy, give money, etc.; 恩恵 onkei = favor, benefit
薄 ₂		^258. combining this water with this plant material from this 田 (rice paddy), this 寸 (sunny guy) and this truncated 犬 (dog) produce 薄い **usu**i (thin) rice tea appropriate for **Usu**rers and **H**ackers-from-**Ku**wait	薄い usui = pale, thin, light, watery, dilute, weak (taste); 薄情 hakujou = cruel, heartless, uncaring
敷 ₂		^865. this 方 (honorable person) on the left has this truncated 犬 (dog) and this 田 (rice paddy) on his mind, but this dancer on the right wants him to explain the use of the **Sh**ift-**Key** to some **Shi**ites who are waiting in a 座敷 za**shiki** (Japanese-style room)	座敷 zashiki = Japanese-style room with tatami flooring; 敷く shiku = to lay out, spread or enact

勧 2		^698. this truncated 矢 (Native American chief) is hugging a net in a zoo, where a wild animal is being kept by 力 (force); the people of **Kan**sas are outraged about this, and the chief 勧める <u>susu</u>meru (recommends) that they **Sue-the-Su**perintendent of the zoo	勧告 kankoku = recommendation, advice; 勧める susumeru = to advise or recommend
観 2		^886. this truncated 矢 (Native American chief) made a 勧 (recommendation) that the people of **Kan**sas 見 (look) in the **Mir**ror and address the problems involving animals in nets like this with 楽観 rak**kan** (optimism)	観光 kankou = sightseeing; 花を観る hana wo miru = flower viewing (this can also be written 花を見る)
権 2		^916. this truncated 矢 (Native American chief) named **Gon**zalez used to work at the **Ken**tucky Derby, where he pruned 木 (trees) like this, but now he has 権威 **ken**'i (authority) over a zoo and hugs this net because he cares about the animals in it	権現 gongen = an incarnation of Buddha, an avatar; 権利 kenri = right, privilege
戻 1		^75. this 大 (big) **Mo**dest-**Do**orman wants to 戻る <u>modo</u>ru (return) to his duties, but he's stuck under this double roof with a layer of snow on top	戻る modoru = to return to a place
涙 1		^649. a certain **Narco-has-a-Midas** touch and plenty of money, but when he 戻 (returns) to see all this water flooding the snow-covered lean-to where his 大 (big) modest doorman stands guard, his 涙 <u>namida</u> (tears) will flow	涙 namida = tears
戸 4		^871. when **Tol**stoy returned to this lean-to covered with snow like this on **Cold** nights, the 戸 <u>to</u> (**Do**or) would always open, and he would go to **Bed**	戸 to = door; 一戸 ikko = one house or household; 井戸 ido = well; 神戸 Koube = a city in Japan
房 2		^1134. in winter, this 方 (honorable person) lives a **Bo**ring life in this lean-to with this double roof and this layer of snow on top, which is heated by a single 暖房 dan**bou** (heater), and his only **Food-is-Sardines**	暖房 danbou = heating, heater; 冷房 reibou = air conditioning; 房 fusa = a bunch, cluster, tassel
編 3		^1052. this 糸 (skeet shooter) is shooting at this snow-covered double-roofed lean-to because he disapproves of the 編者 **hen**sha (editor) inside, who is working on this 冊 (book) about **Hen**s that use **Pen**s to make **Art**	編者 hensha = editor; 短編 tanpen = short story or film; 編む amu = to knit
日 13		^32. 日光 <u>ni</u>kkou (sunshine) flows through this window of a **Cabin** on the **Beach**, bringing **Heat** to the **Jittery-Superstar Nietzche**, who rubs his **Kne**es and **Nose** while **Tanned-Child**ren shoot at **Targets**, watch **Tel**evision, play with **Toys**, drink **Sou**p and eat **Yo**gurt	二日 futsuka = 2nd day of the month, 2 days; 誕生日 tanjoubi = birthday; 日にち hinichi = date; 平日 heijitsu = weekday; 一日 ichinichi = one day; 日光 Nikkou = a town in Japan, sunshine; 昨日 kinou = yesterday; 一日 tsuitachi = first day of the month; 明日 ashita = tomorrow; 明後日 asatte = day after tomorrow, usually written あさって; 一昨日 ototoi = day before yesterday, usually written おととい; 明日 asu = tomorrow; 今日 kyou = today
冊 2		^568. **Sad**ly, only six 冊 <u>satsu</u> (volumes) of **Sat**isfying-**Su**perman novels will fit into this bookcase	冊子 sasshi = a booklet or pamphlet; 三冊 sansatsu = three books
柵 1		^899. when I bought a **Sack** of 冊 (books) like these, I noticed that they had built a 柵 <u>saku</u> (fence) around the store, made of 木 (wood) like this	柵 saku = fence; 鉄柵 tessaku = iron fence
那 1		^669. when my ß (Greek) 旦那 dan<u>na</u> (husband) visited **Nar**nia, he saw this drawing of the 月 (moon), in which the artist had extended all of the horizontal lines to the left	旦那 danna = husband
応 2		^677. my 心 (heart) is in this lean-to with a small chimney in N. Da**Kota**, where I plan to live until I'm **Old**, or at least 一応 ichi<u>ou</u> (for the time being)	応える kotaeru = to respond or affect; 応じる oujiru = to respond or comply with

予 1		^544. since this マ (mother) can balance on this arrow on top of this nail without using a stabilizing leg, she will make 予定 **yo**tei (plans) to start **Yo**ga	予定 yotei = plan, schedule; 予約 yoyaku = reservation
野 2		^545. this sincere guy with these bifocals and this マ (mother), who is balanced on a nail, live in **No**rway, and they have a 予 (plan) to grow 野菜 **ya**sai (vegetables), including **Ya**ms	野原 nohara = field; 野菜 yasai = vegetable; 野球 yakyuu = baseball
柔 3		^546. this マ (mother) from **Nyuu**yooku (New York) practices 柔道 **juu**dou, she balances on this nail with the help of this stablizing leg, she can climb this 木 (tree), although she knows that this activity is **Ju**venile, and she gives her **Yak-Wa**ter after she descends	柔和 nyuuwa = gentleness, mildness; 柔道 juudou = judo; 柔らかい yawarakai = soft, tender, limp
変 2		^553. I just saw a 変な **hen** na (strange) sight: this **Hen** with these four legs swooped down over this dancer with a ponytail and tried to 変える **ka**eru (change) her; let's try to **Ca**tch it	変な hen na = strange; 大変 taihen = terrible; 変える kaeru = to change, transitive
恋 2		^695. this four-legged hen is in 恋 **koi** (love) with this 心 (heart), and it's swooping down to give it a **Coi**n to help pay the **Ren**t	恋 koi = love; 恋人 koibito = lover; 恋愛 ren'ai = romantic love
収 2		^1113. since his 収入 **shuu**nyuu (income) was high, **Osa**ma had 4 又 (tables) like this where he 収めた **osa**meta (put away) his **Shoe**s	収める osameru = to put away in a closet, conclude, pay a bill (this can also be written 納める); 収入 shuunyuu = income
叫 2		^746. after drinking 4 bottles of **Sake** in **Kyou**to, I opened this 口 (mouth), and a 絶叫 zek**kyou** (scream) emerged	叫ぶ sakebu = to shout, yell, scream; 絶叫 zekkyou = a scream or shriek
叶 1		^1076. I had to open this 口 (mouth) 十 (ten) times and beg before they 叶えた **kana**eta (granted) me **Cana**dian citizenship	叶える kanaeru = to grant or answer a request, to meet requirements
劇 1		^1058. this guy リ Ri has a **Guest-Key** for this lean-to in which 七 (seven) people observe the world through this periscope, keep this 豚 (pig) and enjoy going to the 劇場 **geki**jou (theater)	劇 geki = a play; 劇場 gekijou = a theater; 歌劇 kageki = opera
虎 1		^1057. 七 (seven) people who live in this lean-to and observe the outside world through this periscope are holding **To**lstoy-for-**Ra**nsom, and they sometimes dangle these lopsided legs out through a window to entice passing 虎 **tora** (tigers)	虎 tora = tiger
虜 2		^1107. the 七 (seven) **Tory-Co**rporals who live in this lean-to with this periscope have captured this 男 (male) 虜 **toriko** (prisoner of war) named Pope **Leo**	虜 toriko = captive, prisoner; 捕虜 horyo = prisoner of war, captive
慮 1		^1194. when Pope **Leo** revisited the 七 (seven) jailers in this lean-to with this periscope at the top, he 思 (thought) that they should give more 配慮 hai**ryo** (consideration) to the welfare of their 虜 (captives)	配慮 hairyo = consideration, concern; 考慮 kouryo = consideration; 遠慮 enryo = hesitation, reserve, restraint, modesty
虚 1		^966. 七 (seven) people who are known for their 謙虚 ken**kyo** (modesty) live in this lean-to, cook on this 普 (ordinary) four-burner stove like the ones they use in **Kyo**to and observe the outside world through this periscope	謙虚 kenkyo = modesty
嘘 1		^967. these 七 (seven) people cook on this 普 (ordinary) stove, and one of them used this 口 (mouth) to tell an 嘘 **uso** (lie) when he claimed that they have **Ube**r-**So**lar panels	嘘 uso = lie; 嘘をつく uso wo tsuku = to tell a lie
成 4		^633. our **Sa**feway store is guarded by a **Na**sty-**Ri**ng of **Na**zi guards armed with 刀 (blades) and halberds like this, but **Jo**an of Arc says that it is a 成功 **sei**kou (success)	成功 seikou = success; 成田 Narita = city near Tokyo; 成る naru = to consist of; 成仏する joubutsu suru = to enter Nirvana
城 3		^1008. after I had 成 (success), I decided to build a 城 **shiro** (castle) in **Ki**ev, guarded by 刀 (blades) and halberds like this, on this patch of 土 (soil) where **Shee**p-used-to-**Ro**am, in order to impress **Jo**an of Arc	茨城県 ibaraki ken = Ibaraki prefecture; 宮城県 miyagi ken = Miyagi Prefecture; 城 shiro = castle; 荒城 koujou = ruined castle; 名城 meijou = famous castle

骨 3	^832. when I'm in this roof-top apartment on this 月 (moon), I wear several **Coats**, since it's **Co**ld, and I use a **Ho**me-**Net**work to research **hone** 骨 (bone) health, since the moon's low gravity can cause osteoporosis	骸骨 gaikotsu = skeleton; 骨折する kossetsu suru = to break a bone; 骨 hone = bone
滑 3	^981. I rest my 骨 (bones) in this roof-top apartment, which I can afford thanks to my job as a **Sub**-editor, and I have a **N**anny-**f**rom-**Me**xico who takes care of my **Cats**, but this water is leaking, and our floors are 滑りやすい **suber**iyasui (slippery)	滑る suberu = to slide or slip, to fail an exam; 滑らかな nameraka na = smooth, mellow (usually written なめらかな); 円滑 enkatsu = smooth, harmonious
刻 2	^565. after this リ Ri carved up this boar, he stopped to drink a **Co**ke, and to **Ki**d-**Za**ch about not helping him, and therefore he will 遅刻する chi**koku** suru (be tardy)	遅刻する chikoku suru = to be tardy; 刻む kizamu = to cut, mince, carve
影 2	^839. looking at this 景 (view), I saw an **A**pe holding these three cords and using them to cast 影 **kage** (shadows) on a wall, so I **C**alled-a-**Gue**st to investigate	影響 eikyou = influence, effect; 影 kage = shadow, silhouette
形 4	^573. this tower has a symmetrical 形 **katachi** (shape), and it uses these three cords, which can be bought from a **Cata**log, as parts of a machine for **Cata**pulting-**Chee**se, **Gyo**za and **Ca**ke to prisoners in a jail	形見 katami = keepsake, memento; 髪形 kamigata = hair style; 形 katachi = shape; 人形 ningyou = doll; 形態 keitai = form, shape, system
杉 1	^1154. this 木 (tree), which is a 杉 **sugi** (Japanese cedar tree), has these three cords attached to it, which we use to tie up **Su**perman's-**Gee**se	杉 sugi = Japanese cedar tree
屈 2	^927. this 出 (person) under this lean-to with a double roof is Superman and since he's **Co**oped up and suffering from 退屈 tai**kutsu** (boredom), we want to 出 (extract) him, but we must avoid **Cut**ting-**Su**perman in the process	屈服する kuppuku suru = to surrender; 退屈 taikutsu = boredom; 理屈 rikutsu = argument, theory, pretext
思 2	^308. **O**saka-**Mo**squitoes breed in this 田 (rice paddy), and we 思う **omo**u (think) that they sting our **Shee**p, which have 心 (hearts) like this	思う omou = to think/feel; 思想 shisou = thought, idea
峰 3	^938. this dancer, who is a **Ho**stess, dances on top of this telephone **Po**le next to this 名峰 mei**hou** (famous mountain) in **Minn**esota	名峰 meihou = famous mountain; 連峰 renpou = mountain range; 峰 mine = mt. peak
巡 3	^778. this snail is wearing this chevron to indicate its status as a **Jun**ior member of the fraternity of **Men**-with-**Goo**, and as it 巡る **megu**ru (goes around) the neighborhood carrying a grease gun, it behaves like a **Ma**rine-**Wa**rrior	巡査 junsa = patrolman; 巡る meguru = to go or come around, to surround; お巡りさん omawarisan = a policeman
災 2	^1019. this chevron is a **Si**gn that a 災難 **sai**nan (disaster) is likely, since it suggests that **Wa**cky-**Za**mbian-**Wa**rriors are 巡 (going around) in uniforms decorated with chevrons like this and starting 火 (fires) like this	震災 shinsai = great earthquake; 火災 kasai = fire; 災難 sainan = misfortune, disaster; 災い wazawai = calamity, disaster
遭 2	^1073. this snail uses this 日 (sun) for **So**lar power to listen to these 曲 (tunes) as it travels, but a switch in its sound system tends to get this short circuit, and sometimes it 遭う **a**u (gets involved) in Accidents	遭難 sounan = accident, disaster; 遭う au = to be involved (in an accident, etc.), to get caught in
川 3	^250. this 川 **kawa** (river) supplies water for a **Ca**r-**Wa**sh in the **Cen**ter of a town, where there is a **Ga**s-**Wa**r	川 kawa = river; 河川 kasen = river; 小川 ogawa = brook
州 2	^1071. **Su**perman lost a **Sho**e when he rode these three toboggans in 本州 Hon**shuu**	三角州 sankakusu = a delta; 本州 honshuu = Honshu island
訓 1	^1090. a **Ku**ng fu master 言 (speaks) about the 訓練 **kun**ren (training) that he received when he worked on this 川 (river)	訓練 kunren = training; 教訓 kyoukun = moral, teaching, lesson
慢 1	^1127. this guy on the left on the left stands proudly near this 又 (table) in **Man**hattan and 自慢する ji**man** suru (boasts) about these three 目 (eyes) which are never bothered by this 日 (sun)	自慢 jiman = pride, boast; 我慢 gaman = patience, endurance

Chapter 13

違 3		^355. these two feet are 違う **chiga**u (different) in that they face in opposite directions, and both feet have been been bitten up by the **Chigg**ers-and-**A**nts that live in this 口 (box), so that it isn't **Ea**sy for them to walk, but they will **Tag-A**long when this snail goes to the store	違う chigau = different; 違反 ihan = violation, offense; 仲違い nakatagai = disagreement
偉 2		^1174. this man on the left is tilting his hat back to examine this guy with feet like these facing in opposite directions, realizing that the guy's life wasn't **Ea**sy during an **Era** when people had to walk everywhere and that he was an 偉人 **ij**in (exceptional person)	偉人 ijin = an exceptional person; 偉大 idai = great, grand; 偉い erai = great, excellent, eminent, distinguished
衛 1		^918. honest **A**be is in the middle of 行 (going) out to check on the 防衛 bou**ei** (defense) of his capital, and he takes a 違 (different) route every time he goes	衛生 eisei = hygiene, sanitation; 衛星 eisei = satellite; 防衛 bouei = defense
洋 1		^330. 西洋 sei**you** (the western part of the world) is across this water, where a lot of people keep 羊 (sheep) like this and eat **Yo**gurt	西洋 seiyou = the western part of the world; 洋服 youfuku = Western clothes
遅 3		^350. this snail carries this **Old-So**malian 羊 (sheep) under this double roof, but the snail moves slowly, and it appears that the sheep will be 遅い **oso**i (late) to lunch, he will 遅れる **oku**reru (be delayed) to the **Occu**lt museum, and he will 遅刻する **chi**koku suru (be tardy) on his trip to the **Chee**se factory	遅い osoi = late, slow; 遅れる okureru = to be delayed; 遅刻する chikoku suru = to be tardy
鮮 2		^858. a **Sen**ator eats this 新鮮な shin**sen** na (fresh) 魚 (fish), while keeping an eye on this 羊 (sheep) to make sure that it doesn't eat his **Az**aleas	新鮮 shinsen = fresh; 鮮やか azayaka = colorful, bright, vivid, impressive, beautiful
逆 2		^894. this ghost, which is wearing rabbit ears and holding candlesticks, floats and plays **Sakka**a (soccer), which is a 逆説 **gyaku**setsu (paradox) since it has no feet, and this snail on which it rides can outrun **Geeky-Yaku**za (gangsters), contrary to known Universal laws	逆らう sakarau = to oppose or disobey; 逆説 gyakusetsu = paradox; 逆の gyaku no = contrary, opposite, antithetical
純 1		^761. this 糸 (skeet shooter) is shooting at these 七 (seven) Universal Laws because he thinks that they are too 単純 tan**jun** (simple) to ensure survival in a **Jun**gle	純粋な junsui na = pure, pure-blooded, genuine; 単純な tanjun na = simple
衣 4		^1042. エ and Y stand near this tire stop and make Exciting **Eas**ter 衣服 **i**fuku (clothing) to sell from **Cata**logues, and they use their **Coro**lla's-**M**otor for warmth	衣紋 emon = clothing; 衣服 ifuku = clothing; 浴衣 yukata = informal summer kimono; 衣 koromo = coating or breading (food), clothes
巨 1		^689. a 巨人 **kyo**jin (giant) knocked over this swing set in **Kyo**to	巨大 kyodai = huge; 巨人 kyojin = a giant
臣 2		^1039. a **Shin**to priest, who is a 臣民 **shin**min (royal subject), put on his **Jean**s before turning this swing set on its side and tying these swing ropes in order to prevent harm to children	臣民 shinmin = royal subject; 総理大臣 souridaijin = prime minister
姫 1		^1040. the emperor's daughter is a 女 (female) and a 姫 **hime** (princess) who is attracted to **He-Me**n, but she is too young to use this swing set safely, so it has been made inoperable	姫 hime = princess
臓 1		^951. my 心臓 shin**zou** (heart) rates can be classified into four different **Zo**nes associated with my moods, which can be represented by this 月 (moon) which is volatile, these plants which are soothing, this 臣 (inoperable swing set) which is frustrating, and this halberd which is scary	心臓 shinzou = the heart (organ); 内臓 naizou = internal organ, intestines
蔵 2		^1190. my heart rate is classified into three **Zo**nes represented by these soothing plants, this frustrating 臣 (disabled swing set) and this scary halberd supporting this lean-to, and sometimes I move it into a fourth zone by taking a beer from the 冷蔵庫 rei**zou**ko (refrigerator) and turning on the **Kuura**a (air conditioner)	冷蔵庫 reizouko = refrigerator; 蔵 kura = a storehouse (this can also be written 倉)

広 3		^494. this ム (cow) has a 広い **hiro**i (wide and spacious) lean-to; this sign at the top says that it is intended for **Hero**es who eat a lot of **Bean-Ro**lls and drink **Co**la	広い hiroi = wide, spacious; 背広 sebiro = man's suit; 広告 koukoku = advertisement
公 3		^16. in a 公園 **kou**en (park) in **Ku**wait, there are 八 (eight) ム (cows), some **Co**lts, and several **Old-Yak-E**tchings, for 公の **ooyake** no (public) enjoyment	公家 kuge = the Imperial court; 公園 kouen = park; 公 ooyake = public
松 2		^1025. this 木 (tree) is a 松 **matsu** (pine tree), and people sit under it on **Mat**s, **Show** off their legs and watch these 八 (eight) ム (cows)	松 matsu = pine tree; 松竹梅 shouchiku-bai = pine, bamboo and plum, a symbol of good luck
総 1		^1038. this 糸 (skeet shooter) is shooting at these 八 (eight) ム (cows), but he has this good 心 (heart) 総じて **sou**jite (in general) and is employed as a **Soldier**	総じて soujite = in general, on the whole; 総会 soukai = general meeting
比 2		^857. these two ヒ's (**He**roes) both raise **Ku**waiti-**R**abbits, but they look different, prompting us to 比べる **kura**beru (compare) them	比較 hikaku = comparison; 恵比寿 Ebisu = a district in Tokyo; 比べる kuraberu = to compare
批 1		^1082. this guy on the left kneels to examine and 比 (compare) these two ヒ (**He**roes), and he directs 批判 **hi**han (criticism) at the one he finds lacking	批判 hihan = criticism; 批評 hihyou = review, remark, criticism
必 3		^307. if you want the **Cana**dian-**R**at to expire 必ず **kanara**zu (without fail), it is 必要 **hitsu**you (necessary) that you slice this 心 (heart) in two, before it **Hits-yoU** with its tail and bruises your **Heel**	必ず kanarazu = without fail; 必要 hitsuyou = necessary; 必死に hisshi = desperate, frantic
秘 2		^1187. our 秘書 **hi**sho (secretary) **Pee**ks out the window and, seeing this 禾 (ripe grain), realizes that it's 必 (necessary) to take off her **Hee**ls and trample it to separate the wheat from the chaff	神秘 shinpi = a mystery; 秘密 himitsu = a secret; 秘書 hisho = a secretary
密 3		^1188. it's 必 (necessary) that you **Meet-Su**perman on this 山 (mountain), sympathize with this bad haircut, share his **Mea**ls, and **Hear**-his-**S**ordid 秘密 hi**mitsu** (secrets)	秘密 himitsu = a secret; 密会 mikkai = secret meeting; 密かに hisoka ni = secretly, behind the scenes
曲 2		^82. this **Ma**chine is a six-section coop with two wires at the top that I can 曲がる **ma**garu (turn) in order to play various 曲 **kyoku** (songs) for the **Kyo**to-**Kool**-Aid Club	曲がる magaru = to bend or turn; 曲 kyoku = song, musical composition; 音曲 ongyoku = songs with samisen accompaniment
典 1		^1117. we keep CD's of 古典の ko**ten** no (classical) 曲 (tunes) like this, which resemble a coop, on this two-legged table and listen to them while we play **Ten**nis	古典 koten = classical work, classic
現 2		^739. this 王 (king) is named **Gen**ghis, and he tells an **Arab-Wa**rrior to 見 (watch) his horse in return for some 現金 **gen**kin (cash)	現実 genjitsu = reality, fact; 現れる arawareru = to appear or to show up
寛 1		^1205. this guy came to **Kan**sas to 見 (look) around, but this bad haircut and these plants on his head affect his 見 (vision), so please be 寛大 **kan**dai (tolerant)	寛大 kandai = understanding, lenient, tolerant, generous, broad-minded
康 1		^831. after a man was stabbed with this trident, he felt **Co**ld and crawled into this lean-to to get warm, but he needs 水 (water) like this, since this injury is affecting his 健康 ken**kou** (health)	健康 kenkou = health
夢 2		^165. in my 夢 **yume** (dreams), I have three eyes on a platform like this, and **You**thful-**Me**rmaids eat plants like this in the light of this 夕 (half **Moon**)	夢 yume = dream; 悪夢 akumu = nightmare
旧 1		^1017. the # 1 日 (day) of the year is 旧正月 **kyuu** shougatsu (lunar New Year), and it's a good time to eat a **C**ucumber salad	旧正月 kyuu shougatsu = lunar New Year; 旧年 kyuunen = last year
児 3		^1093. this guy with this deformed right **K**nee holds up this rod on 旧 (lunar New Year) to salute a 児童 **ji**dou (child) who can drive a **Jee**p on the **Go**lf course	小児科 shounika = pediatrics; 児童 jidou = child; 孤児 koji = orphan; 鹿児島 Kagoshima = a city in Kyushu

Kanji	Mnemonic	Readings
冒 2	^812. **Occa**sionally, when I go out in my **Boat**, I use this 目 (eye) to look directly into this 日 (sun), but I know that I am taking a 冒険 **bou**ken (risk) in doing so	冒す okasu = to brave or risk, to face or venture; 冒険 bouken = adventure, risk
唱 2	^1152. a 合唱 gas**shou** (chorus) of singers opened 口 (mouths) like this to sing for a **Show** on a planet with two 日 (suns) like these, and their **Ton**al quality was excellent	合唱 gasshou = chorus, singing in a chorus; 唱える tonaeru = to advocate or recite
掛 2	^596. this kneeling guy has a **Ca**bin where he 掛ける **ka**keru (hangs) this ト (toboggan) as he waits for winter, but when he looks out at the **Gar**den now, all he sees is this 土 (soil) piled upon 土 (soil)	掛ける kakeru = to hang (a picture, etc.), to sit on a chair, to take (time or money), to make a phone call, and many other meanings; 心掛ける kokorogakeru = to keep in mind
街 3	^625. when the **Kai**ser is in the middle of 行 (going) around the 街角 **machi**kado (street corner), these two big **Match**ing piles of 土 (soil) block the way, but the 街灯 **gai**tou (street light) **Gui**des him	街道 kaidou = highway, path; 街角 machikado = street corner; 街灯 gaitou = street light
崖 2	^911. **Gallant-Ken** was working as a **Gui**de on this 山 (mountain) when he saw this lean-to which was full of 土 (soil) piled on 土 (soil) like this, due to a landslide under a **gake** 崖 (cliff)	崖 gake = precipice, cliff; 断崖 dangai = precipice, cliff
圧 2	^748. this lean-to **At-Su**perman's house was designed by an **Arch**itect, but this 土 (soil) is putting a lot of 圧力 **atsu**ryoku (pressure) on the walls	圧力 atsuryoku = pressure; 圧倒的 attouteki = overwhelming
弁 2	^1162. this ム (cow) is working at the top of this tower, but it isn't happy with the **Ben**efits the job provides and plans to contact its 弁護士 **ben**goshi (lawyer) and look for a position on a **Be**autiful-**Ran**ch	弁護士 bengoshi = lawyer; 弁解 benkai = excuse, justification; 花弁 hanabira = a flower petal
十 6	^18. we have 十 **juu** (ten) **T**all cans of **T**omato **J**uice for the **Ju**ry in the **Jee**p, in a **Tsu**itcase (suitcase)	二十歳 hatachi = 20 years old ; 十 too = 10; 十 juu = 10; 十分 juppun (10 minutes), which can also be pronounced jippun; 二十日 hatsuka = the 20th of the month
計 2	^434. I 言 (speak) about my 計画 **kei**kaku (plan) to buy a 時計 to**kei** (clock) with these 十 (ten) dollars that I earned in the last **Hacka**thon, which we held in a **Cave**	計る hakaru = to measure; 時計 tokei = clock, watch; 計画 keikaku = plan
汁 3	^900. we drank 十 (10) bottles of 果汁 ka**juu** (fruit **J**uice), made from this water, with a **Shi**ite-**Ru**ler who parks his **J**eep-under-a-**R**oof	果汁 kajuu = fruit juice; 汁 shiru = soup; 鼻汁 hanajiru = nasal discharge
術 1	^808. this woman in the center is in the middle of 行 (going) out to have 手術 shu**jutsu** (surgery) for this lump that **Jut**s out over her right shoulder	手術 shujutsu = surgery; 美術 bijutsu = visual art
貝 1	^83. the **Kai**ser keeps his 貝 **kai** (shells) in this three-drawer money chest with these two legs	貝 kai = shell
敗 3	^793. this dancer, whose name is **Heidi**, got an idea to mail **Pies** to foreign countries, but the idea 失敗した ship**pai** shita (failed), and she had to empty this 貝 (money chest) and sell her **Y**akskin **Boo**ts	敗戦 haisen = a defeat or loss; 失敗する shippai suru = to fail or make a mistake; 敗れる yabureru = to lose or be defeated
賛 1	^1115. these two 夫 (husbands) 賛成する **san**sei suru (agree) to use the money from this 貝 (money chest) to buy **S**andwiches	賛成 sansei = agreement; 絶賛する zessan suru = to praise highly
替 3	^551. since **Carl** and **Garry-E**ricson are these two 夫 otto (husbands) who are almost identical, there is no **Gap** between them as they stand in this 日 (sun), and we can 替える **ka**eru (exchange) one for the other	替える kaeru = to replace or exchange money (this can also be spelled 換える); 両替 ryougae = money exchange; 着替える kigaeru = to change clothes
全 3	^300. a **Mat**ador and a **Sub**editor come to this **Zen** temple to talk about 全部 **zen**bu (everything) with this 王 (king)	全く mattaku = entirely; 全て subete = all, everything; 全部 zenbu = all, everything

決 3		^180. a pilot moves this tiller when he 決める <u>ki</u>meru (decides) to turn his boat in this water and, while eating **Qui**che, he pours tea from a **Ket**tle-into-his-**Sou**p, spilling some onto his **Ke**ds (a brand of shoes)	決める kimeru = to decide or arrange; 解決 kaiketsu = settlement, resolution, solution; 決して kesshite = never
快 2		^734. this man on the left stands tall and proud because he knows that he is training his **Kokoro**-(heart)-with-**Yo**ga, and he is usually 愉快 yu**kai** (cheerful) and often 決 (arranges) to fly **Ki**tes	快い kokoroyoi = pleasant, comfortable; 愉快 yukai = pleasant, cheerful
良 4		^303. Pope **Leo** wears 白 (white) suits at **Ea**ster, he is Light Years ahead of his peers, and he's a 良い <u>yo</u>i (good) person who feeds **Yo**gurt to his **Ra**bbits	良好 ryoukou = favorable, satisfactory; 良い ii = good, usually written いい; 良い yoi = good; 奈良 Nara = a city in Japan
根 2		^741. this 良 (good) 木 (tree) is the 根拠 <u>kon</u>kyo (foundation) of the materials that we use to make the 屋根 ya**ne** (roofs) that we sell in the **Ne**therlands and the **Co**ngo	屋根 yane = roof; 木の根 kinone = tree root; 根拠 konkyo = source or basis (of reasoning, etc.)
浪 1		^805. a 浪人 <u>rou</u>nin (masterless samurai) can find 良 (good) work on this water **Ro**wing boats	浪費 rouhi = waste, extravagance
退 3		^926. a 良 (good) **No**rwegian rode up on this snail and said that, if **Sheep**-could-**Rea**d-the-signs-of-the-**Zo**diac, they might experience less 退屈 <u>tai</u>kutsu (boredom), but then a **Tiger** ate him	立ち退く tachinoku = to evacuate, vacate; 退く shirizoku = to retreat; 退屈 taikutsu = boredom
芝 1		^779. the Queen of **Sheba** used to play croquet on a 芝生 <u>shiba</u>fu (lawn), represented by this plant radical, with Z (zebras) like this watching	芝生 shibafu = lawn, turf
脅 3		^914. I looked up to see these three men of 力 (force) dancing on this 月 (moon), and they 脅した <u>odo</u>shita (threatened) to send some foul **Odo**rs down to us in **Kyou**to, but I just kept on eating **O**ld-**Beans**-and-**Ya**ms	脅かす odokasu = to threaten or startle; 脅威 kyoui = a threat, peril, menace; 脅かす obiyakasu = to menace or threaten
協 1		^940. in **Kyou**to, 十 (ten) policemen 協力する <u>kyou</u>ryoku suru (cooperate) with these three men of 力 (force) to keep the peace	協力する kyouryoku suru = to cooperate; 協同 kyoudou = cooperation
週 1		^346. our **Sho**es arrive 毎週 mai<u>shuu</u> (every week) in this box hidden under this 土 (soil), carried in this tent on this snail	来週 raishuu = next week
周 2		^630. some **Ma**rine-**Wa**rriors live in our 周辺 <u>shuu</u>hen (neighborhood); they have **Sho**es that they hide in this box under this 土 soil in a tent, and they don't need a snail to carry them	周り mawari = surrounding; 周辺 shuuhen = neighborhood, vicinity, circum-ference; 一周 isshuu = round, tour
調 2		^441. people 言 (say) that a detective has been **Cho**sen to 調べる <u>shira</u>beru (check) this box hidden below this 土 (soil) inside this tent to see whether it contains **Sheep**-or-**Ra**bbit food	調子 choushi = condition; 調べる shiraberu = to check
復 2		^527. in **Fuku**oka, this injured dancer works with this therapist with two hats; she uses this crutch, he lends her a hat so that she can sit in this 日 (sun), he gives her good **Food**, and she experiences 回復 kai<u>fuku</u> (recovery) (CSD = crutch, sun, dancer)	復習 fukushuu = review; 回復 kaifuku = recovery; 反復 hanpuku = repetition; 復活 fukkatsu = revival, rebirth, restoration
腹 3		^863. this injured sunny dancer from **Fuku**oka has a **Na**sty-**Ca**t that **Hara**sses her when this 月 (moon) is full, or when it feels 空腹 kuu<u>fuku</u> (hunger) (CSD = crutch, sun, dancer)	空腹 kuufuku = hunger; 満腹 manpuku = full stomach; お腹 onaka = stomach; 腹 hara = stomach, abdomen; 脇腹 wakibara = the flank; 横っ腹 yokoppara = side of the body, the flank
覆 3		^893. an **O**pen-minded-**O**ld surgeon who uses these three eyes in his work met a guy in **Fuku**oka who worked for Superman, and the doctor **Cut-Su**perman's-**Guy**, 覆った <u>oo</u>tta (covered) the wound with a dressing, and achieved 復 (recovery) with the help of this dancer with this crutch sitting in this sun (CSD = crutch, sun, dancer)	覆う oou = to cover, conceal, wrap, disguise; 覆面 fukumen = mask; 転覆する tenpuku suru = to capsize or overturn; 覆す kutsugaesu = to overturn or overthrow

Kanji	Mnemonic	Vocabulary
交 4	^144. this 交差点 **kou**saten (traffic intersection) of 六 (six) roads outside a **Cou**rthouse has **Mag**ic traffic signals with **Mag**nets that keep **Ca**rs from colliding	交通 koutsuu = traffic; 交差点 kousaten = traffic intersection; 交わる majiwaru = to keep company with; 交ぜる mazeru = to mix (this can also be spelled 混ぜる mazeru); 交わす kawasu = to exchange
校 1	^130. a 学校 gak**kou** (school) is near this 交 (crossing) of 六 (six) roads, and it's usually **Co**ld because it's shaded by this 木 (tree)	学校 gakkou = school
郊 1	^145. this ß (Greek) guy lives near this 交 (crossing) in the 郊外 **kou**gai (suburbs) of Athens, and he's **Co**ld, since his house is unheated	郊外 kougai = suburbs
効 2	^1139. the threat of 力 (force) like this is the **Key** to 交 (traffic) code enforcement in **Ko**rea, and it 良く効く yoku **ki**ku (has a good effect)	効く kiku = to be effective; 効果 kouka = an effect
郷 3	^1059. after my 良 (good) ß (Greek) friend saw this lightning hit a **Sa**tellite-**To**wer in **Kyou**to, which is my 郷里 **kyou**ri (hometown), he was afraid to play **Go**lf and went back to Athens	故郷 furusato = hometown, often written ふるさと, or ふる里, # 1060; 故郷 can also be pronounced kokyou, with the same meaning; 郷里 kyouri = hometown; 水郷 suigou = riverside or lakeside location
響 2	^840. when this lightning strikes in **Kyou**to, the 影響 ei**kyou** (effect) of this 音 (sound) on my 良 (good) ß (Greek) friend is to give him the **Hee**bee jeebies, and he's going home to Athens	影響 eikyou = influence, effect; 響く hibiku = to resound, to be heard far away
程 2	^954. this 王 (king) is standing next to this 禾 (ripe grain) on the left, and he says to a servant, "**Hold-the-Do**or while I **Ta**ste this with this 口 (mouth) to determine the 程度 **tei**do (extent) to which it meets my standards"	程 hodo = extent, degree, limits, moderation, approximate time, about so much (usually written ほど); 程度 teido = criterion, standard, extent, degree, amount
部 3	^267. **He**len is a right-wing ß (Greek) 部長 **bu**chou (division manager) who keeps this 立 (**Be**ll) on this 口 (box) in her 部屋 **he**ya (room) for **Bu**ddhist ceremonies	部屋 heya = room; 子供部屋 kodomo-beya = child's room; 全部 zenbu = entirely
音 4	^266. during the **Otto**man era, people discovered that this 立 (bell) on this two-drawer 日 (cabinet) full of **On**ions makes an **In**credible 音 **oto** (sound) which annoys the people **Ne**xt door	音 oto = sound; 音楽 ongaku = music; 母音 boin = vowel; 音色 ne'iro = timbre
暗 2	^268. even when this 日 (sun) shines on this 立 (bell), there are 暗い **kura**i (dark) places in this 日 (cabinet) below it, where we keep **Curry-Ra**men, but **An**ts are getting into them	暗い kurai = dark; 暗示 anji = hint
闇 1	^950. when I'm out shopping for **Yak-Me**at, and the 暗闇 kura**yami** (darkness) increases, my family makes 音 (sounds) in this 門 (gate) to help me find my way home	闇 yami = darkness; 暗闇 kurayami = darkness
意 1	^317. this 音 (sound) in this 心 (heart) sounds **Ee**rie and must have some kind of 意味 **i**mi (meaning)	意味 imi = meaning; 意見 iken = opinion
億 1	^318. this man tilts his hat back in order to examine this bell which can play 一億の ichi**oku** no (100 million) **Old-Kool-Aid** jingles that have 意 (meaning) for people	五億 go oku = 500 million
隠 2	^834. **Karl-the-Kool-**Aid vendor is this ß (Greek) guy who was barbecuing on this grate in Athens when this long hair belonging to him caught fire, causing this 心 (heart) to ache, and then he spent time on the **In**ternet and 隠れた **kaku**reta (hid himself) until his hair grew back	隠す kakusu = to hide or cover up; 隠れる kakureru = to conceal oneself or disappear; 隠元豆 ingenmame = green bean, string bean

暮 3		^641. this is a tale of two 日 (suns): they both 暮らす **ku**rasu (make a living) by shining light on plants like these, and both of them are 大 (big); the top sun drinks only **Koo**l-Aid and is **Bo**ring, but the bottom sun is **Goo**fy (PSB = plants, sun, big)	暮らし kurashi = living, life; 暮らす kurasu = to make a living; 暮れ kure = year end, nightfall; お歳暮 oseibo = a year-end gift; 日暮れ higure = nightfall, dusk; 一人暮らし hitorigurashi = to live alone
幕 2		^653. this 日 (sun) makes these plants grow, but it has caused 大 (big) problems for 巾 (Bo Peep), who has **Macu**lar degeneration and spends her days behind closed 幕 **maku** (drapery) enjoying **Ba**nana-**Coo**kies (PSB = plants, sun, big)	幕 maku = theater curtain, act of a play; 字幕 jimaku = subtitle; 幕府 bakufu = shogunate administration
募 2		^1109. this is a poster designed to 募る **tsuno**ru (recruit) **Ts**uperior-(superior)-**No**rwegians for a **Bo**at trip to a land where these plants are 大 (big), this 日 (sun) shines abundant light, and this 力 (force) is strong (PSB = plants, sun, big)	募る tsunoru = to advertise, recruit, intensify; 応募 oubo = application, subscription
添 2		^841. this 天 (sky) is like a **Tent** above a 小 (small) piece of gum, which will interact with this water on the left until it 添える **so**eru (attaches) to a **So**ldier's boot	添加物 tenkabutsu = an additive (e.g., to food); 添える soeru = to attach to, to garnish a dish, to help or support; 力添え chikarazoe = assistance, support
活 2		^260. in **Ca**lifornia, I watch my **Cats** using 舌 (tongues) like this to drink water like this, and I enjoy their 活気 **ka**kki (liveliness)	活気 kakki = liveliness; 生活 seikatsu = life, livelihood
辞 2		^387. **Ji**mmy Carter showed us this 舌 (tongue), and he also brought out this 辛 (needle), to illustrate the sharp taste of the **Ya**m dishes that he was tasting at work, saying that therefore he will 辞める **ya**meru (resign) from his job	辞書 jisho = dictionary; 辞める yameru = to resign a position
話 3		^433. this 舌 (tongue) belongs to **Hannah**, and when she 言 (speaks) to **Hannah**'s-**Sheep**, who are **Wa**lking around, it 話す **hana**su (talks)	話す hanasu = to talk; 話 hanashi = story; 昔話 mukashibanashi = folklore; 会話 kaiwa = conversation
乱 2		^1020. during a **Mea**l-with-**Da**rwin, when we discussed the evolution of 乳 (breast) feeding, he stuck this 舌 (tongue) out at us, became 乱暴 **ran**bou (violent) and **Ran**sacked the place	乱れる midareru = to become chaotic or windblown (hair); 乱暴 ranbou = violent, disorderly
室 3		^62. I keep this 一 (one) ム (cow) with this bad haircut, my **Sheets** and a **Sheep** in this 室 **shitsu** (room), which features a floor of 土 (soil) like this and **Murderous-Ro**gues for roommates	室内 shitsunai = indoors; 至福 shifuku = supreme bliss; 室町 Muromachi = Japanese era ending in 1573
屋 2		^63. since I live in a land of falling yams, the addition of this heavy **Ya**m-proof 屋根 **ya**ne (roof) and an **Oa**k lean-to has allowed me to convert this simple 室 (room) into a more durable (小)屋 ko**ya** (cabin)	本屋 honya = bookstore; 部屋 heya = room; 小屋 koya = cabin; 屋根 yane = roof; 屋上 okujou = rooftop
倒 3		^563. this man on the left and this リ Ri are using a **Tow**el to clean the **To**rso of this 一 (one) ム (cow) which is **Do**zing in this 土 (soil), and both of them feel 面倒 men**dou** (annoyance), but the man tilts his hat in order to inspect their work	倒れる taoreru = to fall, collapse, drop, fall senseless; 倒産 tousan = bankruptcy; 面倒 mendou = annoyance, difficulty, care
至 2		^609. on the road that 至る **ita**ru (leads) to some **Ita**lian monuments, I saw a 至難の **shi**nan no (extremely difficult) situation: this 一 (one) ム (cow) had collided with a **Sheep** and was stuck in this 土 (soil)	至る itaru = to lead to, to reach, to result in; 至急 shikyuu = immediately, urgently; 至難の shinan no = extremely difficult
到 1		^612. リ Ri 到着する **tou**chaku suru (arrives) riding on this 一 (one) ム (cow) and 至 (immediately) uses this long **Toe** to clean this 土 (soil) from its hooves	到着する touchaku suru = to arrive; 到底 toutei (with negative expressions) = not by any means, not at all
介 1		^659. the **Kai**ser plans to serve as a 仲介者 chuu**kai**sha (mediator) in a moon dispute, but first we need to shoot him up into the sky along a trajectory like this	紹介 shoukai = introduction; 仲介者 chuukaisha = mediator
界 1		^69. we shoot **Ki**tes like this up into the sky, where they will be seen by 世界 se**kai** (the world)	世界 sekai = the world

Books in the *Learn to Read in Japanese* Series

1. *Learn to Read in Japanese,* Volume I. Published in 2016, it teaches 608 target kanji and includes a kanji catalogue, plus 4,200 reading practice sentences.

2. *Learn to Read in Japanese,* Volume II. Published in 2018, it teaches 600 additional target kanji, with an expanded kanji catalogue. It includes 2,900 vocabulary terms and 1,660 sentences for reading practice. It also suggests extensive supplemental reading material.

3. *Learn to Read in Japanese,* Volume III. Published in 2020, it teaches 320 more target kanji, with an expanded kanji catalogue. It includes 2,100 vocabulary terms and 912 sentences for reading practice. It also suggests extensive supplemental reading material.

4. *Learn to Read in Japanese,* Volume IV. Published in 2022, it teaches 560 more target kanji. Due to space limitations, it does not include a kanji catalogue, which is published separately (see Item # 5, below). It includes 3,800 vocabulary terms and 1,623 sentences for reading practice.

5. *Core Kanji, a Catalogue of 2,088 Essential Kanji.* Published in 2022 and expanded in 2024, it includes memorable kanji descriptions, retrieval cues for kanji readings and comparisons among similar characters, as well as an index to 4,300 kanji pronunciations. It also contains tools that can be used for identifying kanji, a technique known as Kanji ID.

6. *Learn to Read in Japanese, a Glossary.* Published in 2020 and expanded in 2022, it lists more than 9,700 Japanese vocabulary terms, with definitions, mnemonics and comparisons among terms.

7. *Kanji Memorization Drills,* Version One. Published in 2025, it contains drills for learning to recognize and pronounce 608 kanji. A supplement to *Learn to Read in Japanese,* Volume I.

8. *Kanji Memorization Drills,* Version Two. Published in 2025, it contains drills for learning to recognize and pronounce 1,208 kanji. A supplement to *Learn to Read in Japanese,* Volume II.

9. *Kanji Memorization Drills,* Version Three. Published in 2025, it contains drills for learning to recognize and pronounce 1,528 kanji. A supplement to *Learn to Read in Japanese,* Volume III.

10. *Kanji Memorization Drills,* Version Four. Published in 2025, it contains drills for learning to recognize and pronounce 2,088 kanji. A supplement to *Learn to Read in Japanese,* Volume IV.

www.ingramcontent.com/pod-product-compliance
Lightning Source LLC
LaVergne TN
LVHW061301060426
835509LV00016B/1673